THE LEGAL EMPOWERMENT AGENDA

In memory of
Arjun Kumar Sengupta
(1937–2010)

The Legal Empowerment Agenda
Poverty, Labour and the Informal Economy in Africa

Edited by
DAN BANIK
University of Oslo, Norway

Routledge
Taylor & Francis Group
LONDON AND NEW YORK

First published 2011 by Ashgate Publishing

Published 2016 by Routledge
2 Park Square, Milton Park, Abingdon, Oxon OX14 4RN
711 Third Avenue, New York, NY 10017, USA

Routledge is an imprint of the Taylor & Francis Group, an informa business

British Library Cataloguing in Publication Data
The legal empowerment agenda : poverty, labour and the
informal economy in Africa.
1. Public welfare--Law and legislation--Africa.
2. Informal sector (Economics)--Law and legislation--
Africa. 3. Labour laws and legislation--Africa. 4. Equality
before the law--Africa.
I. Banik, Dan, 1969-
344.6'0325-dc22

Library of Congress Cataloging-in-Publication Data
The legal empowerment agenda : poverty, labour and the informal economy in Africa / [edited and co-authored] by Dan Banik.
p. cm.
Includes index.
ISBN 978-1-4094-1118-5 (hbk) -- ISBN 978-1-4094-1119-2 (pbk) --
1. Informal sector (Economics)--Law and legislation--Africa, Sub-Saharan.
I. Banik, Dan, 1969-

KQC764.L44 2011
330--dc22

2010050745

ISBN 9781409411185 (hbk)
ISBN 9781409411192 (pbk)

Contents

List of Figures, Tables and Map

Figure

Tables

Map

List of Contributors

Pamhidzai H. Bamu is a researcher and doctoral candidate at the Institute of Development and Labour Law at the University of Cape Town. She completed her LLB in 2004 and then received her LLM in labour law at the University of Cape Town in 2006. Pamhidzai has worked as a researcher on various labour and development issues. Her research interests include the changing world of work, the impact of globalisation on labour regulation, labour migration, social security in developing labour markets, the promotion of decent work, and labour markets and their regulation in the SADC region.

Dan Banik is an Associate Professor and Research Director at the Centre for Development and Environment (SUM), University of Oslo. Dan's research interests include development theory, democracy, inequality, human rights, legal empowerment of the poor, policy studies and implementation, development ethics, undernutrition and famine, civil service reform and media in developing countries. In addition to directing the research programme 'Poverty and Development in the 21st Century' at SUM, he heads the Reference Group of the Norwegian–Finnish Trust Fund in the World Bank for Environmentally and Socially Sustainable Development (TFESSD). His recent books include *Rights and Legal Empowerment in Eradicating Poverty* (Ashgate 2008) and *Poverty and Elusive Development* (Scandinavian University Press 2010).

Blessings Chinsinga holds an MPhil from the University of Cambridge, UK and a PhD from the University of Mainz, Germany. He is based at the Department of Political and Administrative Studies, Chancellor College, University of Malawi as an Associate Professor and the Deputy Dean of Social Science. Blessings specialises in institutions, governance and development, public policy analysis, rural livelihood, democracy and decentralisation and local level politics. He coordinated an MA programme in Development Studies between 2006 and 2008 and currently coordinates a five-year collaborative project on democracy consolidation between the Department of Political and Administrative Studies, University of Malawi and the Department of Comparative Politics, University of Bergen, Norway.

Kanakulya Dickson is a lecturer of philosophy at Makerere University and the Uganda Christian University. He has a Masters degree from the University of Bergen and is currently a doctoral candidate at Makerere. Kanakulya's research interests include ethics and morality, philosophy of medicine, human rights and empowerment, development and politics and cultural philosophy. He has been engaged in various collaborative research projects, written and presented papers at various international forums and published a number of peer reviewed articles. His latest work (co-authored with Paola de Cuzzani), *Making Bioethics Global: Ethical Challenges in Indigenous Medicine* (Verlag Dr. Muller Publishers, 2010), investigates the moral issues in the indigenous medical research industry. Kanakulya is a member of the Makerere Centre for Applied Ethics (MACAE) and the Academic Network on the Legal Empowerment of the Poor (ANLEP).

Ellen Hillbom is an Assistant Professor at the Department of Economic History, Lund University, Sweden. Her primary field of research is agricultural development and transformation in sub-Saharan Africa. Within this broader field, she has studied property rights, access and allocation of water resources, intensification of farming methods, market expansion and rural-urban linkages. In connection to her interests in the agricultural transformation, Ellen has also written on processes of structural transformation and its importance for sustainable national economic development. Within the region, she has studied Botswana and Tanzania, but has also written generally on the economic history of sub-Saharan Africa.

Ngeyi Ruth Kanyongolo is a lecturer in the Faculty of Law and head of the Practical Legal Studies Department at Chancellor College, University of Malawi. She has an LLB (Hons) (Malawi), LLM (London) and PhD (Warwick) and specialises in issues related to labour, social security, and women and law. Ngeyi is a visiting lecturer at the University of Zimbabwe's LLM programme on women's law and is currently the President of the Women Lawyers Association. She has previously served as Vice President of the Malawi Law Society. Her recent and forthcoming publications are on social security, labour and trade unions in Malawi, teaching methods in women and law and women and customary law in Malawi.

Evance Kalula is Professor of Law (employment law and social security), director of the Institute of Development and Labour Law and Deputy Dean for Internationalisation and Outreach in the Faculty of Law, University of Cape Town. He chairs the South African Employment Conditions Commission, a statutory body responsible for setting sectoral conditions of employment and wages. He is also a member of the Ministerial Advisory Panel of the Department of Economic Development, South Africa and President-elect of the International Labour and Employment Relations Association (ILERA). His research and teaching interests are mainly in international and comparative labour law, labour market regulation and social security. He specialises in the jurisdictions of the Southern African Development Community (SADC) countries.

Happy Kayuni is senior lecturer and Head of the Department of Political and Administrative Studies at Chancellor College, University of Malawi. He previously worked as a programme manager for Women's World Banking – Malawi Affiliate. Mr. Kayuni holds a Master of Public Administration degree (MPA) from the University of Stellenbosch and has authored several articles and research reports in the areas of politics, development and public administration/management. He currently teaches courses on international relations theory and regional cooperation and integration.

Lilian Keene-Mugerwa holds a Bachelor of Laws degree from Makerere University, a Master of Arts degree from the University of Sussex and a diploma in legal practice from the Law Development Centre, Kampala. She is currently the executive director of the Platform for Labour Action, a national NGO in Uganda and is Chairperson of the Pan African Platform on Social Protection. Lilian has also worked as a consultant for DFID, DANIDA, UNDP, UN-HABITAT and ILO. Her publications include *Adult Domestic Workers in Uganda, Risks and Vulnerabilities of HIV/AIDS in the Informal Sector* and *The Quest for a Transparent and Accountable Social Security System in Uganda.*

Wilma Sichombo Nchito is a lecturer at the University of Zambia, where she has taught in the Geography Department since 1993. She obtained a BA from the University of Zambia and a MSc in geography from the London School of Economics. Her research interests are small towns, urban water, sanitation and waste management, urban poverty and the informal sector. She is currently a PhD candidate in the Geography department at the University of Zambia.

Ngozi Okorafor is a researcher at the Institute of Development and Labour Law, University of Cape Town. She studied law at the University of Benin, Nigeria and holds a Master of Laws (LLM) from the University of Cape Town. Ngozi specialises in international law and has vast experience in legal research spanning several years with specific interests in human rights and related issues.

Jan Theron completed a LLB at the University of Cape Town and thereafter went to work for the emergent union movement. He was General Secretary of the Food and Canning Workers Union (1976–1986) and the Food and Allied Workers Union (1986–1988). He then completed his articles, and is now a practising attorney. Jan is also a co-ordinator of the Labour and Enterprise Policy Research Group, which is based in the Institute of Development and Labour Law and the Sociology Department at the University of Cape Town. He is the author of numerous articles on labour and development law.

Margareet Visser is a researcher at the Labour and Enterprise Policy Research Group based at the University of Cape Town. She previously worked as a journalist and researcher in the NGO community before completing an MPhil in Development Studies at the University of Cape Town. Margareet's research interests include the impact of trade liberalisation on labour law, the state of collective bargaining in

South Africa, the externalisation of waste management in the City of Cape Town and part-time work in the retail sector.

Marlese von Broembsen is a senior lecturer in the Faculty of Law, University of Cape Town, where she teaches an interdisciplinary Masters programme in Social Justice. Her areas of interest include the informal economy, specifically the interface between rights and other developmental frameworks to secure decent work for the most marginalised. Having worked in the micro-enterprise sector for several years, her work is grounded in a grass-roots perspective. Marlese is both a lawyer and has a Masters degree in development studies. Prior to joining the University of Cape Town, she taught social policy at the University of the Western Cape and was the team leader for the Graduate School of Business's research project on entrepreneurship in the informal economy. She has written many policy documents, including one for the Taylor Commission on Social Security, the South African business rights paper for the UNDP's Commission for the Legal Empowerment of the Poor and is currently working for the South African government's Second Economy Strategy Project.

Acknowledgements

This book is the result of three workshops held in Kampala, Cape Town and Lund in 2009–2010 and organised by the University of Oslo's Academic Network on Legal Empowerment of the Poor (ANLEP) together with local partners. For excellent collaboration in organising these events, I am grateful to Anna-Karin Bergman, Marlese von Broembsen, Evance Kalula, Annika Wetlesen and Sophie Kristoffersen. The participants attending these workshops deserve special thanks for extremely rich and stimulating discussions.

For useful discussions and advice on a range of issues that have helped shape this book, I thank Maren Aase, Bård Anders Andreassen, Lloyd Axworthy, Vibeke Kieding Banik, Tor Arve Benjaminsen, Anna-Karin Bergman, Mona Elizabeth Brøther, Larry Diamond, Frands Dolberg, Boel Flodgren, Francis Fukuyama, Stephen Golub, Siri Gloppen, Ashraf Ghani, Sam Hickey, Evance Kalula, David Kennedy, Erik Jensen, Urban Jonsson, Happy Kayuni, Allan Larsson, Marilou McPhedran, Desmond McNeill, John-Andrew McNeish, Karl Ove Moene, Muna Ndulo, Lennart Olsson, Siddiq Osmani, Mizanur Rahman, Mary Robinson, Arjun Sengupta, Asuncion St. Clair, Kathryn Stoner-Weiss and Annika Wetlesen. In addition, the comments of two anonymous referees have helped improve the final product.

The Royal Norwegian Ministry of Foreign Affairs has provided generous funding to ANLEP and I wish to thank Lajla Brandt Jakhelln and her colleagues in the Ministry who have provided unwavering support and commitment towards furthering critical academic debate on the topic. Much of the editing of this volume was undertaken during my stint as visiting scholar at Stanford University in 2010–2011. I wish to especially thank David Grusky at the Stanford Center for the Study of Poverty and Inequality and Larry Diamond at the Center on Democracy, Development and the Rule of Law for providing a stimulating academic environment that helped me complete work on the manuscript and receive constructive feedback from colleagues at both centres. Sophie Kristoffersen, ANLEP's coordinator, has been an important ally in my work on legal empowerment and she has over the years provided invaluable research and administrative assistance. Kirstin Howgate and her colleagues at Ashgate have been both patient and generous with deadlines and have always been at hand to provide useful advice. I was particularly pleased to have a new opportunity to work with Pam Bertram, senior editor at Ashgate, and am grateful for her assistance. The main credit for this volume goes to my co-authors, who deserve a special vote of thanks for working extremely hard, respecting alarmingly short deadlines and generally for willing to be a part of this project.

Chapter 1
Introduction

Dan Banik

The informal economy is back in the news and there is now renewed interest in its role in promoting growth and in reducing poverty. After an initial period of popularity in the 1970s, and increasing usage of the term in policymaking and academic circles in the 1980s and 1990s, its importance in the development vocabulary has gradually waned. Today, however, it is widely accepted that the informal economy is 'here to stay', in that it is not only growing in size (contrary to earlier assumptions of its demise), but has developed in newer ways and in newer places, thus becoming an entrenched feature of life of people living in poverty in developing countries (Chen 2004). The result of a combination of factors – including successive financial crises and increased flexibility and informalisation of production and employment relationships – large numbers of people (some estimate this number to be almost four billion) around the world struggle to make a living outside the boundaries of the formal economy (ILO 2002; CLEP 2008). And despite providing society with a set of absolutely crucial services, workers in the informal economy are more often than not subject to exclusion and discrimination and their lives are characterised by various types of vulnerabilities that result from a denial of social, economic, political and legal protection.

When it entered the development vocabulary in the early 1970s, influenced by the work of Keith Hart and the International Labour Organisation (ILO), the term 'informal sector' helped identify and highlight various activities of the poor in developing countries that did not fall within the official categories of employment (McNeill 2006). The informal sector has since then been replaced by the broader term of 'informal economy', which reflects the need to analyse the problems and challenges facing a 'dynamic, heterogeneous and complex aspects of a phenomenon' that are not necessarily limited to a particular sector, but that 'encompass the expanding and increasingly diverse group of workers and enterprises in both rural and urban areas operating informally' (ILO 2002: 2).

The informal economy is characterised by its heterogeneous composition – with individuals and groups that include employers, informal wage workers, own account workers, industrial outworkers, homemakers and unpaid family workers – and its complexity in that it is segmented by employment status and by sex (e.g. women are over-represented in lower earnings and higher risk areas).[1] Typical

1 For further details, see the Women in Informal Employment: Globalising and Organising (WIEGO) website: http://www.wiego.org/publications/of_interest.php.

characteristics, as identified by the ILO already in the early 1970s (and still applicable today) include small-scale, labour-intensive and/or family-owned units, that do not require formal skills, and that operate in unregulated markets that have low barriers to entry. A transition from 'sector' to 'economy' thus acknowledges the entire gamut of informality that exists not only in poor countries, but also in transitioning and industrialised economies. And such a focus also entails moving from legally unregulated enterprises to legally unregulated and unprotected employment relationships (Chen 2004: 10, 15).

Among the set of factors responsible for bringing the informal economy back in the limelight of policymaking is the recent focus by the ILO on 'decent work' and the various efforts to promote 'legal empowerment of the poor' (LEP). The decent work agenda involves promoting the 'aspirations of people in their working lives' in four strategic objectives: fundamental principles and rights at work and international labour standards; employment and income opportunities; social protection and social security; and social dialogue and tripartism. According to the ILO, these objectives apply for all workers, not just in the informal, but also formal, economies and to those engaged in salaried employment or working on their own account, including work in fields, factories, offices, and home and in the community.[2]

Defined as a process that increases access to justice and the legal rights of the poor, 'legal empowerment' is slowly but steadily being considered by many international institutions to be an important tool in reducing poverty in developing countries. A major impetus was provided with the publication of the report by the Commission on Legal Empowerment of the Poor (CLEP), *Making the Law Work for Everyone* (2008), which identifies the implementation of labour and so-called 'business rights' in the informal economy as central pillars in the legal empowerment agenda. Key policy recommendations in the CLEP report build on the decent work agenda of the ILO and encompass a wide range of issues. For example, it is argued that urgent steps must be taken to strengthen the identity, voice and representation of the working poor, as well as their dialogue with employers and governments. Further, improving the quality of labour regulation and the functioning of institutions requires radical reforms backed by political support for the application of a minimum package of labour rights in the informal economy. Other recommendations include strengthening access to opportunities for decent work and education; issues related to training and retraining; fighting social and political discrimination; promoting gender equality; and supporting inclusive social protection. Additionally, the CLEP report recommends strengthening informal businesses by reducing the regulatory burden and barriers to formal markets and institutions, and increasing the asset base. The legal empowerment and decent work agendas therefore appear to complement each other and have the potential of making a major impact in reducing poverty and improving the quality

2 For further details, see http://www.ilo.org/global/About_the_ILO/Mainpillars/WhatisDecentWork/lang--en/index.htm (Accessed: 04 October 2010).

of life in developing country settings. But to what extent are such approaches being operationalised on the ground? And what are the main challenges involved and what has been the impact of efforts thus far?

The Purpose

The book discusses opportunities and constraints related to the enhancement of legal empowerment and decent work in the informal economy, with a focus on labour and business rights in Africa. Its conceptual point of departure is that the informal economy is characterised by its linkages to the formal economy as well as its heterogeneity in work arrangements and employment relationships, encompassing wage workers and the self-employed. The characteristics of the informal economy, however, vary in locally specific ways and contextual analyses are therefore urgently needed. Although the informal economy is partly or fully outside formal regulation, it is does not mean an absence of rules and norms. Rather activities in the informal economy are regulated by informal and group rules, arrangements, institutions and structures of mutual trust and help (ILO 2002: 3). In order to understand the potential of, and obstacles to, the realisation of labour rights, we believe it is further important to examine the nexus between formal and informal regulatory mechanisms. In this regard, sensitivity towards structures and relations of power between the formal and the informal economy as well as within the informal economy is a key issue. And analyses of potential regulatory dilemmas, for example in relation to regulation of informal enterprises, are crucial.

The overall issues addressed in this volume relate to the regulatory and operational challenges and dilemmas related to implementing legal empowerment and decent work approaches in selected countries in Africa. More specifically, the volume addresses six broad sets of interrelated issues.

First, several authors discuss definitions, underlying causes and the major theoretical approaches that explain the resilience of the phenomenon. Also included here are critical discussions of the relevance of current conceptual frameworks on decent work and legal empowerment to deal with the empirical complexities on the ground.

Second, this volume discusses the need to move from a focus simply on definitions to a focus on identifying the nature and characteristics of actual linkages to the formal economy. Here it is crucial to not only understand the advantages and disadvantages of strategies that emphasise 'formalisation', but also actual benefits that accrue to the poor, including an examination of why the poor often prefer to remain in the informal economy and thereby resist formalisation efforts.

Third, there is an emphasis on strategies to collectively organise informal workers, producers and traders and examine new initiatives and responses from traditional unions, and common and conflicting interests among various groups of actors in the formal and informal economy. Here the role of civil society organisations is particularly interesting.

Fourth, the book highlights the vulnerabilities and daily struggles of particular groups in the population that are generally neglected by governments and, in some cases, not adequately addressed by civil society organisations. These include waste pickers, home-based business owners, volunteer care-givers, street vendors, food and non-food sellers, domestic workers and health workers in informal sector.

Fifth, some chapters have an explicit focus on current legislative frameworks and the need for better applying legal provisions to encompass the informal economy. There are also suggestions for introducing new legislation to address the needs and problems of particular groups of people that are not covered by existing legal and administrative frameworks. Related to this are discussions on the benefits of social dialogue aimed at improving the conditions of not just workers, but also producers and traders.

Sixth, the book discusses the challenges involved in politically mobilising groups in the informal economy to effectively claim their rights and entitlements. With an overall focus on understanding the links between democracy and development, the case studies critically examine the role of political parties, trade unions and civil society organisations to aggregate and articulate interests and concerns of the poor in the informal economy.

Overview of the Chapters

The contributors to this volume are academics, with a background in the social sciences and law, and members of civil society involved in labour law and action. While Chapter 2 provides an overview of some of the major challenges faced by actors in the informal economy in the fifteen SADC countries, the remaining parts of the book offer detailed empirical evidence from five countries – South Africa, Malawi, Uganda, Zambia and Tanzania. The topics addressed are numerous and varied but have many common elements in their focus on the actors, groups and sectors in the informal economy and the typical policy measures that governments undertake or neglect to do so in response to such challenges. In the ensuing sections, I will briefly highlight the main arguments contained in each chapter.

Kalula, Okorafor and Bamu examine the regulatory framework for labour rights and social protection in the fifteen Southern African Development Community (SADC) countries. Although possessing great potential, the region is characterised by gross inequality and gendered poverty. The situation has further worsened due to the HIV-AIDS pandemic. And with 30–40 per cent of the labour force unemployed, the informal economy is not only dominant, but also steadily increasing. Despite such trends, the authors argue that regulation of labour markets and the provision of social protection remain overwhelmingly focused on the formal economy.

The chapter builds on recent explanations of the role and impact of labour market regulation in East Asia and Southern Africa and examines selected labour rights, bearing in mind their inevitable link to business rights and enterprise, and various approaches to social protection. The authors also examine the relevance and applicability of two recent but complementary approaches – LEP and the decent work – that address different dimensions of work, including employment and its quality, rights at work, representation and voice, social protection and social dialogue. One of the major conclusions is that labour law in Southern Africa continues to be influenced by pre-colonial history, and despite attempts at reforms, it has not yet been adapted to the new realities of 'causalisation' and 'externalisation'. Moreover, labour law institutions, such as trade unions, courts and inspectors, continue to face considerable challenges in their daily work related to lack of resources and absence of qualified personnel. Similarly, social protection remains limited in coverage and is often restricted to groups in the population engaged in the formal economy.

Kalula, Okorafor and Bamu also undertake a comparison of recent efforts by India and Brazil to address regulation in the informal economy. What is particularly interesting here is that while both countries have high levels of informality, they have nonetheless demonstrated relatively strong political commitment to address the problems emanating from their informal economies. And despite the enormity of the challenge – with hundreds of millions of people affected – the authors show that the efforts of successive labour commissions in India have resulted in the design and implementation of ambitious programmes related to employment generation and old age pensions. The Brazilian experience is less impressive in this field, with numerous instances of unenforced legislation. However, the country has made some positive headway by improving access to credit and reduced the time required to register businesses. The authors suggest that rather than proposing new regulatory frameworks, governments should start using those that already exist in order to implement improved social protection, And in this context, the decent work agenda, and particularly its emphasis on 'decent work deficit' analysis, can be particularly helpful.

Marlese von Broembsen explores the implications of the LEP framework for a typical poor woman's informal business in South Africa. She begins with an examination of the CLEP (2008) report on business rights and argues that it largely reflects a legalist understanding of the economy and a narrow view of 'empowerment'. Thus, while the recommendations contained in this report may result in an improvement of living and working conditions of the poor, they may not necessarily be empowering in terms of facilitating greater participation in the formal economy. Accordingly, advocating reforms along these lines will generate policy responses that are of limited value to the poor, particularly those who run 'own-account' informal businesses in South African townships. Activities of home-based businesses, and other activities that operate from small stalls in the fringes of large cities and sell products to other groups of poor, constitute the bulk of the country's informal economy – an estimated 7 to 12 per cent of South Africa's GDP. And such activities will continue to exist and even increase in numbers as long as they remain without regular exposure and access to the formal economy and its markets.

Meaningful participation, or as CLEP would term it 'fair' participation in the formal economy, is hence only achievable if there is structural change, not least to the structure of the economy – a premise of South Africa's Second Economy Strategy Project. A more political understanding of participation, von Broembsen argues, is reflected in Volume II of CLEP's report on business rights. This particular report reflects both structuralist and informalisation perspectives of the informal economy and hints at a broader understanding of empowerment. Thus, policy recommendations based on this volume could potentially advance the struggle of the poor in South Africa to generate sustainable livelihoods and participate more fairly in the formal economy. And in line with Volume II's perspective of the informal economy, von Broembsen reviews two South African cases that aim to improve the livelihoods of the poor and reduce transaction costs by facilitating 'backward' and 'forward' linkages between formal and informal businesses on 'fairer terms'. In general, von Broembsen suggests that any initiative to promote genuine legal empowerment must better understand the process that creates and sustains informality in particular contexts. And responses will depend on one's understanding of the concept of empowerment and process that characterises the formal-informal relationship.

Continuing with a focus on South Africa, *Jan Theron* and *Margareet Visser* study the role of local government in waste management. The traditional roles of collecting and transporting waste to landfill sites on the fringes of a city are gradually changing. With increased urbanisation and growth in population, finding adequate space for landfills is also becoming increasingly difficult and expensive. As a result, South Africa has revised its waste management policies and recently adopted a Waste Management Act. However, with increased attention on waste collection and minimisation (or recycling), enormous challenges remain in protecting the rights of workers in the business. Waste management is a major source of employment in the region, and local authorities play a critical role in determining the type of employment such activities generate. However, as in many other parts of the world, financial constraints have drastically reduced the number of persons directly employed by local authorities as compared to the number actually engaged in the waste management activity.

Theron and Visser suggest ways by which the labour rights of workers in the informal economy can be extended and better protected. They are particularly concerned with the terms and working conditions of so-called 'non-core' workers – i.e. those employed by enterprises engaged in various ways by local authorities – engaged in waste collection for the City of Cape Town. This category includes self-employed individuals (e.g. waste pickers) who are not formally engaged by local authorities but are nevertheless part of the overall waste management system. The general argument is that by reducing the number of people they directly employ, the local authorities have eroded crucial labour standards. However, instead of returning to a system of direct employment by the state – a feature the authors consider unrealistic in the current scenario – the chapter discusses the concept of 'externalisation' as a system of regulation.

Thus, in order to extend labour rights to non-core workers, Theron and Visser argue that one must first differentiate between workers who are ostensibly formally employed, but in practice insufficiently covered by existing legislation, and those that are not protected at all, such as the self-employed. In the case of the City of Cape Town, the former category includes large contractors providing waste management services, and small enterprises that are often owned by emergent entrepreneurs. In both instances, the fundamental obstacle to extending labour rights to the workers they employ is a legislative definition of the 'workplace' that does not recognise ground level realities. At the same time, particularly in the case of the self-employed, labour rights cannot be divorced from business rights, since it may be through associating together as an enterprise that the self-employed and other vulnerable workers are best able to advance their economic interests. And while the City of Cape Town does little to support initiatives that enable the self-employed to establish their own enterprises, it does, in fact, subsidise the enterprises of intermediaries engaged in waste management. Theron and Visser therefore argue that a re-definition of the notion of the workplace – that acknowledges the role self-employed and vulnerable workers play in waste collection and minimisation – could facilitate greater transparency, and a fairer allocation of public resources. And these, in turn, will also help meet the objective of creating opportunities for decent work.

Two chapters in the volume discuss in detail the everyday realities of street vending, a phenomenon that continues to expand exponentially at national, regional and international levels. Street vendors – who mainly sell goods or services in public spaces – have become an integral feature of many African cities and attempts by the authorities to relocate them into purpose-built market buildings are justified variously on the basis of promoting law and order, beautification of urban centres, improving opportunities for sales and profit, and ensuring that streets are not over-crowded and clogged by vending activities.

Wilma Sichombo Nchito looks at how informal rules of engagement in the street trading business raise interesting questions regarding how vendors survive in their 'illegal' businesses and the degree of profitability one can expect when they sit beside each other and sell similar, if not the very same, products. It is estimated that the informal economy in Zambia accounts for almost 88 per cent of the country's labour force. And even in urban areas, the figure is as high as 65 per cent. Women often outnumber men and most are self-employed or unpaid family workers. The case in question is the drive by officials in Lusaka to build new market buildings in order to relocate street traders. Nchito examines the advantages and disadvantages of such a development in terms of space utilisation once a formal system of management is introduced. The regulations as to who should legally have access to the newly created trading spaces changes once the spaces are developed. While the development of modern market infrastructure can appear to be a positive step, it also entails a loss of livelihood for some; for example, a trader may not be allocated a stall even though he/she had previously operated in older markets and spaces. Others may be unable to afford the increased rents or fees that such transitions entail. Still others may prefer to return to the streets in order to capture the attention of customers who prefer easily accessible (e.g. roadside) locations to purchase goods.

Nchito identifies the role played by various actors, including the media and politicians, and the strength of informal 'management' strategies in protecting the rights of traders. In particular, she discusses various coping strategies of those who fail to benefit from such attempts at formalisation either because they have been excluded or because they are not in a position to afford to pay the rent required to use a stall in a formalised market structure. The analysis further questions whether the perceived problems of street vending can be resolved by a process of legalisation and formalisation, particularly when, as her case study from Lusaka shows, traders simply shift businesses to newer (illegal) sites. Thus, Nchito rejects the claim, often drawn from the works of Hernando de Soto, that the informal economy will always best benefit from a process of standardisation, legalisation, formalisation and regulation.

Blessings Chinsinga and *Happy Kayuni* continue with this theme and examine street vending in Blantyre and Zomba in Malawi. Like Zambia, it is estimated that almost 88 per cent of the population earn their livelihoods in the informal economy and street vending, in particular, has been a visible sign of such activity. The authors examine the complexities and paradoxes of governing and regulating the informal economy, especially since one of its perceived major advantages is its flexibility. Just as Nchito did in the previous chapter, Chinsinga and Kayuni question the rationale and feasibility of formalising the informal economy through the creation of designated markets. Such initiatives began to be undertaken in Malawi in the 1990s, following a public debate on the detrimental impacts of street vending on urban congestion, crime and violence. The authors also discuss the extent to which these resulting initiatives have resulted in legal empowerment and protection of the rights of vendors as championed by the ILO's decent work agenda. Based on a theoretical foundation in the human rights-based approach to development (HRBA) and an institutional approach, Chinsinga and Kayuni specifically highlight the interface between formal and informal institutions viewed through the prism of a scheme of interaction.

The case studies of purpose-built flea markets show that the first democratically elected government of Malawi (formed by the UDF party) considered vendors to be important political allies, and hence did not insist on forcibly implementing its policy of relocating vendors to such market buildings. The next government, formed by the DPP party, however, has claimed that it has successfully managed to implement its vendor relocation policy. The authors do not agree with such a view and argue that three years after such a forced relocation, vendors in the two cities continue to complain about the lack of consultation in implementing the relocation strategy, inappropriate market structure designs and the lack of security against theft. Indeed, Chinsinga and Kayuni conclude that the overall welfare of street vendors has generally not improved; rather, it has, in many ways, deteriorated. This is attributed to limited room for growth of enterprises in confined spaces, increased levels of corruption by city officials administering the flea markets, politicisation of the allocation of spaces to vendors, exploitative class formations among the vendors, the capture of emerging trade unions and associations by elites and the absence of supportive environment (policy and legislative) for institutional mechanisms for voice and representation through which to advance the interests of vendors.

Kanakulya Dickson examines the linkages between health and the discourse on empowerment of the poor. In sub-Saharan Africa, he argues, the poor generally perceive the formal health sector as 'disempowering' and cites the World Health Organization estimates that 80 per cent of the world's poor rely on informal medical service providers for their primary health care needs. Dickson takes a starting point in the LEP approach, and discusses the extent to which the recommendations of the Commission on Legal Empowerment of the Poor (CLEP) can be implemented in local contexts. With examples from Uganda, Tanzania and Kenya, he discusses the extent of public funding available for health, including the fact that despite being better off, Kenya spends less on health than Uganda and Tanzania. Applying a LEP approach in the informal health industry also presents considerable regulatory and policy challenges that require revisiting the conception of what constitutes genuine 'empowerment'. Dickson argues that the conception and application of the LEP approach in the informal health industry can be problematic when viewed from alternative development approaches, such as the capabilities approach developed by Amartya Sen and Martha Nussbaum. He examines areas and situations of potential incompatibility between the application of LEP and the capabilities approaches in relation to the informal health industry in the three country cases.

Of particular importance here is the argument that establishing a legal identity – a core recommendation of the LEP approach – is insufficient for addressing the challenges in the informal health sector. Legal identity does not automatically result in access to justice since the existence, maintenance and continuation of informality requires us to understand why the poor prefer the informal to the formal. And the major attraction of informal healthcare providers is their ability to effectively understand the needs of the poor and thereby avoid the misunderstandings and conflicts that often arise when the poor approach the formal (and largely perceived to be arrogant) health care system. Moreover, Dickson suggests that the preference of the informal economy by the poor is not just due to a failure of formal laws and institutions, but because the poor as well as local elites believe they can continue to benefit from the status quo.

Lilian Keene-Mugerwa provides a civil society perspective based on the work of the Platform for Labour Action (PLA) based in Kampala. She discusses the regulatory and operational challenges in collectively organising the poor based on existing research on social injustice among domestic workers and on HIV/AIDS in the informal economy. Of particular concern is the huge representational gap in the country, as over 80 per cent of the population does not belong to a trade union or work-related organisation. The situation is particularly serious for the large group of domestic workers whose freedom of movement and association is often severely undermined by their employers. This is compounded by the relative isolation of such workers from others in society (being largely confined within the house), long hours of work, inadequate time for rest, sexual harassment and with very limited possibilities for alternative employment. And despite not being explicitly excluded from the Labour Union Act, domestic workers have not yet been mobilised by unions.

Keene-Mugerwa goes on to explore how the poor within the informal economy can be better protected by applying and extending existing legislation in Uganda without impeding the country's current rate of economic growth and level of business competitiveness. And civil society organisations can here play a crucial role by making the poor aware of their rights through legal education in general and mobilising them through community-based monitoring systems in particular. Based on studies carried out by the PLA, Keene-Mugerwa discusses the implementation and applicability of existing legislation and enforcement mechanisms to challenges related to minimum wages, privacy, work hours, working conditions (including occupational, health, safety and security) and group formation. One conclusion is that despite current problems in enforcing the wide body of legislation to protect the rights of workers in Uganda, workers in the informal economy workers can indeed be organised through concerted civil society efforts, and that those interviewed in the study were indeed eager to be organised. Moreover, both employers and employees in the informal economy can be supported with legal aid to promote their rights and formalise some of their mutual relationships. And the evidence presented in the chapter shows that civil society organisations can successfully negotiate better working conditions for workers without negatively affecting the employment security of the poor. Despite numerous challenges in reaching out to child labourers and domestic workers, including seeking permission from local leaders, and difficulties in raising sensitive issues with employers, a major conclusion is that issue-based bargaining – such as improved access to services such as water and sanitation facilities and police-provided security in unsafe areas – can work if associations of workers' rights are successfully able to communicate, and gain respect for, the needs of the poor to relevant authorities.

A focus on new, and improved enforcement of existing, legislation is the focus of *Ngeyi Ruth Kanyongolo's* chapter, where she examines the role and practice of care-giving and how care work in Malawi can be regulated to improve the overall well-being of care-givers and their clients. As in most developing countries, labour in the informal economy is generally overlooked, undervalued and poorly regulated in Malawi. In a country with increasing levels of HIV/AIDS and growing demands for community-based care for the sick, Kanyongolo highlights the high societal importance of unpaid labour, which is commonly performed by female volunteers. With a starting point in the ethic of care approach, she discusses the nature of care, which relates to both paid and unpaid work and involves the nurturance of necessarily dependent others (children, the sick and the elderly), as well as non-relational social reproduction work that is necessary to ensure the daily maintenance and ongoing reproduction of the labour force. Despite its growing importance, labour regulation in Malawi focuses on and favours those employed in the formal economy and neglects unpaid care-giving. Volunteer care-givers work for long periods of time in unsafe environments and lack protective care materials and psycho-social support. And care-givers are extremely vulnerable to abuse, exploitation and risk contracting infectious disease. Moreover, caring is often seen as natural, unskilled and a feminine activity and is consequently devalued. Care-givers are generally untrained, lack necessary equipment (e.g. protective gloves that reduces the risk of infections) and work without remuneration.

Despite some attempts at organising training sessions and providing care-givers with medical kits and protective gloves, the government has refused to consider paying salaries and providing general psycho-social support to care-givers. Moreover, and quite surprisingly, the numerous civil society organisations that work in Malawi, have largely ignored the problems faced by care-givers in their daily work. Kanyongolo goes on to argue that legal protection of care-givers requires an understanding of the important role they plan in everyday life in the country, particularly in rural areas. And current legislation, according to her view, reflects a gendered and undervalued construction of the activity. The conclusion is that recognition of the importance of care is not enough without legitimation of care, which combines recognition with a distribution of costs and responsibilities of care across actors and sectors. In addition to enforcing the provisions of the Employment Act of 2000, especially in relation to women employees, Kanyongolo proposes the enactment of a special Volunteer Workers Act, with an emphasis on minimum workers hours, health and safety issues and access to compensation from various employment tribunals in case of injury at work. There is hence a need for protection through specific legislation that addresses the problems and challenges facing such volunteer work by care-givers in Malawi. The argument is that the rights and interests of care-givers should be legally protected and fulfilled in the same way as those of people who are engaged in paid work.

In the final empirical chapter of this volume, *Ellen Hillbom* shifts our focus from labour and informal businesses to another crucial pillar in CLEP's (2008) report, namely the creation of legally protected formal property rights. Hernando de Soto claims that property rights are crucial for economic growth and development and that such rights have developed over centuries in the Western world. The process has included adapting informal rights to assets, recognised by the general public, to a formal economic system under the supervision of a legitimate nation state. Hillbom critically analyses the policy recommendations of the CLEP report as well as de Soto's theory on legally protected formal property rights. And the applicability of policy and theory is tested on the basis of an empirical case – property rights governing irrigation furrows in Meru, Tanzania. Hillbom argues that any grand policy or theory claiming to have the tools for eradicating poverty must be relevant to the places where poverty is foremost prevailing today. And one such place is the agricultural sector in rural sub-Saharan Africa, which exhibits interesting features of property rights formation and power struggles over agricultural resources. She shows that the causal relationship between tenure systems and investments are often more complex than the informal—formal dichotomy and that the major problem with the LEP approach is that it does not adequately address the complexities of power struggles over local resources. Thus, an important conclusion is that while the rule of law in general, and property rights in particular, are undoubtedly important for economic growth and poverty reduction, the LEP approach does not provide a convincing enough answer regarding how good institutions can and should be developed. The way forward is therefore to go beyond CLEP and place greater emphasis on the growing literature of legal pluralism, the success of communal property rights regimes and the complexities involved in redistributing resources.

In Chapter 11, I provide a brief summary of the conclusions that I see resulting from the discussion in the preceding chapters.

This is the second in a series of books that have resulted from events organised by the Academic Network on Legal Empowerment of the Poor (ANLEP), based at the Centre for Development and the Environment, University of Oslo, and comprising a network of academics working on and/or interested in the topic. The first volume (Banik 2008) contained case studies from South Asia, sub-Saharan Africa and Latin America on access to justice and the rule of law and property rights. The focus in this volume has been narrower in terms of labour rights and has had an exclusive focus on selected countries in sub-Saharan Africa. The United Nations Development Programme and the International Labour Organisation have numerous attempts underway to operationalise the concepts of decent work and legal empowerment, and to identify appropriate indicators for measuring success. It is our hope that this volume will contribute towards the further development of such efforts to formulate well formulated and implementable policy by offering a more nuanced understanding of the aspirations and vulnerabilities that characterise the daily lives of people living in poverty.

References

Banik, D. (ed.). 2008. *Rights and Legal Empowerment in Eradicating Poverty*, Farnham: Ashgate.

Chen, M. 2004. Rethinking the Informal Economy: Linkages with the Formal Economy and the Formal Regulatory Environment. Paper presented at EGDI and UNU-WIDER conference, 17–18 September 2004, Helsinki, Available at: http://www.wiego.org/papers/2005/unifem/5_Chen_WIDER_paper.pdf (Accessed: 15 September 2010).

CLEP 2008. *Making the Law Work for Everyone*, Final Report Parts 1–4. Available at: http://www.undp.org/legalempowerment/report/index.html [Accessed 14 October 2010].

ILO. 2002. Decent Work and the Informal Economy. Report VI, International Labour Conference, 90th session, 2002, International Labour Office, Geneva,

Available at: http://www.ilo.org/public/english/standards/relm/ilc/ilc90/pdf/rep-vi.pdf (Accessed: 15 September 2010).
McNeill, D. 2006. The Diffusion of Ideas in Development Theory and Policy. *Global Social Policy*, 6(3), 334–54.

Chapter 2
Towards an Effective Regulatory Framework for Labour Rights and Social Protection in Southern Africa

Evance Kalula, Ngozi Okorafor and Pamhidzai Bamu

Introduction

Scholarly debates around the world show that the informal economy can no longer be considered a temporary phenomenon (Becker 2004). It has therefore become necessary to move from the more popular discussions over the definition of this concept and practice to the more arduous but extremely urgent task of formulating a regulatory and implementation framework to ensure that the actors in the informal economy are given adequate protection under labour and other relevant laws. Although possessing great potential, the Southern Africa sub-region is one of the poorest in the world. Over 40 per cent of its population live in poverty, characterised by gross inequality and worsened by the HIV and AIDS pandemic. The poverty is gender-based in all countries, with women and children bearing most of the burden. Above all, the informal economy is not only dominant but increasing.

This chapter analyses the situation generally in the Southern African Development Community (SADC) comprising fifteen member states, using varying examples of specific countries. We examine selected labour rights, and approaches to social protection. We show that in spite of this preponderance of the informal economy, the domestic regulation of labour markets and provision of social protection is overwhelmingly concerned with the formal economy and excludes actors in the informal economy.

In the absence of strong domestic and regional legislation and policies to address the exclusion of informal economy workers from labour protection in the SADC region, we turn to international approaches that may potentially be adopted. We examine concepts popular in the Decent Work Agenda of the International Labour Organisation (ILO), including employment and its quality; social protection and social dialogue; representation and voice; and rights at work. Thereafter we focus on the conceptual framework of legal empowerment, examining the essence of the work of the Commission on the Legal Empowerment of the Poor (hereafter CLEP). The discussion will consider whether and to what extent the Decent Work Agenda and the legal empowerment of the poor can play a role in bringing about labour and social protection in SADC countries.

This chapter draws mainly on secondary sources, focusing on legislation, policies and scholarly contributions. It is conceived within the recent articulation of theories concerning the role and impact of labour market regulation, including the work of Kalula and Fenwick on Southern Africa (Kalula and Fenwick 2004). We begin by briefly discussing the evolution of the debate around the concept of the informal economy. Then we discuss the regional profile of the SADC and explore the issues of poverty, inequality and exclusion. We also outline the key scope and character of the informal economy in the region. Further, the nature of the world of work and activities are examined. In the next section, we discuss labour markets and their regulation in Southern Africa with a focus on the labour law and regulation of labour rights. The nature and extent of social protection offered within this region are further explored. Thereafter we discuss the ILO's Decent Work Agenda and the work of CLEP in addressing the challenges faced in the informal economy. We have also undertaken a comparative bench marking of Brazil and India – two countries that, though plagued with high numbers of informal workers, have taken steps towards providing a framework for regulating their informal economies. In the final section of this chapter, we consider the lessons that SADC member states can learn from the decent work and legal empowerment approaches, as well as the comparative jurisdictions considered in part five.

Understanding the Informal Economy

Several attempts have been made to identify and define the informal economy since its 'discovery' in the 1970s (Becker 2004). Previously known as the informal sector, the informal economy has been defined by reference to economic units/enterprises found within the informal economy, employment categories based on the location of informal economy actors, and income and employment enhancing potential. All of these definitions are evident of the multi-dimensional nature of the informal economy (ibid.). However, the Resolution Concerning Decent Work and the Informal Economy formulated the most recent and widely recognised definition of the informal economy. It defines the informal economy by reference:

> to all economic activities by workers and economic units that are – in law or in practice – not covered or insufficiently covered by formal arrangements. Their activities are not included in the law, which means that they are operating outside the formal reach of the law; or they are not covered in practice which means that- although they are operating within the reach of the law, the law is not applied or enforced; or the law discourages compliance because it is inappropriate, burdensome, or imposes excessive costs. (ILO 2002)

Initially, and following the 'discovery' of the informal economy, there were mixed reviews about its character (Chen 2004). While some observers saw the informal economy as distinctly separate from the formal economy – and consisting of marginal economic activities – others attributed the upsurge of informal economies especially in developing countries, to underdevelopment and lack of sufficient growth of these economies (ibid.). In addition, some observers argued that it was indicative of an emerging new pattern in industrial development in developing countries, different from the one observed in the already developed countries (ibid.).

Thus far, three schools of thought have emerged in the effort to explain the informal economy and its relationship with the formal economy: the dualists, the legalists and the structuralists. Made popular by the ILO in the 1970s, the dualists see the informal sector as consisting of marginal activities that provide income for the poor and a safety net during crisis and therefore, separate from the formal sector (ibid.).

The legalist account is that the informal economy comprises micro-entrepreneurs that operate informally in order to avoid the costs, time and effort associated with formal registration. It argues that informality is a result of a conscious choice by micro-entrepreneurs faced with cumbersome and costly government regulations. The structuralists, on the other hand, believe that different modes and forms of production co-exist and are inextricably connected and interdependent (ibid.). In terms of the structuralist model, the informal sector is seen as subordinated economic units, and workers – who by reducing input and labour costs – effectively increase the competitiveness of large capitalist firms (ibid.).

It is beyond the scope of this chapter to undertake a full analysis of these three theories. We proceed on the assumption that no single account can give a complete explanation for the existence of the informal economy given the diversity it entails and the different circumstances in which informal activities arise. Moreover, we assume that each account (subject to its limitations) is to some extent applicable to at least a certain segment of the informal economy.

SADC Regional Profile

This section gives a broad overview of the SADC, which provides the context within which the nature of the informal economy and key aspects of labour and social protection therein will be understood. We begin with a historical account of the formation of the SADC, outline some of its key objectives, and then provide an overview of the socio-economic context, with an emphasis on key challenges of poverty, inequality and exclusion. Thereafter, we outline the key aspects of the labour markets in SADC countries and end with a discussion on the informal economy in SADC member states.

History of the Formation of SADC

The Southern African Development Community (SADC) was initially formed as a loose alliance – the Southern African Development Coordination Conference

(SADCC) – on 1 April 1980 and was an economic association of the nine independent states in Southern Africa: Angola, Botswana, Lesotho, Malawi, Mozambique, Swaziland, Tanzania, Zambia, and Zimbabwe (Hanlon 1989: 4). Their main objective as stated in *Southern Africa: Toward Economic Liberation*, also known as the Lusaka Declaration, was 'to pursue policies aimed at the economic liberation and integrated development of our national economies' (ibid.). This objective included the following: the reduction of economic dependence on South Africa; creation of a genuine and equitable regional integration; mobilisation of resources to promote the implementation of national, interstate and regional policies; and promotion of international cooperation within the framework of strategy for economic liberation (ibid.).

However, in August 1992, a declaration and treaty was signed, transforming the organisation from a Coordinating Conference – which operated with a Memorandum of Understanding – into a Development Community, which had taken on a legal character (SADC 2009a). Prominent among the objectives – as stated in Chapter 5 of the SADC Treaty – are to 'achieve development and economic growth, alleviate poverty, enhance the standard and quality of life of the peoples of Southern Africa, support the socially disadvantaged through regional integration', and to 'promote and maximise productive employment and utilisation of resources of the region' – objectives which are of direct relevance to the purpose of this chapter.[1]

To enable it achieve its aims, the SADC has undertaken to harmonise political and socio-economic policies and plans of Member states, as well as to create appropriate institutions and mechanisms for the mobilisation of resources for the implementation of the programmes and projects of SADC and its institutions, among others (SADC 2009b). Currently, the membership of SADC has increased from nine to fifteen member states. In addition to the countries listed above, are the Democratic Republic of Congo, Madagascar, Mauritius, Namibia, Seychelles and South Africa.

Poverty, Inequality and Exclusion

The development of labour laws and social protection in the southern African region cannot be accurately reported on without contextualising it within the factors that have given it its current character. The economies of the Southern African States, though at different levels of growth[2] – reported as an average of 2.7 per cent in 2003 – have been characterised by high levels of poverty, which has been further exacerbated by the disproportion between economic growth and the need for poverty alleviation (Fenwick, Kalula and Landau 2004: 9). According to ILO estimates, Sub-Saharan Africa records the highest incidence of working

1 For the rest of the objectives stated in Article 5 of the SADC Treaty, please refer to www.sadc.int.

2 In comparison with other countries in the region, the highest levels of economic growth have been recorded in Mauritius and Botswana.

poverty among all the developing regions with 55 per cent of those employed earning incomes of about US$1 a day and 76.4 per cent of the population not earning enough to lift them above the poverty line of US$2 day (ibid.). Inequality in SADC is reflected in income, employment and access to social protection. Income inequality and unemployment are thus directly linked to the high levels of poverty in the region (ibid.).

According to the Development Policy Research Unit (DPRU) at the University of Cape Town, sub-Saharan Africa exhibits the highest levels of income inequality in the world. Because of previous colonial domination of the countries in the region, income inequality, unfortunately, continues to be structured along racial lines (ibid.). From the estimates of the DPRU, 30–40 per cent of the labour force in the SADC region is unemployed due to the inability of the formal sector to absorb the economically active population (EAP) (ibid.). This has contributed significantly to the EAP seeking employment outside the formal sector and into sectors that are inadequately protected under labour laws.

The incidence of HIV and AIDS has further increased poverty levels in Southern Africa. Available statistics on the incidence of this pandemic in the region is staggering. In 1997, an alarming 21 million, out of the global total of 30 million, people living with HIV and AIDS were found in sub-Saharan Africa (Cohen 2009). A decade and some years later, it is estimated that adults in many countries in Southern Africa have an infection rate in the range of 20–25 per cent (ibid.). While Botswana and Lesotho fall into this range with infection rates of 24 per cent and 23 per cent respectively, Swaziland's rate of infection rate falls outside this range at 33.4 per cent, all in 2005 (Fenwick, Kalula and Landau. 2007). Conversely, prevalence rates below five per cent were recorded in the same year, in Angola, DRC and Madagascar (ibid.).

As Cohen (1998) argues, there is a need to understand the 'relationship between HIV/AIDS and poverty – understanding the processes through which the experience of HIV and AIDS by households and communities leads to an intensification of poverty'. Some of the effects of HIV and AIDS in the region include the way it changes life expectancy – a sharp drop from 62 years without HIV and AIDS to 47 years – which reduces the size of the labour supply and changes the composition of the labour force (Fenwick, Kalula and Landau 2007). In addition, the stigma attached to the disease and the discrimination suffered by HIV positive employees in the workplace further engenders social exclusion among a population already marginalised by other socio-economic elements.

The Informal Economy in SADC

In Africa, the informal economy makes up a significant proportion of the total economy. Estimates put this proportion at almost 80 per cent of non-agricultural employment and at levels exceeding 60 per cent of urban employment and 90 per cent of new jobs in Africa (ILO 2002: 16). In sub-Saharan Africa, the percentage representing total job opportunities outside the agricultural sector is 92 per cent for women and 71 per cent for men: 95 per cent of these jobs are self employed or own- account jobs and a miserly five per cent as paid employment (ibid.)

In most of the SADC countries, the economic situation (in terms of the level of economic growth) is often indicative of size and importance of the informal economy. For example, only 10 per cent of Zambia's economically active population work in the formal economy, with the rest of the population either unemployed or in the informal economy. In 2000 and 2005, the number of workers recorded in the informal economy in South Africa was four million and 3.7 million respectively, constituting 34 per cent and the 31 per cent of the labour force (Valodia 2007).

In countries such as Angola and South Africa, the informal economy takes on the form of retail trade in which formal retailing establishments, distributors and manufacturers use informal workers as middle men between themselves and the low income groups and rural dwellers (ILO 2002: 16). In Zimbabwe and Zambia, cross border trade with South Africa is common, especially among the women (ibid.). Female traders from Zimbabwe and Zambia travel to South Africa to sell goods such as hand-made crafts made in their home countries. In turn, they purchase household goods and appliances, which they take back to sell back home. And in Tanzania, self employment in the nature of small scale enterprises constitutes 74 per cent of the total informal economy. The nature of the informal economy in the country thus mimes the cultural prescription of roles between men and women in most African societies. While women were more likely to be found in activities that required cooking, weaving of mats and fibre production, men were involved in construction, mining, quarrying and transport services (ibid.).

One of the common traits of the informal economy in SADC is its segmentation by gender. For women, more than men, it represents a significant percentage of the total job opportunities.[3] Another notable feature of the informal economy globally is the high prevalence rate of child labour. Children are most vulnerable to all the negative aspects of informality and in sub-Saharan Africa, the highest relative number of working children – about 29 per cent of children between the ages of 5 and 14 – is present (ILO 2002: 26).

Further, the informal economy in the SADC region has grown in size, in response to poverty, underdevelopment, high rates of unemployment and such other harsh economic realities as there are. It is pertinent to state that the informal economy in South Africa has not conformed to this last trend. Here, one of its salient features is the volatility in the nature of its informal economy[4] and the small

3 According to Hunter R. Clarke (quoted in Miller 2006), women have benefited from the expansion of the informal economy in Africa because it allows them the opportunity to escape discriminatory employment practices associated with formal employment.

4 Available data showed an increase in the size of the informal economy between 1997 and 2001, and then a rapid decline by 1 million workers between 2001 and 2002. According to Devey et al. (2003), this might be due to irregularities in data collection methods at the time.

size of the informal sector in comparison with the extremely high unemployment rate (Devey, Skinner and Valodia 2006).

With regard to the informal economy in South Africa, the former South African President Thabo Mbeki implied that its existence is the result of poverty and underdevelopment – introducing the notion of the existence of a dual economy in which there is a de-linkage between the formal and informal economies. He suggested that the 'second economy'– the informal economy – is 'structurally disconnected from both the first and the global economy and is incapable of self generated growth and development' (ibid: 1). Research undertaken by the Human Sciences Research Council in Johannesburg, however, disagrees with this view with what it calls the 'early dualist notions of developing economies' consisting of a modern capitalist sector and a traditional sector. Rather, the Council argues that there is an increasing recognition of the informal sector as having been integrated into the formal sector (ibid.).

Current trends in labour markets may, however, be suggestive of a co-existence between the two divides. In countries such as Angola and South Africa, formal retail establishments, distributors and manufacturers such as Unilever and Coca Cola, are capitalising on the large size of the informal economy to expand their markets to locations too remote for their market strategy (ILO 2002). In such instances, it can be argued that a complementary relationship exists between the formal and informal economies, with the formal economy providing employment for a large segment of workers in the informal economy. However, Valodia (2007) argues that this relationship may not necessarily be complementary, and may be characterised by competition between the informal and formal economies or exploitation of the latter by the former. He suggests another type of relationship between the two economies, which might be anti-cyclical and/or pro-cyclical, i.e., a scenario where the informal economy absorbs workers displaced by a shrinking formal economy, or where the informal economy grows as the formal economy grows due to extensive subcontracting arrangements that may exist, or both scenarios at the same time (ibid.).

Labour market transitions evident in some SADC countries such as Namibia, Zimbabwe and South Africa in the form of casualisation, externalisation and informalisation of labour, also, point to the fact that the informal economy exhibits some features of the formal economy and vice versa.[5] To end this section, the report on Decent Work and the Informal Economy earlier cited, recommends that in developing policy issues for decent work, the focus should be shifted from establishing linkages (that already clearly exist) between the formal and informal

5 Casualisation refers to the 'displacement of standard employment by temporary or part-time employment or both, externalisation refers to a process of economic restructuring in terms of which employment is regulated by a commercial contract rather than a contract of employment, and informalisation refers to the 'process by which unemployment is increasingly unregulated and workers are not protected by the labour law', See Kalula et al. (2007: 18).

economies to determining whether these linkages are 'benign, exploitative or mutually beneficial' with the purpose of enhancing and incorporating the positive linkages (ILO 2002: 38).

This section discussed the history of socio-economic context in the SADC region and outlined the key aspects of labour markets in member states. Importantly, it highlighted key challenges such as poverty, unemployment and inequality, which are largely structured along racial and gender lines. It then highlighted diversity of the informal economy in the SADC, which comprises self-employed traders and workers in casualised, externalised and informalised working arrangements with their employers. It noted the existence of linkages between the formal and informal economies. Having painted a broad picture of key aspects of the socio-economic context, labour markets and the informal economy, we now turn to examine the labour and social protection systems in the SADC.

Labour and Social Protection in the SADC

This section gives an overview of labour regulation and labour rights in SADC countries. It also gives an overview of the social security systems in SADC member states. It highlights the fact that both labour and social protection primarily cater for workers in the formal economy to the exclusion of those in the informal economy.

Labour Law and Regulation of Labour Rights

Labour law in Southern Africa is heavily influenced by its pre-colonial history – a period which was characterised by racially discriminatory policies and laws that sought to regulate temporary labour migration and, impose punishment for non-compliance with these laws (Fenwick, Kalula and Landau 2007). The emergence of labour law in the region, immediately after independence, was still un-tripartite in nature. In Malawi, Lesotho and other then single party ruled states, the State's power of control extended to limiting social organisations and ensuring that their activities conformed to the political ideals of these states (ibid.). With democratisation also came significant reform in the labour law systems, in which individual and collective labour rights became entrenched in the constitution of countries such as Angola, Malawi, Mozambique, Namibia and South Africa, as a reflection of their adoption of multi-party systems (ibid.).

Currently, labour laws in SADC generally embody a range of legislated minimum rights related to wages, hours of work, leave, workplace health and safety, freedom of association, collective organisation and action by workers and employers, and prohibition of child labour and discrimination (ibid.). In addition, a system of dispute resolution, either through mediation, conciliation and/or arbitration, has been introduced in countries such as South Africa, Lesotho, Malawi and Swaziland, with social partners playing a significant role in formulating platforms for dispute resolution and facilitating consultation between social partners (ibid.).

At the regional level, the social partners include National Economic Development and Labour Council (NEDLAC) in South Africa, the Labour Consultative Council in Zambia and Malawi, a tripartite forum in Mozambique, Labour Advisory Committee in Botswana and the Labour Advisory Council (LAC) in Namibia. Internationally, SADC member states, except Madagascar and Namibia, have ratified the entire core ILO Conventions. The ILO has also been instrumental in providing technical assistance and developing technical capacity in the region. Further, Codes of practice covering a wide range of employment related issues, such as under the Labour Relations Act of 1995 adopted first by South Africa, and similar ones subsequently enacted by Botswana and Lesotho, have been introduced. The Codes have been commended because they allow for greater working flexibility than regulation or legislation (ibid.).

These reforms regardless, several challenges continue to plague the successful development of labour law in Southern Africa. First, most current labour legislation and regulation still do not reflect the transitions that have occurred in labour market trends (Kalula, Ordor and Fenwick 2008). In the light of 'new' employment relationships that have emerged, such as casualisation and externalisation, the standard employment relationship as a means of effective labour legislation is inadequate. Second, there is a glaring lack of capacity – in the form of qualified personnel, finances, among other resources – in labour law institutions (trade unions, courts and inspectorates) to meet the challenges that are a necessary outcome in regulating labour markets (ibid.). Other problems include unemployment and income inequality, HIV and AIDS in the workplace and the resulting decline in available work force and resources that would otherwise have been channelled towards economic development that instead go to ameliorating the effects of the virus (ibid.).

Nature and Extent of Social Protection

The concept of social protection encompasses the provision of social security. Beyond this, it extends to access to assets, services such as energy, water, health and education, which assist in asset development, asset replacement and active labour market policies that address labour market failures through employment creation and skills development (NEDLAC 2006). Against this backdrop, social protection in most SADC countries falls short. In practice, social protection is often limited to the provision of social security benefits, which are largely contributory in nature and restricted to a small category of employees in the formal sector who can contribute to such schemes from their earnings.

Countries such as Mauritius, Mozambique, Namibia, South Africa, Zambia and Zimbabwe run on the social insurance schemes, which are available to workers who are formally employed.[6] Even so, these employees do not receive

6 See Pieris Fultz, 'Employment Injury Schemes in Southern Africa: An Overview and Proposals for Future Directions', Available at: www.ilo.org/public/english/region/afpro/harare/download/.../pps7.doc (Accessed: 16 August 2010).

complete coverage – including maternity benefits and health insurance – from such schemes. Though the essence of protection is targeted at vulnerable groups in society, most of who exist in the informal economy, this category of persons does not receive any social protection. For example, in Zambia, where the majority of the population lives in extreme poverty, the provision of social security is based largely on the social insurance model[7] and covers only loss or reduction of income resulting from retirement, disability and death for the formally employed (ILO 2008). By the nature of this system, workers in the informal economy, particularly women and young people,[8] are excluded (ibid: 90). The ambit of the coverage of Zambia's social security system thus currently does not measure up to the ILO prescribed minimum standards Convention (1952, No. 102) of social security (ibid: 68).

In South Africa, the social security system consists of private savings for contingencies; social insurance comprising joint contributions by employers and employees to pension and provident funds; a non-contributory social assistance scheme, which provides income-tested benefits to indigent groups such as the disabled, elderly people and unsupported parents and children; and the provision of a non-contributory social relief which is a short term measure for people who are in distress (Olivier et al. 1999: 122).[9] Except for the means tested universal pension scheme, social security in South Africa is largely characterised by the absence of a national pension scheme and a reliance on the private sector to provide benefits on an optional basis, which in turn has yielded unevenness in the coverage of the workforce (ibid.). Though the scope of coverage in South Africa is wider than it is in Zambia and some other countries in the region, with its inclusion of social assistance and social relief measures, South Africa continues to discriminate against people in the informal economy who do not meet the criteria necessary to qualify for these schemes.

In this section, we examined the extent to which the SADC member states' labour and social protection systems address the needs of workers in the informal economy. We found that despite the growing prominence of the informal economy, access to labour rights and social protection is largely restricted to formal economy workers, with informal economy workers being ignored and excluded. In the absence of national and regional instruments to protect informal economy workers,

7 This comprises joint contributions by employers and employees to pension, provident and medical aid funds.

8 This applies to young people who have completed their secondary or tertiary education and are entering the labour market. It excludes children below the relevant minimum age for employment.

9 The South African Social Security Agency (SASSA) defines a person in distress as a person who is unable to meet their or their family's most basic needs. This may be the result of inability to work, death of the breadwinner, or a natural disaster. See 'Social Relief of Distress', available at http://www.sassa.gov.za/SOCIAL-RELIEF-643.aspx (Accessed: 12 September 2010).

it is necessary to look at international approaches to addressing the challenges faced by workers in the informal economy.

The Conceptual Framework for Decent Work and Legal Empowerment

This section outlines two international approaches to address the labour and social protection challenges experienced by informal economy workers in the SADC region. The first is the Decent Work Agenda, which was developed by the ILO in the late 1990s, and aims to ensure that decent work is a reality for workers in both the formal and the informal economy. The second is the work of the Commission of Legal Empowerment of the Poor (CLEP), which encompasses the notion of decent work but also calls for the recognition and protection of the broader legal rights of the poor to ensure their empowerment and access to economic opportunities.

The International Labour Organisation's 'Decent Work Agenda'

The Decent Work Agenda was developed by the ILO in response to the challenges experienced by people throughout the world, including unemployment and underemployment, poor quality and unproductive jobs, unsafe work and insecure income, gender inequality, exploitation of vulnerable workers and lack of representation and voice (ILO 2006a).

Decent Work is a concept that envisions a workplace environment where the following are protected and promoted: opportunities for work and fair income, security in the workplace, social protection for families, better prospects for personal development and social integration, equality of treatment and opportunity for all, and freedom to express their concerns, organise and participate in decisions affecting workers (ibid.). The Decent Work Agenda can be narrowed down to four strategic objectives – rights at work, employment, social protection and social dialogue.

The ILO in partnership with its tripartite constituents pushes for the integration of these objectives into strategies for poverty reduction and a fair and inclusive globalisation. At the national level, Decent Work Country Programmes (DWCPs) have been developed to translate the Decent Work Agenda into their specific national policy environments, taking into consideration, of course, each country's peculiar economic, social and political situation (ibid.). Although the content of DWCPs will vary from country to country, certain key principles must be adhered to in the process of defining this content.

First, the DWCPs are organised around a few selected country programme priorities and outcomes, which are further detailed in an implementation plan (ILO 2008). Second, the implementation plan must facilitate policy coherence and resource integration through, for instance, identifying action in different technical areas, identifying various means of actions (ibid: 4–7). In addition, social dialogue and tripartism are central to the formulation and implementation of the plans. DWCPs must also support performance management and more transparent accountability through monitoring, reporting and evaluation. They must also be dynamic, reflecting the circumstances in which they are developed, but responsive to changes affecting the member state (ibid.).

The ILO provides member states with financial and technical support for the drafting, implementation, monitoring and evaluation of DWCPs. To date, a number of ILO member states have participated in the Decent Work Country Programme, and are at various stages of formulating and implementing their DWCPs.

The Commission for Legal Empowerment of the Poor (CLEP)

As the first global initiative of its kind – with specific focus on the link between poverty, exclusion and law – the Commission of Legal Empowerment of the Poor (CLEP) was launched in 2005, by a team of policymakers and, practitioners from a pool of developing and industrialised countries,[10] to seek practical solutions to the worldwide scourge and challenges of poverty (UNDP 2008).[11] The working principle of CLEP was that poverty reduction is achievable, if proper legal mechanisms that recognise and protect the rights of the poor are formulated and entrenched (UNDP 2006a). As stated in its mission statement, the Commission 'aims to make legal protection and economic opportunity not the privilege of the few but the right of all' (UNDP 2006a).

Two key features of the work of CLEP in seeking to develop laws favourable to the poor made its work unique and are worthy of mention. The first was its willingness to partner with relevant stakeholders, such as grassroots organisations, governments and institutions including the International Labour Organisation and the United Nations Development Programme. The second was its emphasis on working through groups comprising world experts in the area of legal empowerment (ibid.).

The mandate of these working groups was to produce final reports that would inform and guide policymaking. The working groups focused on four pillars of legal empowerment of the poor: rule of law and access to justice; property rights; labour rights, and business rights (CLEP 2008: 4). CLEP's key conclusions and recommendations regarding these four pillars are outlined below.

Access to justice is essential for legal empowerment of the poor. Making access to justice a reality for the poor requires more than merely ensuring that the legal system is technically inclusive and fair (ibid: 5–6). It requires the commitment of state and public institutions to take positive and substantive measures to ensure

10 These countries include Canada, Denmark, Egypt, Finland, Guatemala, Iceland, Norway, Sweden, South Africa, Tanzania and the United Kingdom.

11 'Unlocking Human Potential', available at: http://www.undp.org/legalempowerment/who/ [Accessed: 19 August 2009].

that the legal system is sensitive to the needs and circumstances of the poor (ibid.). Such measures include the facilitation of organisations and institutions that work in the interest of the poor and taking measures to ensure that the poor know about laws and can take advantage of them.

Property rights are also critical for legal empowerment because they facilitate the inclusion of the poor in the formal economy and are a tool for their upward social mobility. Securing and protecting the property rights of the poor involves taking measures to ensure that their individual and collective rights (including customary rights) to property are formally recognised and are enforceable (ibid: 6–7). Measures should also be taken to ensure security of tenure of the poor by limiting the circumstances in which evictions can take place and requiring that they be executed according to due process (ibid.).

CLEP recognises that legal empowerment of the poor also entails that their labour and human capital be effectively recognised and protected (ibid: 7–8). This entails upholding the 'emerging global social contract', which has three components. The first entails the enforcement of the minimum core of labour rights enshrined in the ILO's Declaration on the Fundamental Principles and Rights at Work of 1998. The four fundamental principles are freedom of association and the right to collective bargaining; the elimination of forced labour, the elimination of child labour and the elimination of discrimination.

The second component of the emerging global contract relates to the promotion of the ILO's Decent Work Agenda, which is discussed in more detail below (ibid: 8–9). The third component relates to measures to protect and promote the rights of workers in the informal economy, including measures to ensure that they have access to social protection and to health care, medical insurance and pensions (ibid.).

The fourth pillar in the legal empowerment framework recognises that the poor are entitled to rights when developing their own businesses. Legal measures in the business rights domain include guaranteeing basic business rights such as the right to trade, to have a workspace and to have access to infrastructure. In addition, measures must be taken to ensure the ease and affordability of setting up a business, accessing markets and exiting a business. Measures should also be taken to promote inclusive financial services that offer savings, credit, and insurance and pensions facilities to entrepreneurs in the developing world (ibid.).

The Commission also charted a road map for the implementation of the measures discussed above. It recommends that the four pillars be implemented as a comprehensive strategy and not in piecemeal fashion. It further acknowledges the importance of political leadership in driving the agenda and creating political momentum. It also emphasises that the participation of citizens and grass-roots organisations can create valuable momentum and improve the lives of the poor (ibid: 9).

Though the mandate of the Commission was for three years and ended in 2008, the significance of its work still resonates in academic, legal and policymaking circles.[12] The findings and publications of the Commission on poverty alleviation have become a useful resource for countries, researchers, policymakers and the public.

Significance of the Decent Work Agenda and the Work of CLEP for the Informal Economy

The informal economy is characterised by unemployment, underemployment, poor working conditions, little or no social and legal protection in places of work. Relevant, also, is the relationship between poverty and the informal economy. As the International Labour Organisation suggests, 'Decent Work Deficit'[13] provides the most consistent way of analysing the situation of people in the informal economy.[14] The Decent Work Agenda and the Commission for Legal Empowerment have undertaken initiatives geared towards poverty alleviation and instituting mechanisms that ensure proper conditions of work and living – initiatives that are crucial to 'eliminating the negative aspects of informality (and) ensuring at the same time survival and entrepreneurial opportunities and fostering the protection and incorporation of workers and economic units of the informal economy into the formal economy'.[15] To support the regulation of the informal economy, the Resolution Concerning Decent Work and the Informal Economy was adopted by the International Labour Conference in 2002 at its 90th Session in Geneva.

The ILO's Decent Work agenda goes further than merely articulating ideals that countries must strive towards. Its Decent Work Country Programme requires states to take carefully developed and concrete measures to ensure that member states make decent work a reality in the lives of all workers, including those in the informal economy. By allowing for flexibility and the participation of all interested stakeholders in the development of DWCPs ensure their relevance to the labour market and enable them to tailor them to meet the distinct challenges faced by informal economy workers.

The work of CLEP can be seen as including and building upon the Decent Work Agenda. While endorsing the need to take targeted measures to address vulnerability in the labour market, the Commission adopts a broader approach to

12 The UNDP has continued with several aspects of the CLEP's work on legal empowerment of the poor.

13 Decent Work Deficit includes the gaps and exclusions in the form of unemployment and underemployment, poor quality and unproductive jobs, unsafe work and insecure income, gender inequality, exploited migrant workers, lack of representation and voice and inadequate social protection. See ILO 'Decent Work FAQ: Making Decent Work a global goal', http://www.ilo.org/global/About_the_ILO/Media_and_public_information/Feature_stories/lang--en/WCMS_071241/index.htm (Accessed: 20 August 2009).

14 See 'Informal Economy-Decent Work-Poverty', Available at: http://www.ilo.org/public/english/region/ampro/cinterfor/temas/informal/tdecpob/index.htm, (Accessed: 20 August 2009).

15 Ibid.

poverty and exclusion. It emphasises the need to address lack of access to other rights that bring about vulnerability of the poor, including workers in the informal economy. It argues that increasing access to property rights and business rights of the poor will ensure that they become part of the mainstream economy and comply with relevant laws. Arguably, these include labour and social protection laws. It also requires that states ensure that the poor have access to justice through legal reforms that ensure that they are accommodated in the justice system. This would ensure that the poor, particularly those in the informal economy, would be empowered to enforce their labour and social protection rights.

To conclude, both approaches are useful to countries needing to ensure the social protection of workers in the informal economy. Although adopting different approaches, they are not mutually exclusive and can be adopted in conjunction with each other to ensure the protection of workers in the informal economy. We now turn to a comparative analysis and consider the measures taken by two developing countries to address challenges in the informal economy.

Comparative Benchmarking: Brazil and India

It is important to consider lessons learnt in other jurisdictions aiming to address challenges in the informal economy. In this section, we consider two leading developing jurisdictions, namely India and Brazil, which both have a significant proportion of people working in the informal economy. We give a brief profile of the informal economy in the respective jurisdictions and then discuss the extent to which they have been successful in efforts to ensure the labour and social protection of workers in the informal economy. Using India and Brazil for our comparative benchmarking is intentional. They both have high prevalence rates of informality in their countries with less than adequate labour and social protection laws, and are both located within developing country contexts. The possible lessons that SADC countries may glean from these are considered in the section six of the paper.

India

The National Commission for Enterprises in the Unorganised Sector estimates that 50 per cent of India's Gross Domestic Product was contributed by the informal economy in 2004–5 (NCEUS 2007). There has been a continued increase in size of the informal economy even when its Gross Domestic Product (GDP) reflected an increase in economic growth (Chen 2006), and the informal sector is largely responsible for absorbing the influx of workers from the formal economy during the reform period (Harris-White 2002).

The size of the informal economy – otherwise known as the 'unorganised sector' in India – is just as significant as its population size, comprising 370 million workers and about per cent of its total workforce, the majority of whom are poor (NCEUS 2007; 2009). Like informal economies in other developing countries, it is segmented by nature of work, especially in the areas of agriculture, trade and construction (Chen 2006). It is structured according to informal employment in agriculture (small farmers and agricultural labour), informal employment in informal enterprises (employers, own account workers and employees), and informal employment outside informal enterprises (industrial home workers subcontracted by formal firms and domestic workers engaged by households) (ibid.). The sheer magnitude of India's informal economy undoubtedly presents significant challenges for the government to ensure the labour protection and social protection of the affected workers.

Regardless of these challenges, India has made efforts to bring its informal economy within the purview of state regulation. An important initiative to provide social security to vulnerable workers is the workers welfare boards established by the national government from as early as 1946. These are organised according to industries such as construction, mining and the *beedi* (Indian cigarettes) industry (Chatterjee 2008: 108–9). These boards are funded through a cess or tax levied on the final product and paid by employers. The government administers the funds, but worker and employers' representatives are members of the board and play a role in planning, developing and implementation of social protection measures. Benefits typically include health insurance, child-care, maternity benefits and housing (ibid.).

The government has also made efforts to regulate all workers in the informal economy, regardless of sector or industry. These efforts date as far back as 1969, when the First National Commission on Labour devoted its attention to the informal economy (NCEUS 2007). Currently, India stands as one of the two or three countries in the world that has collected data as a basis for measuring all informal employment in the economy, both inside and outside informal enterprises (Chen 2006). The National Commissions on Self Employed Workers, and Labour, set up by the Indian government, have been instrumental in drafting legislation and recommending policies in recognition of the informal economy; more specifically, a National Policy for urban street vendors which was adopted by the Ministry of Urban Development and Poverty Alleviation in 2004 (Government of India 2004; Chen 2006). One of the primary objectives of the latter policy is to provide and promote a supportive environment for the earning livelihoods of street traders (Government of India 2004).

In addition, the Second National Labour Commission, set up in 1999, worked in partnership with organisations of informal workers to draft legislation for the informal workforce (ILO 2002: 51). It proposed the enactment of comprehensive legislation to cover social security and welfare, regulation of employment and conditions of work, as well as promotion of livelihoods for workers in the informal economy (NCEUS 2007). The proposed legislation would cover issues such as social security, health and safety, working hours, holidays, prohibition of child labour, unfair labour practices and training and skills development (ibid.). A central board at national level and state boards at the state levels would administer these. The proposed legislation was modified by the government and subsequent commissions, but forms the basis of the current legislation governing social security for workers in the informal economy, which is discussed below.

The national government also established the National Commission for Enterprises in the Unorganised Sector (NCEUS), which falls under the Ministry of Small Scale Enterprises. It is an advisory body and watchdog for the informal sector, and aims to improve the productivity of informal enterprises to ensure the sustainable generation of employment opportunities.[16] Through its various task forces, it addresses and makes recommendations on the definition and measurement of the unorganised sector, social security for workers in the unorganised sectors, skill formation in the unorganised sector and the impact of labour laws on the labour market.

The Unorganised Sector Workers' Social Security Scheme was similarly introduced by the national government, on a pilot basis, in 50 districts.[17] The scheme covers old age pension, personal accident insurance and medical insurance and applies compulsorily to registered employers who are required to contribute to the scheme with their employees (CLEP 2008). Self employed workers may also become members of the scheme on a voluntary basis and are required in this case, to pay worker and employer contributions, the governments also pays contributions.

In 2008, the Indian government enacted the Unorganised Workers' Social Security Act 33 of 2008, which provides for a framework within which the social security rights of workers in the organised sector are to be promoted and protected. It delineates responsibility for social security schemes for unorganised workers between the central government and state government.[18] It also provides for the establishment of a National Social Security Board and State Social Security Boards for unorganised workers.[19] These boards must make recommendations and advise the respective governments on suitable schemes and monitor and review the implementation of social security schemes in terms of the Act.[20]

India provides some valuable lessons for SADC countries wishing to address the challenges in the informal economy. Chief amongst these is the need to foster partnerships between government and grass roots organisations that represent those in the informal economy. The participation of informal economy workers in the development and implementation of social schemes ensures that these programmes are relevant to their intended beneficiaries (Chatterjee 2008: 110). In addition, the state government of Gujarat is further working in partnership with

---

16 Information obtained from the website of the NCEUS, www.nceuis.nic.in (Accessed: 12 September 2010).

17 Directorate General, Labour Welfare, 'Salient Features of the Unorganised Sector Social Security Scheme', http://labour.nic.in/dglw/welcome.html (Accessed: 12 September 2010).

18 See sections 3 and 4 of the Act.

19 See sections 5 and 6 of the Act.

20 See sections 5 and 6 of the Act.

the Self-Employed Women's Association (SEWA) in monitoring the conditions of home workers and establishing minimum piece rates that would be consistent with minimum wage provisions (ILO 2002: 52). SEWA has one of the largest contributory social security schemes for informal workers in the world, covering about 93,000 insured members, being women workers and their husbands (Chatterjee 2008: 107).

Another lesson is the need to develop innovative solutions that take cognisance of the circumstances and needs of those in the informal economy. One example of this is the provision of child care in welfare funds, which is not usually a component of social security in the formal economy, but is nevertheless a pressing need for those in the informal economy (ibid: 110).

India has also developed a Decent Work Country Programme with the support of the ILO for the period 2007–12. The key objectives in the DWCP include enhancing the capacities of partners to contribute more effectively in policy-making; strengthening implementation of policy; restructuring training and employment services, especially within the informal economy; strengthening sector and area-based approaches for sustainable livelihoods and the formulation and extension of social protection policies (ILO 2007b).

Despite the strides that India has made in trying to protect workers in the informal sector, significant challenges remain. One relates to the Unorganised Workers Social Security Act, which is merely procedural. Critics have argued that it does not go far enough to bring about the NCEUS' recommendations, which made provision for substantial and enforceable rights for unorganised workers (Sankaran 2008). An additional challenge relates to the regulation of terms and conditions of work. The NCEUS reports that existing labour legislation only covers informal economy workers in a piece-meal and inadequate manner (NCEUS 2007). Another shortcoming is that present legislation and policies do not go far enough to protect enhance the earnings and livelihood of informal economy workers (ibid.). We now turn to Brazil, which has adopted a different approach to addressing the challenges in the informal economy.

Brazil

In Brazil, work in the informal economy implies work outside the regulation of the state and is therefore devoid of any form of labour or social protection (UNDP 2006b). Most of the workers in the informal economy do not have formal identification, i.e. neither identity cards nor birth certificates. Persons without birth certificates therefore do not benefit from social services such as education, health plans and pensions, or participate in social processes such as formal employment and voting. Lack of any formal identity also excludes informal workers from formally owning property and accessing full credit (ibid.). Self-employed workers are grouped together with illegal or unregistered employees for purposes of defining and measuring the informal economy (ILO 2002: 52). Currently, over 60 per cent (about 48 million people) of the entire Brazilian workforce are employed in its informal economy and the majority can be found in the textile and transport sectors.[21] As has been the trend with informality around the world, a higher percentage of women (66 per cent) than men (59 per cent), work in this economy (ILO 2002: 18).

Child labour and forced labour are prevalent in Brazil, and in order to keep them invisible, are largely relegated to the informal economy. Child labour is a significant challenge in Brazil, although its incidence has reportedly declined from 8.42 million to 4.85 million between 1992 and 2007 (ILO 2009: 25–6). These figures account for 19.6 per cent and 10.8 per cent of the total number of children between the ages of five and 17 years respectively for those years (ibid.). The proportion of children between the ages of 10 and 14 who work declined from 20.5 per cent in 1992 to 8.5 per cent in 2007. Forced labour takes various forms, for instance, the use of violence, or threats of violence or death, confinement, punishment of a financial nature or the withholding of the victim's personal documents (ibid.).

The growth of the informal economy has been attributed to high taxes imposed on formal businesses, and the high costs and bureaucratic difficulties of starting a business (Ernst 2008: 31).[22] Having one of the world's fastest growing urban population means that a greater percentage of Brazil's population live in urban areas, most of whom are wage earners and can only afford to live in slums (UNDP 2006b). Furthermore, poor educational and skills levels in the labour market have also contributed to low-productivity, particularly in the informal economy (Ernst 2008: 31).

A recent ILO assessment of Brazil's progress towards making decent work a reality for workers in Brazil demonstrates that workers in the informal economy are largely excluded from labour and social security protection. Legislation relating to working hours and leave are largely unenforced in the informal economy (ILO 2009: 15–16). Maternity leave and the accompanying social security benefits are restricted to workers with signed employment contracts and who have contributed to the relevant social security fund (ibid: 21). This effectively excludes the vast majority of working women who work in the informal economy. The provisions governing dismissal and the provision of unemployment insurance are also restricted to workers who have signed employment contracts and who have contributed to the insurance fund, thus restricting it to workers in the formal economy (ibid: 31). The position is similar for laws providing for employment injury benefits, which exclude own-account workers.

Furthermore, informal economy workers are *in law* covered by protections for freedom of association and the right to organise, but are not protected in practice

21 See, 'Brazil's Informal Economy Absorbs 60% of Workforce', MercoPress-South Atlantic News Agency, 31 July 2006, http://en.mercopress.com/2006/07/31/brazil-s-informal-economy-absorbs-60-of-workforce (Accessed: 29 August 2009).

22 Also see http://en.mercopress.com/2006/07/31/brazil-s-informal-economy-absorbs-60-of-workforce (Accessed: 29 August 2009).

(ibid: 50). Moreover, most of the legislation excludes domestic and agricultural workers, who form a significant proportion of the informal economy and are constitute vulnerable segments of the informal economy.

The above shows that Brazil has done very little to make labour and social protection provisions accessible to the workers in the informal economy. The only measures Brazil has taken in the informal economy are improving access to credit, rights to ownership of property and reducing the bureaucracies associated with registering and owning formal businesses (UNDP 2006b). It is clear that Brazil has not taken a comprehensive approach to addressing the challenges of the informal economy. We submit that without direct measures targeted at extending labour and social protection rights to workers in the informal economy, the measures adopted in Brazil cannot bring about substantive change in their lives.

Having considered the different approaches taken in these developing country jurisdictions, we now draw together the lessons emerging from this comparative analysis and from discussions in preceding sections.

Addressing Informality: What Lessons for the SADC?

This section aims to draw together the discussions in the foregoing sections in order to draw lessons for the SADC. What emerges from the preceding sections is that the SADC is a region that, while having lot of potential, faces many challenges in relation to the informal economy and the legal empowerment of the poor. Extreme poverty, an increasing informal economy and the scourge of HIV and AIDS beset Southern Africa. Although there is some indication that some policies are being developed to tackle poverty and enhance social protection, legal empowerment of the poor in the context of labour market regulation is not systematic.

There is, however, an increasing realisation that the informal economy is a permanent feature of labour markets in Southern Africa. There are also apparent efforts to reform labour market regulation in pursuit of better implementation of labour rights, social dialogue and social protection. Efforts are being made at both regional and individual country levels. What is nonetheless distinctly absent is the realisation to extend the current frameworks of labour market regulation to include the informal economy and legal empowerment of the poor.

We observe in this chapter that one of the factors that hamper the provision of decent work especially in the informal economy is the content of current national labour laws that do not go beyond the formal economy. The exclusion of the informal economy inevitably denies the poor legal empowerment. In order to begin to address this deficit, it is necessary to utilise the existing regulatory frameworks to implement the legal empowerment of the poor and provide social protection. What is needed in all SADC jurisdictions is the realisation to embark on such programmes in a systematic way.

The Decent Work agenda of the ILO, and, in particular, the Decent Work Country Programme could play a meaningful role in enabling SADC countries to take concrete measures to protect workers in the informal economy, taking into consideration the peculiar socio-economic factors in each country. India provides many valuable lessons in this regard, having enacted legislation and implemented policies aimed at protecting informal economy workers from as early as the 1950s. We conclude that India has taken on a more systematic approach in dealing with its informal economy by adopting different policy and legislative approaches in dealing with the different components of its informal economy, and we dare say, has recorded relative success because it recognises and works in partnership with different informal organisations. India has also adopted a DWCP, which it is hoped, will strengthen existing mechanisms to ensure the protection of workers in the informal economy.

However, the work of CLEP has shown that targeted labour legislation and policies aimed at protecting informal economy workers is not enough and that a broader approach of legal empowerment is necessary. Importantly, these should ensure that more enterprises operate on a formal basis and that workers have access to the justice system to enable them to enforce their labour and social protection rights. While Brazil has adopted these reforms, they have not been adopted labour market reforms to improve conditions of work and social security, and as a result have been unsuccessful in protecting workers in the informal economy.

While a number of lessons can be gleaned by SADC countries, a number of challenges to the implementation of these measures remain. Chief amongst these is the lack of financial and technical capacity to design and implement reforms to ensure that workers in the informal economy are recognised and adequately protected.

Conclusion

In this chapter, we have provided an overview of legal empowerment of the poor in the informal economy in the context of labour markets in Southern Africa. It is necessarily an eclectic effort giving no more than an overview at best. The approaches of the Commission on the Legal Empowerment of the Poor and the ILO Decent Work Agenda have informed the paper. We have also discussed the feasibility of utilising the emerging comparative experience in two leading jurisdictions in the developing world, Brazil and India.

One of the factors that hamper the provision of decent work, especially in the informal economy, is that the content of current national labour laws does not recognise work relationships outside the formal economy. The scope of labour laws and social protection should therefore be made more inclusive to reflect the 'new' forms of employment relationships that have emerged in the region.

The ILO has taken the initiative by expanding the scope of workers who come within the definition of the informal economy with its resolution concerning Decent Work, and reiterating the need for countries to adopt poverty reduction and gender inclusive strategies in formulating laws that support decent work. We also believe that basic minimum standards on substantive matters should be extended to include workers in the informal economy. Areas to be given priority include conditions of work, safety and health, income security, and basic rules for fair treatment relating to job security and vulnerable groups.

Apart from legislation and ILO standards, this analysis (based mainly on secondary sources) shows that there is a need for more empirical research in the different SADC jurisdictions to validate the findings. Such work needs to adopt a multi-disciplinary approach, drawing on the knowledge of experts in fields including labour law, sociology and economics.

References

Becker, K.F. 2004. *The Informal Economy from http://www.sida.se* [Online]. Available at: http://rru.worldbank.org/Documents/PapersLinks/Sida.pdf [Accessed: 24 September 2010].

Chatterjee, M. 2008. Social Protection in the Changing World of Work: Experiences of Informal Women Workers in India, in N. Kudva and L. Beneria, *Rethinking Informalization: Poverty, Precarious Jobs and Social Protection*, Cornell University Open Access Repository. Available at: http://www.wiego.org/publications/Rethinking_Informalization.pdf [Accessed on 12 September 2010].

Chen, M. 2004. Rethinking the Informal Economy: Linkages with the Formal Economy and the Formal Regulatory Environment, EDGI and UNU-WIDER Conference paper Unlocking Human Potential: Linking the Informal and Formal Sectors. 17–18 September 2004, Helsinki, Finland.

Cohen, D. 2009. Poverty and HIV/AIDS in Sub-Saharan Africa, *HIV and Development Programme Issues* Paper No. 27, 2009. UNDP. Available at: http://www.undp.org/hiv/publications/issues/english/issue27e.html [Accessed 18 August 2009].

Commission on Legal Empowerment of the Poor. 2008. *Making the Law Work for Everyone*, Final Report Parts 1–4, Available at: http://www.undp.org/legalempowerment/report/index.html [Accessed 24 September 2010].

Desmond, C. 1998. Poverty and HIV/ AIDS in Sub-Saharan Africa', *HIV and Development Programme Issues* Paper No. 27, Available at: http://www.undp.org [Accessed on 12 August 2009].

Devey, R., Skinner, C. and Valodia, I. 2003. Informal Economy Employment Data in South Africa: A Critical Analysis, Paper presented at the TIPS AND DPRU FORUM 2003, The Challenge of Growth and Poverty: The South African Economy since Democracy, 8–10 September 2003, Indaba Hotel. Johannesburg, Available at: http://www.wiego.org/publications/devey%20skinner%20valodia%20Informal%20Economy%20employment%20data%20in%20ZA.pdf [Accessed: 27 August 2009].

Devey, R., Skinner, C. and Valodia, I. 2006. Second Best? Trends and Linkages in the Informal Economy in South Africa, Development Policy Research Unit Working Paper 06/102. Available at: www.commerce.uct.ac.za/research_units/...//WorkingPapers/.../WP06-102.pdf [Accessed: 24 September 2010].

Directorate General, Labour of Welfare. Date Unavailable. Salient Features of the Unorganised Sector Social Security Scheme. Available at: http://labour.nic.in/dglw/welcome.html [Accessed: 12 September 2010].

Ernst, C. 2008. Recent Dynamics in Brazil's Labour Market, Available at: http://ideas.repec.org/p/ilo/empelm/2007-10.html. [Accessed: 20 September 2010].

Fenwick, C. and Kalula, E.R. 2004. Law and Labour Market Regulation in East Asia and Southern Africa: Comparative Perspectives, *Development and Labour Monograph Series*, 2: 1–42. Institute of Development and Labour Law, University of Cape Town, Occasional Paper 2 of 2004.

Fenwick, C., Kalula, E.R. and Landau, I. 2007. Labour Law: A Southern African Perspective, *Discussion Paper Series*, DP/180/2007, the International Institute for Labour Studies, IILS. Geneva.

Fultz, P. Date unavailable. Employment Injury Schemes in Southern Africa: An Overview and Proposals for Future Directions, in ILO/SAMAT Policy Paper No. 7. Available at: www.ilo.org/public/english/region/afpro/harare/download/.../pps7.doc [Accessed: 16 August 2010].

Government of India. 2004. National Policy for Urban Street Vendors; [Online]. accessed from http://mhupa.gov.in/policies/natpol.htm [Accessed on 12 September 2010].

Hanlon, J. 1989. *SADCC in the 1990s: Development on the Front Line*, Economist Intelligence Unit, London; New York.

Harris-White, B. 2002. India's Informal Economy-Facing the 21st Century. Paper for the Indian Economy Conference, Cornell University, 19–20 April, 2002.

ILO. 2002. *Decent Work and the Informal Economy, Report VI*, International Labour Conference 90th Session 2002, Available at: www.ilo.org/public/english/standards/relm/ilc/ilc90/pdf/rep-vi.pdf [Accessed 24 September 2004].

ILO. 2003. Charter of Fundamental Social Rights in SADC adopted on 5 August 2003. Dar-es-Salaam.

ILO. 2006. *Decent Work FAQ: Making Decent Work a Global Goal*, Available at: http://www.ilo.org/global/About_the_ILO/Media_and_public_information/Feature_stories/lang--en/WCMS_071241/index.htm [Accessed 20 August 2009].

ILO. 2007a. *The Decent Work Agenda in Africa 2007–2015: Report of the Director General*, Eleventh African Regional Meeting Addis Ababa, April 2007, International Labour Office Geneva from http://www.ilo.org [Online]. Available at http://www.ilo.org/global/What_we_do/Publications/Officialdocuments/Director Generalsreports/lang--en/docName--WCMS_082282/index.htm. [Accessed on 21 August 2009].

ILO. 2007b. *Decent Work Country Programme: India (2007–2012).* Available at: http://www.ilo.org/public/english/bureau/program/dwcp/download/india.pdf [Accessed on 1 August 2009].

ILO. 2008. *Decent Work Country Programmes A Guidebook, Version 2* from http://ww.ilo.org [Online]. Available at: http://www.ilo.org/public/english/bureau/program/dwcp/download/guidev2.pdf I [Accessed 12 September 2010].

ILO. 2008. *Zambia-Social Protection Expenditure and Performance Review and Social Budget*, ILO. Harare.

ILO. Date unavailable. *Informal Economy-Decent Work-Poverty* from http://www.ilo.org [Online]. Available at: http://www.ilo.org/public/english/region/ampro/cinterfor/temas/informal/tdecpob/index.htm [Accessed 20 August 2009].

ILO. 2006. *Declaration on Fundamental Principles and Rights at Work – International Organisation of Employers (IOE)* Position Paper, January 2006 [Online]. Available at: http://www.wilsoncenter.org/events/docs/pos_2006_ilodeclaration.pdf [Accessed 30 August 2009].

Kalula, E.R., Ordor, O. and Fenwick, C. 2008. *Labour Law Reforms that Support Decent Work: The Case of Southern Africa. Issue Paper No. 28.* ILO. Harare.

MercoPress–South Atlantic News Agency, 31 July 2006. Brazil's Informal Economy Absorbs 60% of Workforce. [Online]Available at: http://en.mercopress.com/2006/07/31/brazil-s-informal-economy-absorbs-60-of-workforce [Accessed 29 August 2009].

Miller, B.J. 2006. Living outside the Law: How the Informal Economy Frustrates Enforcement of the Human Rights Regime for Billions of the World's Most Marginalized Citizens. *NorthWestern Journal of International Human Rights*, Vol. 5(1), 127–52.

National Commission on Enterprises in the Unorganized Sector (NCEUS). 2007. Report on Comprehensive Legislation for Minimum Conditions of Work and Social Security for Unorganised Workers [Online]. Available at: http://www.nceuis.nic.in/Report_Bill_July_2007_index.htm [Accessed on 12 September 2009].

National Commission for Enterprises in the Unorganised Sector (NCEUS). 2008. Contribution of the Unorganised Sector to GD Report of the Sub Committee of a NCEUS Task Force [Online]. Available at: http://nceuis.nic.in/Final_Booklet_Working_Paper_2.pdf. [Accessed 9 September 2010].

National Commission for Enterprises in the Unorganised Sector (NCEUS). 2009. *Growth Pole Programme for Unorganised Sector Enterprise Development* [Online]. Available at: http://www.nceuis.nic.in/Growth_Pole_Programme.pdf. [Accessed on 12 September 2010].

NEDLAC Community Constituency Position Paper. 2006. *Impact of Labour Market Policy on the Informal Economy- Analysis and Recommendations* [Online]. Available at: http://www.streetnet.org.za/wp-content/pdf/Nedlacpaper.pdf [Accessed 26 June 2009].

Olivier, M.P, Okpaluba, C., Smit, N. and Thompson, M. 1999. *Social Security Law – General Principles, xxxvii.* Durban: Butterworths.

SADC. 2003. *Charter of Fundamental Social Rights in SADC.* Dar es Salaam

SADC. 2009a. *SADC Profile* fromhttp://www.sadc.int [Online], Available at: http://www.sadc.int/index/browse/page/52 [accessed: 17 August 2009].

SADC. 2009b. *SADC Objectives* from http://www.sadc.int/ [Online], Available at: http://www.sadc.int/index/browse/page/52 [Accessed 17 August 2009].

Sankaran, T.A. 2008. Critique of India's Unorganised Workers' Social Security Act, 2008 [Online], Available at: http://www.sacw.net/article658.html [Accessed on 12 September 2010].

UNDP. 2006a. *From Concept to Action: Outcome Document from the Second Meeting.* From http://www.undp.org [Online]. Available at: www.undp.org/legalempowerment/reports/concept2action.html [Accessed on 19 August 2009].

UNDP. 2006b. High Level Commission on Legal Empowerment of the Poor (HLCELP) from www.undp.org [Online]. Available at: www.undp.org/legalempowerment/pdf/HLCLEP_Overview.pdf [Accessed 26 September 2010].

UNDP. 2008. *Unlocking Human Potential* from http://www.undp.org [Online]. Available at: http://www.undp.org/legalempowerment/who/ [Accessed 19 August 2009].

Valodia, I. 2007. *Informal Employment in South Africa*, Human Sciences Research Council. South Africa from http://www.hsrc.ac.za [Online]. Available at: http://www.hsrc.ac.za/Research_Publication-20193.phtml [Accessed 24 September 2010]

Chapter 3
Poverty, Legal Empowerment and Informal Business in South Africa

Marlese von Broembsen

Introduction

Nomfundo Maka sells groceries from a small tuck-shop, referred to in South Africa as a 'spaza',[1] from a room in her 'shack'[2] in Khayelitsha, a dormitory 'town' approximately 30 kilometres outside Cape Town. Her customers are her neighbours, who also live in the informal settlement.

The premise of the Commission for the Legal Empowerment of the Poor (hereafter CLEP) is that Nomfundo chooses to operate her business informally because there are 'regulatory hurdles' – such as the cost of necessary licenses – that prevent her and other poor people from registering as, and meeting the compliance requirements of, a formal business (CLEP 2008a). Consequently, the CLEP argues for legal reform in two broad areas. The first area of legal reform is the attenuation of regulatory 'red tape', that CLEP argues is the primary reason why poor people's businesses remain informal. The second is to develop a 'package of business rights' that include the rights to vend, to a workspace and access to basic infrastructure such as shelter, electricity, water and sanitation (ibid.).

In South Africa, these recommendations have traction for informal traders, who sell their goods from pavements and stalls in city centres. However, while informal traders are the most visible of informal businesses, they constitute a small minority. Home-based businesses and businesses that operate from stalls and premises in dormitory suburbs, such as Khayelitsha, and that sell their goods and services to their local markets, namely other poor people, constitute the majority of informal businesses in South Africa.

While the CLEP's 'package of rights' would improve the living and working conditions of Nomfundo and others like her, neither these rights, nor reducing regulatory red tape would enable these businesses, that often constitute little more than marginal economic activities, to sell their goods and services to formal

1 Spaza means 'camouflage' in Zulu. During the apartheid era, it was illegal for black Africans to own a business. Businesses operated illegally nonetheless. A Coca Cola sign erected on the wall of a house signalled to customers that a grocery store or 'spaza' operated from the house.

2 'Shacks' are informal homes made of corrugated iron and wood.

markets. As the Development Bank of Southern Africa notes, there is no demand for Nomfundo's products in the sophisticated formal sector:

> One of the key constraints on small business – and in particular on small business towards the micro-end of the scale – appears to be lack of effective demand for the products and services they sell. (Aliber 2005: 45)

What then would be legally empowering for Nomfundo and others like her? The answer to the question depends on three factors. First, as the CLEP recognised in its founding documents, it is critical to understand the factors that create and sustain informality in the particular context (UNDP 2006). In the case of South Africa, with its particular history, such an enquiry is particularly pertinent. Second, the response to the question would depend on one's perspective of the informal sector – why it exists, what its characteristics are and the nature of its relationship with the formal sector. Third, the answer would depend on what one understands by the term 'empowerment'.

The first part of this chapter contextualises the question of what an appropriate LEP response to South African informal business owners, such as Nomfundo, would be. I start by discussing the different schools of thought that characterise the informal sector discourse, and discuss how these relate to current policy responses in South Africa. Thereafter, I discuss the CLEP's exposition on the informal sector and its understanding of empowerment. I argue that Volumes I and II of the CLEP report reflect different views of informality and of empowerment and that the views expressed in Volume II will make a difference to Nomfundo, both in terms of her daily existence and in terms of challenging some of the structural barriers to her participating more 'fairly' in the formal economy. By contrast, I argue that some of the suggestions in Volume I will make a difference to her wellbeing, but none is likely to impact on her ability to participate in the formal economy. Finally, I consider the legislative framework that created and still sustains informality and inequality in South Africa today.

The second part of the chapter describes the informal sector in South Africa in terms of its size, diversity and sectoral distribution. I discuss two dominant groups of informal businesses and outline the regressive legal framework within which they operate. The first group is comprised of people whose businesses' only interaction with the formal sector is as consumers. They have backward linkages with the formal sector, as they source the inputs for their businesses from the formal sector, but no forward linkages. Like Nomfundo, they sell their goods and services to other poor people. The second are people who operate informal businesses in particular sectors, such as agriculture, manufacturing, craft and tourism, and who, with the assistance of intermediaries, are able to forge forward linkages with the formal sector.

The CLEP advocates for building backward and forward linkages between formal and informal businesses on 'fair terms' (2008b: 201). Hence, in the third section, I review two South African case studies, one that is of relevance to the first group of informal businesses, like Nomfundo's, that only have backward linkages with the formal economy, and the other is of relevance to the second group, who operate in sectors where forward linkages with the formal sector are possible. My hope in doing so is to contribute to the body of 'lessons on the ground' needed to inform the much needed 'institutional innovation' necessary to facilitate fairer participation of informal businesses in the formal economy (CLEP 2008b).

These interventions make a difference to poor people's livelihoods, despite the fact that they do not address the structural reasons for informality and seldom reach the most marginalised. They constitute empowerment in the narrow sense of the word, in that they facilitate marginalised people's agency, and thus a sense of control over their lives.

Informality, Empowerment and Factors that Create and Sustain Informality in South Africa

Understanding different schools of thought on the informal sector, different understandings of empowerment and the legislative framework that has resulted in the inextricable link between race, informality and poverty in South Africa, are all important facets to forging a meaningful answer to the question of what would be legally empowering for Nomfundo and the many others like her.

Understanding Informality

Since Keith Hart coined the term 'informal sector' in 1973, it has been the subject of extensive deliberation. The International Labour Organization (ILO)'s definition contained in its Kenya Report, which is still used as a point of reference, describes the informal sector as businesses characterised by seven specific traits, including: low barriers to entry, small-scale, labour intensive, family owned, reliant on skills acquired outside of formal schooling and operating in unregulated and competitive markets. More recently, the term 'informal economy' has gained currency, which has broader connotations. It incorporates all activities that are not recorded by formal labour market data, not only informal businesses. Thus, it includes street traders, home-based businesses, casual and contract workers, domestic workers and farm workers.

Different terminologies reflect different views on the reasons for the existence of the informal economy, its characteristics and the nature of its relationship with the formal economy. Chen et al. (2004: 17) describe three 'dominant schools of thought' – the dualists, the structuralists and the legalists.

The dualists, represented by early 1970s ILO papers, viewed the informal economy as distinct and separate from the formal economy, providing income generation opportunities for those unable to find employment in the formal sector. They argued that the informal sector persists because the formal economy does not create sufficient jobs to absorb the surplus labour, either because it is not growing fast enough or because population growth is outstripping growth rates. This view has been discredited (Chen et al. 2004).

The structuralists, such as Caroline Moser and Alejandro Portes, gained ground in the late 1970s and early 1980s. They view the informal economy as 'a set of subordinated economic units which serve to reduce the input and labour costs of the large, formal enterprises' (Devey et al. 2007: 5). In other words, the informal economy is not separate from the formal economy. Rather, the relationship between the formal and informal economy is symbiotic and different modes and forms of production are 'inextricably interconnected and independent'. The informal economy's existence is not ascribed to lack of economic growth, but to the nature of capitalist development (Chen et al. 2004: 17).

The legalists, the most prominent being Hernando de Soto, argue that the informal sector is prevented from formalising because of the high costs associated with formalising. Basing his thesis on empirical work in Peru, De Soto (1998) argues that the informal sector is characterised by entrepreneurs who operate informally by choice, as compliance with the regulatory 'red tape', such as licensing requirements, demands too much time and money. Thus, over-regulation is a primary cause of informality.

A fourth school has emerged during the late 1990s, popularised by Guy Standing. This view asserts that informalisation is a growing trend in all economies. Employment contracts are being replaced by less secure relationships, such as subcontracting and casual labour, which erode both the protection and rights of workers. This has given rise to a new form of informalisation (Standing 1999).

In South Africa, legalist views have dominated the popular press. The expanded view of informality, as represented by Standing, has engaged South African economists and labour lawyers, but is primarily confined to labour market policy debates. The structuralist view, however, is the most the most prominent view reflected in policy documents on small business.[3]

In 2003, President Thabo Mbeki introduced the terminology of 'first' and 'second economy' into the South African informal sector discourse in his annual 'State of the Nation' speech.[4] He argued that since the government's monetary policies had successfully transformed the first economy, it was now time to focus on the second economy. This terminology caused uproar in scholarly circles. Critics argued that the President's construct reflected outdated dualist interpretations and that the myriad of backward and forward linkages between the so-called first and second economies disproved his thesis that the two economies functioned as separate economies.[5] But as du Toit and Neves (2007: 6) observe,

---

3 See for example, Chandra et al. (2001) and DBSA (2005).

4 State of the Nation Address of the President of South Africa, Thabo Mbeki, Cape Town (6 February 2004).

5 See Dewar (2005) and Skinner and Valodia (2003). These articles cite case studies of linkages in particular sectors and proceed to extrapolate these examples to the informal sector as a whole.

> [The] power and importance [of second economy discourse] does not lie in the literal accuracy of what it says about the South African economy – clearly the notion of the second economy as an entirely separate economic realm with its own internal flows, boundaries and central institutions is rather easy to discount—but in its ability to provide a powerful and suggestive shorthand that can serve to name or frame the deeply segmented nature of South African society.

The reality is that the majority of informal businesses, such as Nomfundo's tuck-shop, constitute little more than marginal economic activities that represent survival strategies, rather than entrepreneurial activity. South Africa is so deeply 'segmented', that people like Nomfundo are 'manifestly unprepared to make the transition to the first economy or to link to it somehow' (DBSA 2005). They are unprepared because they are poorly educated. They may be illiterate and may not speak English, which is the language necessary to access markets outside of their community. They are unprepared because they have no formal sector employment history and are unskilled, which is why they operate in sectors where the barriers to entry are very low and engage in mostly retail or simple service or manufacturing activities, which are not in demand by the formal economy.

Thus, the Second Economy Strategy Project was initiated by the government and is located in the President's Office. Whereas the National Small Business Strategy that was launched by the Department of Trade and Industry in 1996 focuses primarily on supply-side interventions, such as credit and training, for small (including informal) businesses, the Second Economy Strategy Project recognises that supply-side interventions do not challenge the inherent inequality of the structure of the market and society in general. These inequalities, argues the principal author of the Strategy, Kate Philip, are the reason why informality persists. I allude to the legislative framework that created these inequalities in the section below.

Philip (2009: 17) argues that 'our strategies cannot rely on the most marginalised 'self-employing 'their way out of poverty'. Thus central to the second economy strategies, is a commitment to engage with structural inequality. Structural change takes time, and attempts will be encountered with resistance from those privileged by existing structures. In the meantime, practical strategies are needed that improve the material conditions of those most marginalised and nurture people's 'sense of economic agency':

> The argument in the Second Economy Strategy Framework is for another level of economic strategy that aims to build the incomes and assets of poor people in ways that do not depend on markets to achieve their intended outcomes, although they will have market effects. While it will take time to overcome the structural factors described, there's no time to lose in building people's sense of economic agency – their ability to change their material conditions through their

> own actions. This requires that we facilitate their economic participation even where markets fail to do so. (Philip 2009: 19)

The Second Economy Strategy Framework thus incorporates macro and micro perspectives, or in the language of Caroline Moser (1989),[6] 'strategic' and 'practical' interests. Macro or 'strategic' interests refer to strategies that challenge embedded power relations. Micro or 'practical' interests are strategies that improve the daily lives of poor, marginalised people, who are engaged in informal income generation activities as part of their livelihood strategies. These practical strategies include 'non-market' interventions, which facilitate their agency.

I will argue that Volume I of CLEP's report on business rights reflects a legalist understanding of the economy and a narrow view of empowerment, which are of limited value to South African informal businesses, such as Nomfundo's. By contrast, Volume II reflects both structuralist and informalisation perspectives of the informal economy and hints at a broader understanding of empowerment, and thus its policy recommendations advance Nomfundo and others' struggle to generate sustainable livelihoods.

The CLEP: Informality and Legal Empowerment of the Poor

Stephen Golub, commonly recognised as the architect of LEP, first introduced the concept of Legal Empowerment of the Poor in 2003, in the context of his work for the Asian Development Bank. Golub (2003: 3) defines LEP as 'the use of legal services and related development activities to increase disadvantaged populations control over their lives', which Golub argues, 'is ultimately about poverty alleviation'.

Golub's understanding of empowerment as a process of expanding poor people's control over their lives, reflects Amartya Sen's (1999) understanding of development as a process whereby each person's 'freedoms' are expanded to enable each person to live with dignity the life he or she values and to participate in the social, political and economic life of his or her community. Inherent in Sen's understanding of development is the eradication of 'un-freedoms', such as 'poverty, poor economic opportunities and social deprivation', that constrain equal participation (ibid: 4). Thus empowerment and participation are interrelated concepts.

The CLEP's conception of legal empowerment is one that focuses primarily on the role of governments, law and legal reform in empowering the poor. Its

6 Moser (1989) differentiates between practical gender initiatives and strategic gender initiatives. Practical initiatives are those interventions that are identified by women themselves that will improve their lives e.g. access to clean drinking water, literacy programmes and childcare. Strategic gender initiatives challenge gender relations. The distinction is a useful analytical tool in this context.

process of empowering the poor is thus largely 'top-down' (Banik 2009; Golub 2009; Stephens 2009):

> It appears that the CLEP has relied heavily on convincing governments (i.e. politicians) of the merits of the Report's recommendations which, in turn, will result in the formulation and implementation of ambitious legal empowerment programmes. And such programmes will consequently involve consultations with the poor and support from civil society. In this crucial sense, the CLEP's recommendations remain very top down, state-centered and orthodox in nature. (Banik 2009: 129)[7]

Unlike legal reform that is a product of 'bottom-up' activism or participation, top-down, state-centred legal reform seldom empowers people, in the sense that it results in their participation in the socio-economic and political life of their community. The reason for its limited impact is twofold.

First, legal reform in and of itself does not necessarily translate into change. Many countries in Africa have justiciable socio-economic rights included in their Constitutions. Only two or three have any jurisprudence on socio-economic rights. States (or private actors) do not deliver, poor people seldom know their rights and if they do, they have negligible access to justice.

Second, 'top-down' legal reform which is not 'grounded in local realities and experiences of the poor' (Stephens 2009: 133) may be progressive, but have little bearing on their lives, or more seriously, result in unintended consequences. For example, as I have argued, a key recommendation of the CLEP in the section on business rights is to reduce compliance requirements. Compliance requirements in South Africa include measures for the protection of employees, such as payment of unemployment insurance, a skills development levy, workman's compensation, and protections that relate to hiring and firing. The 'cut the cost of red tape' lobby in South Africa argues that labour inflexibility retards the growth of small business and the administrative costs associated with compliance with labour and other legislation prejudice the growth of the small business sector. Should CLEP's recommendation be implemented in South Africa, not only will it make no difference to the majority of informal business owners like Nomfundo, but may result in less protection for employees in formal businesses, including domestic workers. An additional limitation of top-down legal reform is that it does little to shape marginalised people's identities as citizens, who have rights and who can exercise power as citizens (Miller et al. 2005).

Golub argues for a different, 'bottom-up' approach, which starts not with institutional reform, but with poor people and their lived experience. Poor people

---

7 The irony of these critiques is that the LEP framework was birthed in response to what Golub (2003) calls the 'Rule of Law Orthodoxy', the dominant modus operandi of law in development, that he argues is top-down, state-centred, and which marginalises poor people.

are partners with lawyers, advocacy specialists, development practitioners (and the state), and the objective is 'to increase the control of poor people over their lives'. This is achieved by integrating legal activities with development activities, such as literacy programmes, building social capital and social movements, and micro-enterprise programmes. He seems to suggest that such programmes build people's capabilities, which increase their ability to claim rights and to participate in decisions that affect their lives. He envisages the relationship between poor communities, civil society and government as follows:

> In contrast with the dominant paradigm, legal empowerment is more balanced in nature. It is grounded in grassroots needs and activities, but can translate that community-level work into impact on national laws and institutions. It generally strengthens civil society and the legal capacities and the power of the poor to address their priorities, but wherever possible involves cooperation with government. (Golub 2003: 5)

Golub argues that empowerment is more about power and freedom, than it is about law. Elsewhere I have argued that it is unfortunate that Golub did not give more content to 'empowerment' and 'power' and that he did not draw on the scholarship and experience of development and rights-based activists.[8] The conceptual development of the LEP framework may then have been less vulnerable to 'orthodox' interpretations, concomitant with a market-based reform approach (Sengupta 2008). LEP may as a result have been framed in more political terms that recognise the necessity of engaging with power relations and structural inequalities that deny poor people the possibility of participating fully in social and political life, as well as in economic opportunities. Perhaps too, the LEP framework would have been more conceptually coherent, which may have called for less interpretation and more application by the CLEP. It is against this backdrop that I examine the sections in the CLEP's report on business rights.

'Making the Law Work for Everyone' Volume I's section on business rights reflects 'the central theme of the report, [namely] the extension of formality into the formal sector' (Stephens 2009: 134). The report suggests that 'heavy handed regulation' (CLEP 2008a: 70) and regulatory environments that are not inclusive, means that people 'choose low risk businesses that often yield low returns (ibid: 71). Such regulatory environments make it costly and difficult for informal businesses to meet registration and compliance requirements. Reforming economic policies, as well as the legal framework, to be more inclusive i.e. to make it easier for informal businesses to formalise, will lead to 'a flourishing market economy that will create growth and formal jobs' (ibid: 71). Thus, Volume I appears to subscribe to the legalistic view of the informal economy.

Volume I's reform agenda includes the following: First, the introduction of economic rights. There seem to be two tiers of rights. The first tier includes the

8 See von Broembsen (2010).

right to vend, to have access to a workspace and the necessary infrastructure and services, such as electricity, water and sanitation. The report concludes that these rights would 'facilitate the success of small and medium enterprises'. Once the business is more established, a second tier of economic rights becomes important. This tier includes tax breaks, export licences and commercial rights such as 'entity shielding, limited liability and protection of minority shareholders' (ibid: 72).

The second reform initiative is to reduce complex administrative and regulatory requirements that keep informal entrepreneurs from formalising – 'red tape and the costs involved in registering … need to be slashed' (ibid: 73). The third item on the reform agenda is to increase access to finance and to invest in innovative financial products that will increase such access. The fourth reform measure is to increase the consultation and participation of informal businesses by supporting representative bodies. The fifth reform item is property reform. The section concludes that 'the more inclusive and attractive the formal market becomes' the less likely that informal enterprises will *choose* to remain informal or return to being informal (my italics, ibid.).

Thus Volume I espouses a largely procedural fairness approach. Once businesses have the right to vend, are provided with infrastructural support and access to finance, and regulations are simplified, one hopes they 'choose' to become and remain formal as their 'success' will have been facilitated. The report does not address the issue of the how unequal distribution of resources and opportunities impacts on poor people, nor does it address the challenges of structural inequality, and thus does not engage in debates that would bring about a more substantive notion of fair participation by informal businesses in the economy.

Volume II comprises the reports of the four working groups – access to justice, property rights, labour rights and business rights. The chapter on business rights reflects a different perspective on informality to that of the first report. While the introductory section, which summarises the reform agenda, is not very different to the timbre of Volume I, the remainder of the report seems to reflect both a structuralist and informalisation interpretation of the informal economy.

Volume II argues that the formal and informal economies are interconnected in a myriad of ways and notes that people move between the two economies. Unlike Volume I, which implies that the goal should be to eradicate the informal sector, Volume II recognises that the informal sector is here to stay. Thus, the challenge is not to remove barriers to formalisation, but rather 'to reduce the decent work deficits of those who work informally' and to optimise 'sustainable linkages'. It argues for affording people legal protection, even if they remain informal (CLEP 2008b: 199).

Volume II reflects a different policy agenda to that of Volume I. This is reflected in at least three areas. First, the report raises issues of inequality and distribution of resources. It argues that 'sound economic governance is built upon principles of equity and equality of opportunity' (ibid: 198). Equality is not understood as procedural reform – such as reducing regulatory requirements – but as something far more substantive. This is reflected in several ways. First, the report argues for 'access to and distribution of assets, economic opportunities and political voice'.

Thus, participation is understood as more than a representative body that is to be consulted on decisions that affect informal businesses. Participation is understood as political voice, as citizenship participation, which infers potential participation in decision-making relating to the distribution of national resources and economic opportunities.

Second, the report recognises that substantive or 'fair' participation in the economy involves 'level(ing) the playing field', which involves government investment in human resource development of poor people, and 'guarantee(ing) business rights and fairness in markets' (ibid: 199).

References to power and inequality are absent in Volume I's sections on business rights, except indirectly. Volume II states unequivocally that countries characterised by an unequal distribution of wealth, tend to be characterised by institutional arrangements that 'favour the interests of the influential and the privileged' (ibid.).

While Volume I argues for 'systemic changes', it describes these in general terms and frames 'the political process' and 'economic policy' as 'facets of the legal framework' (ibid: 200). As Kennedy (2004) argues, law has played a largely instrumentalist role in supporting the economic development agenda, which has favoured 'the influential and privileged'. The reference to business rights indirectly touches on power, but whether that is intended, depends on the CLEP's understanding of rights.

Miller et al. (2005) capture the tension between different discourses on rights, which reflect 'competing voices and agendas' (Gready 2008: 739):

> The notion of rights as universal standards of human dignity [which is the dominant discourse] belies their inherently political and conflictual nature. [A different discourse argues that] rights do not come in neat packages, but rather are part of dynamic, sometimes messy processes of resistance and change that work to engage and transform relations of power (Miller et al. 2005: 36).

Volume I seems to represent the dominant rights view, that accessing rights are technical legal processes, rather than the result of hard won political struggles that involve the contestation of access to resources and opportunities. As Pettit and Wheeler (2005: 7) observe,

> For rights to become meaningful, they must be claimed and realised by real people engaged in specific struggles related to urgently felt needs. And to be sustainable, the process for securing those rights needs to be one which squarely addresses the structural inequalities and power relations which deny them in the first place. Rights are both about physical needs and personal experiences about power.

Volume I's business rights are about physical needs i.e. they constitute practical strategies that will make the daily struggle of earning a living easier. Volume II's reference to the right to 'political voice' suggests a notion of rights as 'experiences of power'. Volume II does not discuss power, but implicit in the discussions on inequality and unfair distribution of wealth and opportunity, is an allusion to power. It is hoped that Volume II's premises and recommendations will be used as the foundation for future work.

Volume II also argues that sustained business linkages between formal and informal business and skills development for informal sector operators are critical. Building sustainable business linkages resonates with South Africa's Second Economy Strategy Project's aim to facilitate greater participation of informal businesses in the economy and at the same time to build agency by poor people, thereby exercising one form of power, 'power to'.[9]

The following section describes the legacy of South Africa's apartheid laws for poor, marginalised black South Africans in general and for informal businesses in particular. Thereafter I discuss the nature of the informal economy. Finally, I discuss two case studies that illustrate how linkages between the informal and formal businesses can be facilitated. One case study focuses on reducing the transaction costs of spaza businesses in their backward linkages with wholesalers. The other involves forward linkages between craft producers and the formal economy. Volume II underlines the need for 'contextual specificity' and for basing policy and 'institutional innovation' on 'lessons from on the ground' (CLEP 2008b: 199). My hope is that these 'lessons from the ground' will contribute to the 'institutional innovation' that is so necessary.

Factors that Create and Sustain Informality in South Africa

The apartheid government's systematic exclusion of black people from participating in the formal economy means that informality and race are inextricably linked in South Africa. Between 1913 and 1989, the government promulgated many racist laws that embodied the ideology that black people's contribution to the economy was solely to provide unskilled labour to white owned businesses. Black Africans, who constitute approximately 79.6 per cent of the total population, were targeted specifically.

Legislation controlled the influx of black Africans from rural 'homelands' (poorly resourced rural areas assigned to black nations) to so-called 'white' urban areas. Disenfranchised people were granted temporary licenses to live in urban centres in order to provide labour.[10] These 'temporary' residents had to live in 'townships', dormitory suburbs situated outside cities and towns.

9 In *Legal Empowerment of the Poor: The Re-emergence of a Lost Strand of Human Rights?* (see footnote 8), I draw on Lukes' and Gaventa's work on typologies of power, as a contribution to the conceptual development of 'empowerment' within the LEP framework.

10 Three pieces of legislation, known as 'influx control' laws, The Native (Black) Urban Areas Act No. 21 of 1923; The Black (Natives) Laws Amendment Act No. 54 of 1952 and the Native (Urban Areas) Consolidation Act No. 25 of 1954 restricted the influx

One of the cornerstones of apartheid was differentiated education for different population groups. An education curriculum was designed to educate black Africans for manual labour. The Bantu Education Act No. 43 of 1953 was promulgated to give effect to this grotesque racist ideology. The architect of differentiated education, Hendrick Verwoerd, expressed this ideology as follows:

> … there is no place for him (blacks) in the European community above the level of certain forms of labour. Until now he has been subjected to a school system which drew him away from his community and misled him by showing him the green pastures of European society in which he was not allowed to graze. Who will do the manual labour if you give the Natives an academic education? Education must train and teach people in accordance with their opportunities in life (Irogbe 2003: 14).

In addition, black Africans were denied individual title to land or ownership of a business.[11]

The legacy of these repressive laws is manifold. Two key implications for poor people's livelihoods are: First, as black Africans were excluded from participating in the formal economy, except as unskilled labour, in the case of the majority, their education and skill levels are therefore vastly inferior to their white counterparts. This inequality in education persists today (van den Berg 2005), which has far-reaching implications in terms of the ability of the poor to enter sophisticated formal markets, either as employees or as business owners. As black Africans were not allowed to own businesses, skills were not passed from generation to generation, as they were amongst artisans in sections of the 'Coloured' community or as is the case in other developing countries. Skill levels are therefore very low, which influences the kinds of businesses people are able to establish and their ability to access formal markets.

Second, all 'black'[12] population groups were spatially separated from towns and cities. While freedom of movement is protected in the Constitution, most of the country's urban poor still live in these dormitory suburbs. As a result, most informal businesses operate from homes or informal structures at transport nodes and informal markets in the townships, sometimes far away from town or city

---

of black people into urban areas, by establishing criteria in terms of which black people qualified live in an urban area (so called 'section 10' rights). Black people who did not qualify for a permit were not permitted into an urban area for longer than 72 hours. The influx control laws were repealed by the Abolition of Influx Control Act No. 68 of 1986.

11 The Group Areas Act No. 41 of 1950 prohibited black Africans from living in areas that were zoned for white citizens without a pass book; from owning a home-based business or from acquiring immovable property.

12 'Black' in the broad sense refers to all population groups that were not classified as white i.e. Black Africans, mixed race or 'Coloured', Indian and Chinese.

centres. This means that these businesses operate in over-traded markets, servicing their local community, which is poor and often buys on credit.[13] In addition, spatial separation affects the transaction costs of accessing inputs for businesses.

The democratically elected government in South Africa has promulgated many laws to remedy the legacy of inequality[14] and the country has one of the most progressive Constitutions in the world. The legal empowerment challenge for small business in South Africa is thus not one of advocating for broad based legislative reform or to reduce 'red tape', but rather, as fore grounded by the Second Economy Strategy Project, the long-term challenge is to address inequality. The challenge in the short-term is to explore ways in which poor people can participate more 'fairly' and 'sustainably' (CLEP 2008b) in the formal economy.

Understanding South Africa's Informal Sector

Estimates of the size and contribution of informal businesses in South Africa vary considerably. It is estimated that there are between 1 and 2.3 million informal businesses, which contribute between 7 and 12 per cent to South Africa's GDP (Dewar 2005; Altman 2008). Micro-level studies – seven in total – suggest that between 3 and 7 out of every ten household in informal settlements are involved in some kind of informal income generation activity (Valodia 2000; Napier and Liebermann 2001).

For the purposes of this chapter, informal businesses are defined as unregistered, unregulated economic activities that contribute to the gross domestic product. Just over a third of the people in the informal economy in South Africa, own and

13 Rogerson (1997) refers to eight articles that support this finding. Also see Ruiters et al. (2004: 148); Kesper (2000); Rogerson (2002); Tipple (2005); Berry et al. (2002) and Napier and Mothwa (2001).

14 These include, but are not limited to the following: The Constitution of 1996; Upgrading of Land Tenure Rights Act 112 of 1991, which restores rights to land use and tenure; The Schools Act 84 of 1996, which provides for differentiated funding that is biased towards poor schools; The Preferential Procurement Policy Framework Act 5 of 2000, that committed government to preferentially procure goods from black-owned business and to break down tenders into smaller units, to enable smaller businesses to tender for contracts; The Competition Act 89 of 1998, which aims to address anti-competitive behaviour of white-owned corporations that have a monopoly on local markets; The Broad-Based Black Business Empowerment Act 53 of 2003, in terms of which any business that wants to tender for government work or applies for government assistance or licences, must comply with 5 areas of black empowerment; and The National Small Business Act 102 of 1996, which established institutional structures to give effect to the government's National Small Business Strategy.

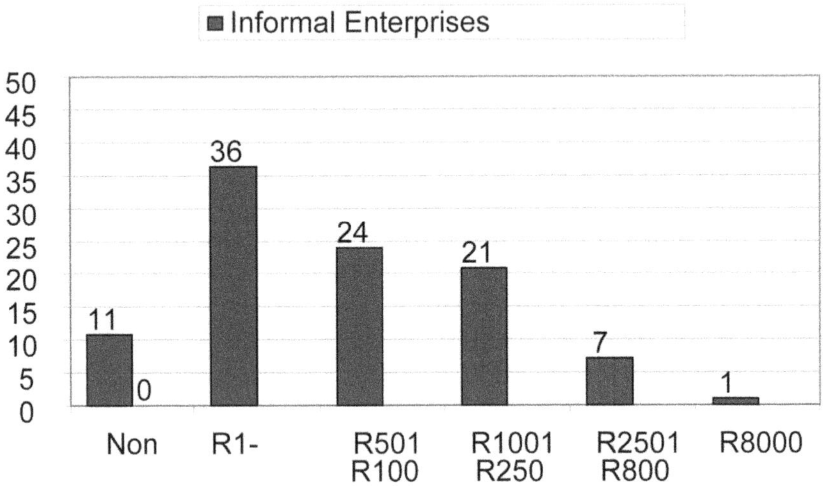

Figure 3.1 Monthly earnings of survivalist and micro-enterprises

Source: Skinner (2007). Calculations based on Labour Force Survey 2005.

manage a business (Valodia 2000). A small percentage of the remaining two thirds are paid or unpaid employees of these businesses.[15]

An estimated 45.5 per cent of informal enterprises are owned and managed by women and approximately 54.5 per cent by men. An estimated 91.3 per cent are owned and managed by black Africans (Statistics SA 2005).[16]

Nevertheless, informal businesses are diverse in terms of their scale and the sector in which they operate. Figure 3.1 shows the scale of informal businesses, using the monthly earnings of both owners and employees as a proxy for scale.

Ninety two per cent of owners and employees of informal businesses earn below R2,500 a month. A significant 71 per cent earn below R1,000 per month. The 11 per cent that do not earn anything, most likely refers to family members who work in micro-enterprises as unpaid employees. It is estimated that only

15 Skinner (2007) analyses five years, 2000–5 of Labour Force Statistics to show that two thirds of the labour force are employed in the formal non-agricultural sector.

16 I use the most recent 'official' statistics reported by Statistics South Africa in its 'Survey of Employers and the Self-Employed (SESE)'. The reason for this choice is that SESE surveys informal businesses, whereas the Labour Force Survey is a population survey, from which informal business statistics can be extrapolated, as is the Global Entrepreneurship Monitor (GEM). The latest SESE survey is the 2005 survey, which was conducted in September 2005. The report was released in November 2006. SESE defines informal businesses as those not registered for Value-added-tax (VAT).

three per cent of the employees of informal businesses are paid (Napier and Liebermann 2006).

Informal businesses are diverse in terms of sector. More than half of informal businesses are in the retail sector (Statistics SA 2005). Typically these businesses include 'spaza' shops that sell groceries and pubs, commonly known as 'shebeens' second-hand furniture shops, sweet, meat and fruit sellers. Retailers include street traders, who sell their goods from pavements or stalls in urban centres.[17] Approximately nine per cent of informal businesses are located in the service industry (Skinner 2007), which typically includes hairdressers, phone booths, car repairs, hiring companies and radio and TV repair.

The vast majority of the approximately 12 per cent of manufacturing enterprises manufacture 'soft' goods, such as dressmaking, shoe-repair and beer brewing. 'Hard' manufacturing such as wood and wood processing, printing and publishing, paper, chemicals and plastics are unusual (Stats SA 2005). Only a small percentage of informal businesses in the craft, agricultural, construction, textile and tourist sectors can potentially create forward linkages with the formal sector, but almost without exception only if mediated by an intermediary that lowers the barriers to entry.

Each sector incorporates several sub-sectors. Businesses in the building sector are constrained by different factors to those in the retail, hospitality or craft industries. Sector-specific studies are therefore important to design optimal legal strategies for the legal empowerment of businesses in the respective sub-sectors.

The most recent statistics suggest that trade and private household sector together account for 2.5 of the 4.9 million people who are categorised as working in informal employment (Quarterly Labour Force Survey 2008).

Larger businesses operate from business premises in black metropolitan areas, but the majority operates from homes or tables at transport nodes. Approximately 60 per cent of all informal businesses are home-based (Statistics SA 2005).

Those that are owned by poor black men and women are therefore located in 'townships', dormitory suburbs outside towns and cities. Some of these townships have formal housing, others are informal settlements characterised by 'shacks' (homes built from corrugated iron) with an outside tap and toilet ('site and service'). And still others are totally informal: shacks are often built on land to which the owner does not have title, there is no sanitation (people relieve themselves in bushes) and communal taps provide the only water for these residents of backyards, farms and communal land. Approximately 500,000 households are 'backyard-dwellers', who live in a structure built onto the back of a 'site and service' shack, which they rent from the owner of the shack (Chirwa 2008).

---

17 Street traders, construction and agricultural businesses, businesses involved in mining and quarrying and the transport industry represent sectors that seldom trade from businesses premises in black metropolitan areas or from homes, and require compliance with legislation specific to the respective industries. They are not the focus of this chapter.

Home-based businesses may be 'survivalist' or more sophisticated micro-enterprises. Studies show that businesses in townships that have more formal housing and access to electricity and running water (as opposed to a communal tap) are more sophisticated and sustainable than those where homes are 'shacks' and where the household have access to few amenities (Napier and Liebermann 2006). Thus the CLEP's 'bundle of rights', specifically access to water, sanitation and electricity would not only improve the well-being of poor people, but also increase the sustainability of their economic activities.

Unlike many other countries, home-based businesses in South Africa do not need a licence to operate legally, unless they trade in perishable food, medicines or liquor (or adult entertainment). Since the majority of home based businesses sell perishable food (such as bread and milk), this merits some discussion.

In terms of the Business Act of 1991, the owner of a business trading in perishable food is required to have a licence. In addition, health regulations require the business to apply for a 'certificate of acceptability' in order to trade legally. This licence is obtained from a local authority, which sends five different departments – Environmental Health; Noise and Air Pollution Control; Metropolitan Public safety and Emergency Services, Fire Safety; Urban Planning; and Building Control – to assess compliance, before granting the licence.

Should the business trade without a licence, the trader may be taken to court and fined or imprisoned for three months. The regulation thus relies on criminal rather than administrative law sanctions. A more progressive approach, in line with viewing these activities as economic activities, would be a move away from a criminal to an administrative legal framework. Business owners would be encouraged to comply through a range of incentives but the ultimate sanction would be the removal of the right to trade rather than fines and imprisonment (Skinner 2007). In reality, however, the regulations are rarely enforced in townships. Nevertheless, they are enforced against street traders who trade in inner cities.

In terms of Schedule 4B of the Constitution, trading and building regulations are local government responsibilities. Home-based businesses in communities that are characterised by formal housing are subject to zoning regulations in terms of Land Use Planning Ordinances, local authority by-laws as well as building regulations. As this is a local authority responsibility, there is little uniformity across the country in terms of whether the by-laws are enforced and how they are implemented. Few local authorities have the capacity and the commitment to implement by-laws at all in townships and if they do, only one or two do so in a pro-poor way. The Durban local authority is an exception. It has piloted a programme which educates people on the purpose of particular by-laws and assists them to comply with the by-laws (Skinner and Valodia 2003).

But these measures are designed to protect the neighbours of informal businesses, or the consumers – the customers of the many informal businesses that sell meat, fruit and vegetables, milk and bread. What, then, of measures to facilitate greater participation by informal businesses in the formal economy?

Home-based Businesses: Participating in the Formal Economy

A range of government interventions, including legislation such as the Preferential Procurement Act and the Broad Based Black Empowerment Act envisage that micro-enterprises should be able to establish forward linkages with the formal sector, by selling their products or services into the formal sector. In reality, such forward linkages are 'almost non-existent' in South Africa (Napier and Mothwa 2001; Smith. et al. 2005; Tladi and Pedro 2007; James 2007).[18]

With the exception of a tiny minority of manufacturing businesses and street traders, informal businesses have very few forward linkages with the formal sector (Napier and Mothwa 2001). As Kesper (2000) notes, where formal sector businesses do have linkages with informal business, these are often with former employees. Corporate companies change the employment status of employees and outsource non-core activities. Thus, the activities that were previously performed as employees are now undertaken by the same people but as 'small businesses' without the protection and rights they enjoyed as employees. This illustrates the new form of informalisation identified by Standing (1999), Chen et al. (2004) and others:

> There has been little systematic evidence on the incidence of micro-enterprise 'graduation' or growth into larger ones in Africa. Indeed, one-person operations constitute the majority of small-scale industry in Africa, and only about 1% succeeds in graduating to an intermediate-size[19] ... Corporate subcontracting to small and mostly 'informal' firms in Africa is more than often a means to reduce costs by exploiting labour-surplus conditions and circumventing regulations and trade union organisations (Kesper 2000: 4).

The national network, the Business Opportunities Network (BON) launched in the late 1990s in order to facilitate linkages between formal and informal business has largely folded, as the practical outworking of formal businesses subcontracting non-core businesses to informal business, proved to be too ambitious.[20] John James, who heads up the USAID Southern African Linkage Programme and SABLE (The South African Business Linkage Programme), argues that the transaction costs for big business in transacting with a number of very small contractors is too high to be feasible; and consequently is no longer

18 I interviewed Tladi and Pedro, directors of a non-profit organisation, The Triple Trust Organisation, that has done extensive research across sectors they work in to determine the extent to which informal businesses participate in the formal market. I also interviewed John James of ECI Africa, who heads up the USAID Southern African Linkages Programme, as well as the Business Opportunities Network, that was established to facilitate linkages between big and small informal business and has abandoned that area of their work. These interviews took place in September 2007

19 Kesper (2000) cites five studies to support this view.

20 Interview with the Acting MD of BON, September 2007.

a model that is pursued at a policy level. Even the government preferential procurement programme in practice supports formal black-owned businesses, as opposed to informal businesses.[21]

A small percentage of informal businesses are able to establish forward linkages. But for the vast majority, forward linkages are impossible, predominantly because the lack of investment in human capital is such that people do not have the education, skills (technical, language or business management) or exposure that would qualify them to know how to start a business that could meet the demands of the formal sector (Aliber 2005). How then does one facilitate fairer participation in the economy through their backward linkages? Below I discuss a civil society organisation, The Triple Trust organisation, which in its work with spaza owners has facilitated the reduction of the transaction costs of backward linkages with the formal economy, which has had other multiplier effects on the local informal economy.

Reducing Transaction Costs in Backward Linkages: A Case Study

While few home-based businesses are able to access formal markets and do not therefore have forward linkages with formal businesses, they do have backward linkages, in that they purchase inputs from formal wholesalers. The Triple Trust Organisation (TTO), a national NGO in the micro-enterprise sector, shows that by intervening in the backward linkage, transaction costs are reduced, which improves the livelihoods of informal retailers.

TTO has adopted the Making Markets Work for the Poor (M4P) conceptual framework. Essentially the M4P framework works as follows: The starting point is the market, not the business (or the poor themselves). Initially called 'sub-sector' analysis and now 'value-chain analysis', the particular value chain is analysed to ascertain who supplies who and what value is added in each stage of the process. Their analysis examines how informal business participates in the particular market, where there is market failure (barriers to the poor participating), and possible strategies to overcome such constraints. The objective is to facilitate more effective participation of informal businesses in the market.

Business Development Services (BDS) refers to non-financial interventions that, based on the above analysis, are developed to facilitate more effective participation of informal business in the particular value chain. Such interventions should ultimately become a sustainable business that services informal businesses. The intervention is supply rather than demand-led. Gibson, a proponent of M4P in the UK articulates the role of the intervening organisation as follows:

21 Catherine Wijnberg, who manages twelve projects across South Africa that mediates entry to formal markets for informal craft businesses, argues that small producers are not sophisticated enough to deal directly with formal markets; and the transactions costs are too high for individual contracting (Interview, October 2008).

> As a general rule, the risks of distortion (of the market) are reduced if organisations are not subsidised directly in the delivery of a service or a product, but are supported through assistance, for example, to develop capacity, new products, new business linkages or collaborative working arrangements. Direct transaction subsidies – "invading" the heart of market processes – run the risk of distorting prices and incentives more than less direct routes. Ideally also, actions should work with a number of players so that unfair competitive advantage does not accrue to one player at the expense of the market system as a whole. (Gibson et al. 2004: 21)

In 2000, TTO commissioned a study of 'spazas' in ten townships outside Cape Town. The study found that spazas predominantly source their supplies from large wholesalers such as Macro, Metro and Cash and Carry. The owners travel by taxi, do not benefit from discounts, are only able to purchase what they are able to accommodate on their laps and the opportunity cost is considerable – a couple of hours away from the business (Smith et al. 2002).

TTO's major strategy was twofold: TTO adopted a horizontal strategy, which was to move away from interventions with individual businesses, by organising the spaza owners into a network, called SHOPNET. Business owners (approximately 800) were mobilised around a common cause – their supply chain. TTO's vertical strategy was for SHOPNET to intervene in the supply chain. While initially managed by TTO, SHOPNET is now managed by spaza owners themselves. SHOPNET negotiates on behalf of its members with wholesalers, thereby shifting the power relationship between spaza owners and wholesalers. It places bulk orders with wholesalers. As a result, wholesalers now compete for SHOPNET's business and offer discounts. In addition, distributors deliver goods to shops. This has had a multiplier effect on the local economy, as SHOPNET has:

- Negotiated with manufacturers to produce products for the home shop market e.g. half loaves of bread, smaller quantities, specific packaging. This means that people are less likely to buy bigger quantities from competing formal sector outlets, and their income thus stays in the local economy;
- Assisted people in the community who own small trucks to start a business transporting goods for home owners;
- Assisted a local book-keeper with a business plan to keep the books for spazas, on a paid basis;
- Offered businesses basic business skills, such as understanding an invoice or a statement; and
- Negotiated with the local authority to partner it in establishing a warehouse facility for its members.

On a 'horizontal' level, members see real benefit: they no longer have to travel to buy goods. Their profit margins have increased, as their input costs have been lowered and as they benefit from economies of scale. In addition, once a business reaches a certain size, distributors offer revolving credit. TTO sees growth in terms of a diversification of products and a bigger turnover.

Members of SHOPNET start as voluntary buying group member. As members experience the benefit of the network, TTO intends for the SHOPNET to become a franchise and for members to pay a monthly fee to belong to it and use its services. In other words, SHOPNET will become a sustainable business.

In this context, the value chain analysis coupled with Business Development Services (BDS) interventions illustrate that effective institutions offer economies of scale that reduce the transaction costs for informal businesses. The form of these institutions may differ from context to context. The Second Economy Strategy Project is currently investing the feasibility of different types of intermediaries, and consumer co-operatives, a similar concept to SHOPNET in that they enable informal businesses to buy their inputs through a co-operative, is one these.

Facilitating Forward Linkages: A Case Study

As discussed in earlier, few micro-enterprises are able to access formal markets. This section focuses on those that do access such markets, by virtue of the fact that they operate in sectors that can meet the demands of the formal sector. Specifically, some informal survival and micro-enterprises in the construction, manufacturing, craft and agricultural sectors have the potential to create forward linkages with the formal sector. I shall discuss the case of The Cape Craft Design Institute (CCDI), which through its intervention, lowers the barriers to entry for informal businesses in the craft sector.[22]

The CCDI, an organisation funded by provincial government, is active in the craft sector in the Western Cape Province, one of nine provinces in South Africa. Its focus is to facilitate the access of formal markets by informal micro-enterprises in the craft sector.

The CCDI recognises the myriad of problems that informal businesses face: local markets are poor, mark-ups are therefore small and selling on credit is norm. In addition, producers lack technical skills, information, finance, storage space, transport and their businesses suffer from the effects of crime. Yet, CCDI argues that even if one were to solve all of these problems, producers would still not be able to access what are sophisticated external markets, where 'design is key, quality and consistency is vital and trends shift rapidly'.[23] The business rights

22 The craft sector it provides income and employment to approximately 38,062 people who own or are employed by approximately 7,028 micro and small enterprises, who participate in the craft value chain (DTI 2005).

23 This extract from a power-point presentation by someone from CCDI does not cite an author or a year. In interviews with the Cape Craft and Design Institute the views of the presentation were echoed.

suggested by the CLEP would thus not solve the inability of craft producers to access formal markets by themselves.

CCDI's response is demand- rather than supply-led. It starts with an analysis of the market demand, not the problems of the producer. As was the case with The Triple Trust Organisation, the conceptual model that the CCDI bases its approach on is Value Chain Management. This entails an analysis within a particular sector of the journey of a particular product – from the raw materials stage to the final consumption of the product – and the role that informal economy workers play in the value chain.

An analysis of the craft supply chain shows that 'the expectation that the crafter must be the designer, the product developer, the producer, the marketer, the agent and the exporter is not realistic'.[24] The producer becomes part of a supply chain and other parties fulfil the different specialist roles in the supply chain. The producer therefore does not interact directly with the market, but does so through an intermediary. This intermediary (in this case a non-profit organisation) lowers the barriers to entry by providing the following services to micro-enterprises: Information about the market and design input; consolidation of volumes from small producers; the ability to secure large export orders and divide them between small producers; and mostly importantly, the organisation assumes the financial risk.

The critical pay-off for informal business is that it reduces the complexity of producing for external markets, which lowers the barriers to entry. The reality of producing for external markets is captured by this comment from Woolworths, a large retailer in South Africa – 'by all means cut red tape, but our buyers need compliance with business protocols and practices that mitigate their risks'.[25] Value chain management means that these business protocols and practices are mediated for the small producer by other market players, which otherwise would disqualify such producers from participating in the market.

The CCDI functions as an intermediary for approximately 800 businesses in the craft sector, of which 22 per cent are from outside the metropolitan area. This means that a holistic approach that assesses the level of business and designs appropriate interventions with partner organisations to move the business to the next level is possible. In the process, micro-enterprises are required to register as formal businesses, in order to access state subsidies to attend trade shows.

Several organisations assist business to register as formal business, which includes acquiring a tax compliance certificate and possibly registering as a Close Corporation with the Registrar of Companies. What is more difficult is that the newly formalised micro-enterprises do not always understand what is required from them and struggle to comply.[26] Compliance is thus not about costs or time, but knowledge. Any formal entity has to satisfy a host of legal requirements

24 Interview with Anne Weyer of CCDI in August 2007.

25 Relayed to me by Anne Weyer; documented in internal CCDI reports.

26 Interview with Anne Weyer, CCDI, August 2007.

– audited financial statements, labour requirements and most critically to pay tax, to mention three. In addition, micro-enterprises subcontract their orders and have little understanding of appropriate contractual arrangements with their subcontractors. Frequently there has been no prior agreement regarding price or quality and conflict ensues.

Thus, legal empowerment needs to go beyond reducing red tape or even other rights-based activities, such as 'know-your rights' programmes and include critical developmental activities such as skills transfer, literacy (including numeral literacy), knowledge transfer and hands-on mentoring to understand and comply with business and legal norms.

This value chain model is being applied in several other contexts: for example in the traditional medicines sector in the Kwazulu-Natal Province, which is supported by Provincial government and by COMMARK, an organisation in the Eastern Cape Province that facilitates rural subsistence farmers selling their cotton and cattle to formal markets. These case studies illustrate that an effective intermediary offers economies of scale that reduces the costs for producers to transact in markets and provides developmental services that enable producers to transact in more sophisticated ways, and in the case of some, to establish formal businesses.

The question of intermediaries raises a number of policy issues. Which legal forms are acceptable – not-for-profit *and* for profit? If not-for-profit, how will such institutions be funded? If for-profit, how will informal business be safeguarded from potentially exploitative relationships? Should we be considering M4P as the conceptual framework, which privileges market-based interventions over other developmental activities, financial sustainability over sustainable livelihoods and reaching numbers rather than those most marginalised? Or should we consider more democratic models such as consumer co-operatives?

South Africa's Second Economy Strategy Project is currently engaging with these questions. Perhaps the issue is not one of for-profit versus non-profit, but rather one of devising mechanisms to protect against exploitation by intermediaries of producers, and to incentivise intermediaries to transfer skills to the producers. Increased capacity on the part of producers translates into gains for the business, which should be facilitated by a range of institutional mechanisms.

One potential mechanism which could facilitate accountability by intermediaries, is to establish a sector-based industry association (as is the case for builders, travel agents, estate agents etc.), which would regulate the behaviour of intermediaries. Government funding for export, attending trade shows, etc. could be linked to membership of the association, which could require developmental interventions, such as transferring skills to producers – on how to contract with subcontractors, how to design products, how to comply with formality requirements, etc. In addition, an administrative tribunal run by the association could address complaints by producers. A source of funding for the human resources development of producers could include leveraging the one per cent after tax profit that big business is required to spend on small enterprise programmes, in order to secure Black Economic Empowerment (BEE) compliance in terms of the Broad-based BEE Act.

Conclusion

This chapter has been concerned with the participation of poor people in economic opportunities in South Africa, specifically poor people that run 'own-account' informal businesses from their homes, stalls, tables or premises in townships. I have tried to show that meaningful participation, or as CLEP would term it 'fair' participation in economic opportunities is only achievable if there is structural change, not least to the structure of the economy. This is a premise of South Africa's Second Economy Strategy Project.

This chapter has shown that to conceive of legal empowerment as primarily a commitment to assist informal businesses to formalise, has limited value for the majority of informal businesses in South Africa. I have argued that empowerment of poor and marginalised people should be both about *strategic* change – that enables people to participate themselves ('bottom-up processes') in challenging embedded power relationships, through 'political voice' – and about *practical* change – that supports strategies that develop poor and marginalised people's 'power to' exercise some control over their lives, as envisaged by the founding vision of Legal Empowerment of the Poor. Volume II of the CLEP's report lays the foundation for future scholarship on the relationship between inequality and poverty in the context of the informal economy. It is to be hoped that future work on conceptualising the Legal Empowerment of the Poor framework and its application to the informal economy, builds on these foundations.

References

Aliber, M. 2005. Synthesis Report of the 2005 Development Report: Overcoming Development in South Africa's Second Economy. Available at: www.sahrc.org.za/sahrc_cms/downloads/6th%20ESR%20report.pdf [Accessed: 13 August 2006].

Altman, M. 2008. Formal-Informal Linkages, Human Sciences Research Council. Available at: http://www.hsrc.ac.za/research/output/outputDocuments/5263_Altman_Formalinformaleconomylinkages.pdf [Accessed: 5 September 2010].

Banik, D. 2009. Legal Empowerment as a Conceptual and Operational Tool in Poverty Alleviation. *Hague Journal on the Rule of Law*, 1, pp. 117–31.

Berry, A., von Blottnitz, M., Cassim, R., Kesper, A., Rajaratnam, B. and van Seventer, D. 2002. The Economics of SMMEs in South Africa. Trade and Industrial Policy Strategies. Available at http://www.tips.org.za [Accessed: October 2003].

Chen, M. Vanek, J. and Carr, M. 2004. *Mainstreaming Informal Employment and Gender in Poverty Reduction: A Handbook for Policy-makers and other Stakeholders*. London: Commonwealth Secretariat.

Chandra, V., Moorty, L., Nganou, J.-P., Rajaratnam, B. and Schaefer, K. 2001. Constraints to Growth and Employment in South Africa: Report No. 2: Evidence from the Small, Medium and Micro Enterprise Firm Survey, Discussion Paper No. 15. The World Bank Southern Africa Department, Washington DC.

Chirwa, D. 2009. Legal Implications of the Proposed Comprehensive Policy on Backyard Dwellers, unpublished paper, University of Cape Town.

Commission on Legal Empowerment of the Poor (CLEP) and United Nations Development Programme. 2008a. Making the Law Work for Everyone, Report of the Commission on Legal Empowerment of the Poor, Volume I. New York. pp. 1–96. Available at: www.undp.org/publications/makingthelawworkforeveryone%20(final20rpt).pdf [Accessed July 2009].

Commission on Legal Empowerment of the Poor (CLEP) and United Nations Development Programme (UNDP) 2008b. Making the Law Work for Everyone, Report of the Commission on Legal Empowerment of the Poor, Volume II. New York. pp. 195–253. Available at: www.undp.org/legalempowerment/publications/concept2action.html [Accessed 27 August 2010].

Department of Trade and Industry (DTI) Sector Development Strategy for the Craft Sector. Available at http://www.capecraftanddesign.org.za/research_folder/pdf/dti_cust.pdf. [Accessed September 2010].

De Soto, H. 1989. *The Other Path: The Economic Answer to Terrorism*. New York: Harper and Row, pp. 3–365.

Development Bank of South Africa (DBSA). 2005. Overcoming Underdevelopment in South Africa's Second Economy. Development Report ISBN 1-919692-71-1.

Devey, R., Skinner, C. and Valodia I. 2006. The State of the Informal Economy in *The State of the Nation 2005–2006* edited by S. Buhlungu, et al. Human Science Research Council Press: Cape Town.

Dewar, D. 2005. A Conceptual Framework for the Formulation of an Informal Trader Policy for South African Towns and Cities. *Urban Forum*, 16(1), 1–16.

Du Toit, A. and Neves, D. 2007. In Search of South Africa's Second Economy: Chronic poverty, vulnerability and adverse incorporation in Mt. Frere and Khayelitsha. Unpublished paper prepared for the Living on the Margins Conference, PLAAS, Stellenbosch.

Gibson, A., Scott, H. and Ferrand, D. 2004. Making Markets Work for the Poor: An Objective and an Approach for Governments and Development Agencies, unpublished paper prepared for Commark Trust. Available at: http://www.tips.org.za/organisations/commark (Accessed: 13 August 2006).

Golub, S. 2003. Beyond Rule of Law Orthodoxy The Legal Empowerment Alternative. *Rule of Law Series, Democracy and Rule of Law Project, Carnegie Endowment Working Papers*, pp. 1–41.

Golub, S. 2009. The Commission on Legal Empowerment of the Poor: One Big Step Forward and A Few Steps Back for Development Policy and Practice. *Hague Journal on the Rule of Law*, 1(1), pp. 101–16.

Gready, P. 2008. Rights-based approaches to development: What is the value added? *Development in Practice*, 18(6), pp. 735–47.

Igrobe, K. 2003. Transformation in South Africa: A Study of Education and Land. *International Third World Studies Journal and Review*. Volume XIV, Available at:http://www.unomaha.edu/itwsjr/thirdXIV/Irogbe.Transformation.14.htm#life [Accessed: 5 September 2010].

Johns, L. 2007. Western Cape Schools Fail the Big Test: Education department paints a grim picture. *Weekend Argus Newspaper*. 8 September, edition 1.

Kennedy, D. 2006. The 'Rule of Law', Political Choices and Development Common Sense, in *The New Law and Economic Development: A Critical Appraisal*, edited by D. Trubeck and A. Santos. New York: Cambridge University Press, pp. 95–173.

Kesper, A. 2000. Failing or not aiming to grow? Manufacturing SMMEs and their contribution to employment growth in South Africa, *TIPS Working Paper* 15, Trade and Industrial Policy Strategies. Available at: http://www.tips.org.za [Accessed: August 2002]

Kingdon, G. and Knight, J. 2002. Quality of Schooling and the Race Gap in Labour Market Outcomes in South Africa. Paper presented at the Development Policy Research Unit (DPRU) and Friedrich Ebert Stiftung Second Annual Conference on *Labour Markets and Poverty in South Africa*, Muldersdrift, Johannesburg.

Mbeki, T. 2004. State of the Nation Address of the President of South Africa, Cape Town.

Miller, V., VeneKlasen, L. and Clarke, C. 2005. Rights-based development: Linking Rights and participation – challenges in thinking and action, in *Developing Rights?*, edited by J. Pettit and J. Wheeler. *IDS Bulletin*, 36(1) pp. 20–41.

Moser, C. 1989. Gender Planning in the Third World: Meeting Practical and Strategic Gender Needs. *World Development* 17(11), pp. 179–82.

Napier, M. and Liebermann, S. 2006. Investigation into entrepreneurs and small scale landlords, unpublished paper prepared for Shisaka Development Services in Association with the Centre for Scientific Industrial Research, Pretoria, South Africa.

Napier, M. and Mothwa, M. 2001. Push and Pull Factors in the Initiation and Maintenance of Home Work in Two Pretoria Settlements: The Myths and Realities of South African Home-Based Enterprises. *Urban Forum* 12(3–4).

Nqelo, N. and Malan, L. 1998. Comparative Study for Impact Assessment and Course Design. Unpublished paper prepared for the Triple Trust Organisation.

Pettit, J. and Wheeler, J. 2005 Developing Rights? Relating discourse to Context and Practice. *IDS Bulletin*, 36(1).

Philip, K. 2008. How the Structure of the Economy Impacts on Opportunities On the Margins, paper presented at Working on the Margins Conference, PLAAS and Chronic Poverty Centre, Cape Town, 23–24 March 2009.

Rogerson, C., Reid, K. and Wicksteed, S. 1997. Towards a Framework for Rural Small Business Support in South Africa, unpublished paper prepared for Ntsika Enterprise Promotion Agency.

Rogerson, C. 2002. Rural SMME Development in South Africa: Contemporary Directions and Policy Frameworks, unpublished paper prepared for the GTZ Project: Models for Rural Job Creation.

Rogerson, C. 2004. The Impact of the South African Government's SMME Programme: A Ten Year Review (1994–2003). *Development Southern Africa*, 21(5).

Ruiters, A., China. A, and Spicer, S. 1994. The functioning of micro enterprises and support services in the Western Cape, unpublished paper prepared for Community Agency for Social Enquiry (CASE), Cape Town.

SEDA (Small Enterprise Development Agency) 2004. Annual Review of Small Business in South Africa. A Department of Trade and Industry Publication.

Sen, A. 1999. *Development is Freedom*. New York: Random House. pp. 1–361.

Sengupta, A. 2008. The Political Economy of Legal Empowerment of the Poor, in *Rights and Legal Empowerment*, edited by Dan Banik. Farnham: Ashgate, pp. 31–45.

Skinner, C. 2007. Laws Governing Street Trading in South Africa: A Critical Commentary Paper, produced for the Commission on Legal Empowerment for the Poor for the South African Study on Business Rights.

Skinner, C. and Valodia, I. 2003. Government Support for Women in the Informal Economy in Durban, South Africa. *International Journal of Politics, Culture and Society*, 16(3), pp. 431–44.

Smith, M. et al. 2002. Survey of Spaza Shops in the Greater Cape Town. An unpublished research paper prepared for the Triple Trust Organisation.

Standing, G. 1999. *Global Labour Flexibility: Seeking Distributive Justice*. London: Macmillan Books. pp. 3–429.

Statistics South Africa. 2005. The Contribution of Small and Micro Enterprises to the Economy of the Country: A survey of non-VAT-registered Businesses in South Africa. Available at http://www.statssa.gov.za [Accessed: September 2010]

Statistics South Africa. 2008. Quarterly Labour Force Survey, 3rd quarter. Pretoria: Statistics South Africa. Available at http://www.statssa.gov.za/publications/statsdownload.asp?PPN=P0211&SCH\ [Accessed 5 September 2005].

Statistics of South Africa, 2005. Survey of the Employers and the Self-Employed. Available at http://www.statistics.gov.za [Accessed August 2007].

Stephens, M. 2009. The Commission on Legal Empowerment of the Poor: An Opportunity Missed. *Hague Journal on the Rule of Law*, 1, pp. 132–57.

Tipple, G. 2005. The Place of Home-based Enterprises in the Informal Sector: Evidence from Cochabamba, New Delhi, Surabaya and Pretoria. *Urban Studies*, 42(4), pp. 611–632.

UNDP. 2006. High Level Commission on Legal Empowerment of the Poor (HLCLEP). *Overview Paper*. Available at: http://legalempowerment.undp.org/ [Accessed: September 2007].

Valodia, I. 2000. Economic Policy and Women's Informal and Flexible Work in South Africa. Paper presented at the TIPS Annual Forum, Glenburn Lodge, 18–20 September.

Van der Berg, S. 2005. The Schooling Solution: Primary School Performance is the Key, in *Economic Transformation Audit 2005: Conflict and Governance*, edited by S. Brown, Institute for Justice and Reconciliation, South Africa.

Von Broembsen, M. 2010. Legal Empowerment of the Poor: The Re-emergence of a Lost Strand of Human Rights? Unpublished paper presented at a conference hosted by the Academic Network of Legal Empowerment of the Poor (ANLEP) and the Institute of Development and Labour Law (IDLL), at the University of Cape Town, 6 May.

Chapter 4
Waste Management and the Workplace[1]

Jan Theron and Margareet Visser

Section 1: Introduction

Waste management refers to collection, transport, processing, recycling or disposal of waste materials produced by human activity. The focus of this chapter is on the role local government plays in waste management. Traditionally this has been the collection and transport of waste to landfill sites, created on the edges of urban areas. However, as a result of urbanisation, population growth, and increased consumption, the volume of waste generated by cities has become bigger, and the space for landfill sites has become scarcer and more expensive. Consequently, governments in different parts of the world have been compelled to revise their waste management policies. South Africa is no exception in this regard. Recently a Waste Act was adopted with the aim of ensuring that local government, which is entrusted with the responsibility of implementing such policies, reduces, reuses, recycles, and recovers waste so as to send less waste to landfill sites.[2] Increased attention is now being paid to the recycling of waste materials, as part of a waste minimisation strategy. At the same time the government cannot be oblivious to the fact that large numbers of people are employed both in the collection of waste and in various processes of recycling.

Three broad categories of persons employed in waste management can be identified. The first are those directly employed by local authorities. The second are those employed by private contractors or intermediaries providing waste management services to local authorities. The third category comprises those who collect, sort and sell recyclables in order to survive.[3] In some countries, they are

1 The research on which this article is based was supported by the UK Department for International Development (DFID) and the Research Committee of the University of Cape Town. The views expressed are not necessarily those of DFID or the University.

2 Section 5, National Environmental Management: Waste Act, No. 59 of 2008. Waste management is a local government competence in terms of Schedule 5B of the Constitution of South Africa (Act 108 of 1996). The Local Government Systems Act (No. 32 of 2000) specifies the obligations of local government in this regard.

3 The range of what materials waste pickers collect varies from city to city. However, the broad categories of what is normally collected by waste pickers include scrap metal, glass, cans, plastic and paper because they are in demand with recyclers.

called 'waste pickers'. In what follows, we shall simply refer to them as the 'self-employed'.

The self-employed, it must be noted, may include family units or small emergent enterprises. Invariably the self-employed also cooperate with one another in various ways. In some countries cooperation has developed to the point where the self-employed have formed cooperatives and community-based associations in order to advance their interests, notably in Latin America (Medina 2005: 20, Bonner 2008: 7, Tejani 2003). This development is in its infancy in South Africa. One of the questions raised in this analysis is whether it should be more actively promoted.

Consistent with a notion of work as encompassing all forms of employment, including self-employment, our point of departure is to regard all persons engaged in the collection, sorting and selling of recyclables as workers. As in other developing countries (Coad 2003: 12), we argue that the self-employed supplement municipal waste management services. Their role should therefore also be seen as integral to the waste management function of local government. Local government in turn determines what kind of employment opportunities exist in waste management, and for which categories of worker.

The 'informal economy', as defined by the ILO, refers to 'all economic activities by workers and economic units that are- in law or practice- not covered or insufficiently covered by formal arrangements'.[4] This definition of the informal economy would certainly encompass the self-employed. It is also broad enough to include workers employed by private contractors that are not covered, or are insufficiently covered, by labour legislation, or other protective regulations. But how, practically, is it possible to extend rights to workers such as these?

To address this question, we take as a case study waste management in the City of Cape Town (hereafter 'The City'). In section 2 of this chapter, we consider the waste management strategies of the City and how it has determined what employment opportunities exist through these strategies. What these strategies boil down to is externalisation, by which we mean a restructuring of employment so that it is actually (or in effect) regulated by a commercial contract, rather than a contract of employment (Theron 2005).

Externalisation, we argue in section 3, is a system of regulation. To appreciate this it is necessary to lift the 'contractual veil' externalisation creates. Its outcome is to establish a hierarchy of rights, in which workers directly employed by local authorities are protected by formal regulation, workers employed by contractors and private agents are partially protected and the self-employed are unprotected. Increased inequality is thus another outcome.

Merely lifting the 'contractual veil', however, does not provide workers who are partially protected or unprotected with a remedy against the entity that ultimately determines their conditions of work, namely the local authority. The mechanism

4 See ILO (2002) resolution concerning decent work and the informal economy, adopted by the General Conference at its 90th Session, 2002.

we propose to do so is to extend the existing notion of the workplace, to include employees of employers other than the local authority, and the self-employed. This is the subject of section 4.

There are two ways in which organisations can engage with local authorities, on the basis of this extended notion of the workplace. The first involves essentially a trade union strategy: to address the issue of inequality in the extended notion of the workplace we have proposed. The other is to do what is being done in Latin America, through the self-employed associating in cooperatives or similar entities to provide services to the local authority. A case study of such an initiative in the City is outlined. An overall conclusion is provided in the last section.

Section 2: The Waste Management Strategies of the City

The strategies adopted by the City to manage waste conform to a conception of the role of the state that has been in vogue globally, and is associated with the promotion of 'public-private partnerships' (PPPs) as a method of having public goods wholly or partially produced by the private sector (Kihato and Schmitz 2002: 6).[5] These strategies must also be understood in the context of the political transition in South Africa post-1994.

In 1997, the 39 municipalities serving its various racially segregated suburbs were restructured into 7 municipal service structures, and in 2000, the so-called 'Unicity' was established (Ferrara et al. 2008). Yet the legacy of institutional fragmentation and social inequality (coupled with differential tariff structures) remained. No doubt, ongoing political tensions within the City have made it more difficult to address this legacy.[6] Yet the fundamental problem is one affecting all local authorities: existing budgets have been insufficient to meet increased demands for service delivery.

This situation was exacerbated by a change of macro-economic policy in 1996. The Reconstruction and Development Programme (RDP) provided a lifeline tariff[7] to give all citizens access to the most basic services. The Growth Employment and Redistribution (GEAR) policy that supplanted the RDP emphasised the

---

5 Some (in our opinion, correctly) regard any agent who is not public as 'private', including for instance CBOs and NGOs (Ahmed and Ali 2004: 469). Others regard 'private' as comprising the comparatively large, for-profit, commercial organisations.

6 The current mayor leads a multi-party political coalition led by the Democratic Alliance. Tension both within this coalition and between the coalition and the ruling ANC has at times been high, a situation that persists at the time of writing.

7 A lifeline tariff (also called a 'social tariff') is a pricing strategy designed to provide minimal amounts of water and electricity either for free or at very low prices to households. Additional amounts carry increasing per-volume prices. (From: Water and Sanitation for All: A Practitioner's Companion, http://web.mit.edu/urbanupgrading/waterandsanitation/resources/definitions.html)

full recovery of costs from all users (Miraftab 2004: 877). As a result, central government financial assistance to local government diminished drastically.[8]

To cope with this situation local governments invoked the concept of PPPs, and increasingly engaged external service providers to provide municipal services (Miraftab 2004: 276, 877). The authors argue that the term should only be used in the context where there is an ongoing set of interactions, which require 'real partnership' between the state on the one side and the private sector and civil society on the other side. A 'real partnership' in turn assumes that the parties have combined forces to define and/or accomplish an objective (Mitchell-Weaver and Manning 1991: 48–9).

In this instance, we argue, PPPs are simply a euphemism for privatisation, which in turn is no more than externalisation in the context of the public sector. The Local Government Municipal Systems Act, which seeks to regulate the appointment of external service providers, does not appear to have constrained local government in this regard.[9]

In Cape Town, this process began with the introduction of a scheme to provide cleaning services in Khayalitsha, its largest township. The parties to this scheme, initially known as the Billy Hattingh Scheme,[10] were the local authority, township-based entrepreneurs and a private company ostensibly acting as a mentor to the entrepreneurs. Each entrepreneur was allocated a truck, and paid a monthly fee to provide a waste collection service. The fee was intended to cover the costs of the vehicle, and the wages of the workers employed to assist him (Miraftab 2004: 881, Samson 2004: 35).

While the scheme achieved significant savings for the City,[11] it was mired in controversy. The SA Municipal Workers Union (SAMWU) saw it as threatening the employment security of their members. After a protracted dispute, the Labour

8 The Financial and Fiscal Commission reported that by 2001 the amount of intergovernmental grants from central to local levels in real terms had fallen by 85 per cent compared to 1991 (Ilrig 2001, cited in Miraftab 2004: 876).

9 The Municipal Systems Act sanctions the appointment of 'appropriate' external service providers to provide municipal services only after a fairly rigorous process, including consultation with the community where the service is to be provided, an assessment of the various service delivery options, including 'the direct and indirect costs and benefits' associated with the proposal, and a feasibility study. Further research is needed to establish to what extent this process is complied with. See section 11(3)(f) and 78 (3) of Act 32 of 2000.

10 The scheme was initially established under the jurisdiction of City of Tygerberg, which was one of the seven local authorities that formed the Unicity. It was later renamed The Entrepreneurial Development Corporation (Tedcor) scheme.

11 Before the introduction of the Billy Hattingh Scheme, the City of Cape Town was spending R11m per year to clean up Khayelitsha. The Billy Hattingh scheme would cost the council only R4.7m per year (Qotole and Xali 2001: 8).

Court upheld local government's right to introduce such a scheme.[12] There was also controversy regarding the company's role in acting as a financial intermediary between the entrepreneurs and the City (Miraftab 2004: 881, Samson 2004: 35), and about the fees paid to entrepreneur (Visser and Theron, 2009: 8). Significantly, this fee was referred to as a 'salary' (Samson 2004: 35). Ultimately, the scheme was abandoned.

However, abandonment of the scheme did not mean abandonment of the strategy of engaging private contractors. Instead the City began entering into – what has been referred to in the literature as – 'one-man' contracts with entrepreneurs from informal settlements who were supposed recruit and hire workers to clean up the area where they reside (Miraftab 2004: 882). Subsequently the City scrapped the requirement that entrepreneurs have to reside in the area in which the service operates. Instead, it has been contracting with established firms providing waste management services and black-owned enterprises that comply with the objectives of government's black economic empowerment (BEE) policies.

Consequently, all waste collection in informal areas, where a significant proportion of the City's population stays, is carried out by private contractors.[13] Private contractors in turn employ the workers who collect the refuse, in black bags that are then deposited either in an open skip or in a shipping container. These contractors are paid per dwelling serviced.[14] A more established contractor then transports the waste refuse from there to the municipal dump.

By comparison, primarily local government employees carry out waste collection in the formal (residential) areas of the City. 'Formal' in this context refers to residential areas that have paved streets and sidewalks, where the comparatively sophisticated system of 240-litre wheeled containers (commonly referred to as 'wheelie bins') can be deployed. These are emptied once a week by compactor trucks fitted with hydraulic lifts.

About 25 per cent of waste collected in these formal areas is collected by private contractors. It is not entirely clear on what basis the City opts to appoint private contractors, but it appears to relate to the City's capacity to provide the service. In commercial and industrial areas, waste may be collected either by private contractors or by arrangement with the City.[15]

---

12 City of Tygerberg v SA Municipal Workers Union and Others (1999) *Industrial Law Journal*, Vol. 20: 1032–43.

13 The total number of informal households serviced by the City was 195,185 in 2008, compared with 787,489 formal households. However, the number of informal households serviced is not the totality of informal households, and it does not appear the City knows the number living in informal households.

14 Dwellings are counted on a six-monthly basis because of the fast pace of migration.

15 If a business chooses to make use of a commercial waste collection company, the City can request proof of the contract entered with the waste collection company. According to a City official such proof is required to deter companies from cutting costs by merely dumping their waste.

Although recycling (or waste minimisation) is acknowledged to be a local government responsibility,[16] very few resources have been allocated to this function. The City has established drop-off centres, where residents may deliver garden refuse, building rubble and recyclable material. It also owns a Material Recovery Facility where recyclable material is salvaged, as well as the equipment utilised to do so. However, the lion's share of the capital budget is still spent on landfill infrastructure and associated services (Sustainability Institute 2007: 75).[17]

In part, this is because the City relies on private contractors to fulfil its responsibilities. Out of a total of twenty drop off centres, eight are operated by private contractors. A private contractor also operates the Material Recovery Facility. However, a more fundamental problem is that the drop-off centres rely on the public to deliver recyclables, and this is only a fraction of the waste that is sent to land-fill sites.

The City has also been piloting a scheme to separate recyclables 'at source', by requesting home owners in the formal, predominantly middle-class areas to put recyclables in a separate bag on top of their 'wheelie-bins'. The effect of this scheme will be to eliminate opportunities for the self-employed that make a living from separating recyclables. It will also help keep them out of middle class areas. This may even be a selling point for the scheme in these areas.

In summary, the City has not created direct employment through its waste management strategies. It has also not directed its strategies at enhancing opportunities for the self-employed. The indications are rather that it intends shutting down such opportunities. Where it has created opportunities of employment is with private contractors, and intermediaries such as temporary employment agencies, or labour brokers, as they are commonly called in South Africa. In some instances, such intermediaries are engaged by the City and in some instances by the private contractor, in terms of a subcontracting agreement or to supplement the contractor's own workforce.

Section 3: Lifting the 'Contractual Veil'

Miraftab (2004), Samson (2004) and Qotole and Xali (2001) all concur that by engaging private service providers, local government has eroded labour standards. What is less clear is whether this is something that can be reversed, and if so, how.

---

16 The objective is to achieve 'zero waste'. The National Environmental Management Act (NEMA) and the Waste Act stipulate that municipalities should minimise waste in order to achieve a long-term 'zero waste' goal. See Act No. 39 of 2007 and Act 59 of 2008. See also the website of the City of Cape Town's Solid Waste Department (http://www.capetown.gov.za/en/solidwaste/Pages/default.aspx) as well as the City's Integrated Waste Management Policy.

17 This is despite the fact that only three of the City's six landfill sites are still in operation, and are estimated to reach capacity within the next five to 13 years.

It would be simplistic to demand that the City directly employ all those that are currently employed via contractors and intermediaries without considering all the implications. These include the implications for the self-employed, and indeed the potential for work opportunities in waste management.

The point of departure, we suggest, is to consider externalisation as a system of regulation. The subject of regulation is the employment relationship, and the means utilised is the contract between the person procuring goods or utilising services, in this case the City, and the person providing goods or services, in this case the contractor or intermediary. The advantage of a case study of externalisation in the public sector is that it is easier to lift the 'contractual veil' externalisation creates than in the private sector, where the terms of such commercial contracts are as a rule not disclosed to non-parties, in accordance with notions about the 'sanctity of contract' that private sector lawyers fiercely defend.

It appears there is no precedent for regarding the contracts entered into between a local authority and a service provider as public documents, to which interested parties such as trade unions and others have a right of access.[18] Nevertheless, the conditions on which service providers tender for contracts, are published. It is therefore possible to know, in the case of the City, with what requirements a contractor or intermediary must comply. It is also possible to infer from this what requirements the City does not regard as important.

It must be said in this regard that there is a general requirement that all contractors comply with labour legislation.[19] This, it might be argued, disposes of the allegation that local government has been complicit in eroding labour standards. The labour legislation in the post-1994 period is often portrayed as representing the state of the art, and effectively protecting the security of employment of employees, as well as their rights to associate and to organise. It is also assumed that it effectively deals with the issue of inequality in the workplace. However, at best such an argument misconceives the extent to which externalisation has eroded the approach to regulation this legislation embodies. At worst it is disingenuous, since one of the objects of an employer externalising a part of its operation, if not the primary object, is to limit the application of labour legislation.

To illustrate, consider the question of 'employment security'.[20] Without adequate employment security, it is difficult, if not impossible, for workers to associate, or organise. It is also difficult to exercise other rights. Workers employed

18 Everyone has the right of access to any information held by the State in terms of the South African Constitution, and the Promotion of Access to Information Act (No. 2 of 2000) was adopted to give effect to this right. In terms of this Act, any person may lodge a formal request for information. However, it remains to be seen, were such a request pursued, whether the courts would compel the terms of a private contract to be disclosed.

19 Specific reference is made to the Labour Relations Act and Basic Conditions of Employment Act.

20 This term is used in the same sense that Standing refers to 'income security', to refer to both the employed and self-employed. See Standing (2000).

by contractors have the right not to be unfairly dismissed by the contractor that employs them. However, this right does not ensure employment security. That is because most contracts between the City and private contractors are for three years and almost invariably the workers employed by private contractors are employed for fixed term contacts of shorter duration. In most instances, these are for one year.[21] Indeed the tender specifications for waste collection in informal areas require that workers only be appointed on one-year contracts. The legal effect of this situation is that once the term expires, the worker is not dismissed, and has no claim against his employer.[22]

Therefore, employment by a private contractor is highly insecure. Similarly, although in theory these workers have the right to associate and to organise, in practice they are unable to exercise these rights. This is both because their employment is insecure and because to exercise the organisational rights provided in labour legislation they first have to establish they are sufficiently representative in the workplace of the employer.[23] Many of the black-owned enterprises contracted to the City are home-based or do not have anything resembling a workplace, in the sense of a place where workers work. Moreover, to the extent that the workers have any bargaining power, it is in any event in respect of the work they do in and for the City. In fact the efficacy of all important labour rights which workers engaged by contractors and others have, with few exceptions, depends on the City. Health and safety, for example, is a major consideration in a work environment in which there are real and immediate risks. Tender documents require that workers employed by private contractors must be provided with the necessary personal protective equipment, and that contractors must provide proof of registration for the purposes of compensation for occupational injuries and diseases.[24] In the case of the 'community-based' contracts, the City even stipulates how many workers and supervisors the contractor should employ;[25] their working hours as well as

---

21 Only one contractor that was interviewed in the course of this study – a major waste collection company – employed workers on a permanent basis. However, this company also made extensive use of two labour brokers (or temporary employment agencies): about 60 per cent of its wage bill consisted of payments to labour brokers.

22 The only circumstance in which the worker could allege he was dismissed was if there was a reasonable expectation the contract might be renewed.

23 See Chapter 3, Part A of the Labour Relations Act (No. 66 of 1995). The term 'sufficiently representative' is not defined, but the workplace means the place(s) where the employees of the employer work.

24 In terms of Section 80 of the Compensation for Occupational Injuries and Diseases Act, 130 of 1993. See also Tender document number: 495S/2007/2008. In fact the indications are that the personal protective equipment issued by private contractors was insufficient. Some workers interviewed in the course of this study reported that they were only issued with gloves and no overalls, safety boots or masks. One worker bought his own mask.

25 It is significant that the City is far more prescriptive in respect of the 'community-based' contracts than in its tender requirements for formal areas.

the minimum wage for general workers.[26] Although the City does not have any effective system of monitoring compliance with these conditions, the risk of losing a contract must operate as a powerful deterrent in the competitive circumstances in which contractors operate.

In interviews with the City's Solid Waste Department, the justification for engaging external service providers is, as one would expect, operational in nature. In the case of waste collection, private contractors are said to be less constrained by red tape, and therefore able to deliver a speedier service.[27] It is also argued that the costs of maintaining a fleet of collection trucks are lower, because the vehicles owned by private contractors are newer and less prone to breakdowns than the City's fleet.[28] But arguments such as these do not stand up to scrutiny. It may be that the City has to follow more cumbersome procedures to acquire new vehicles, but the more fundamental question is why the City has not invested resources in upgrading its capacity.

Clearly, cost is the primary consideration. Since waste collection is pre-eminently a labour intensive operation, undoubtedly the most important cost is that of labour. Workers directly employed by the City are covered by a bargaining council agreement for local government that is negotiated nationally (the SALGBC). Workers engaged by private contractors are not regarded as falling within the scope of the SALGBC, and in practice earn about half what the counterparts in the City earn, not taking into account the fringe benefits the latter enjoy, which are a significant proportion of their total wage. We do not know the number of workers employed by contractors. However, there are indications that it could be as much as forty per cent of the number employed directly by the City. In any event, it clearly represents a massive cost saving to the City to have contractors employ these workers, which will not easily be reversed.

The operational arguments for externalisation in respect of recycling (or waste minimisation) appear, at first blush, somewhat more persuasive. Specialised equipment is required to recycle and the Department does not have it. For instance, the City's Solid Waste Department argue that at drop-off centres specialised, expensive recycling equipment is required to recycle garden waste and building rubble. In addition, the compactor trucks used for waste collection are not suitable for collecting recyclables, because they crush refuse indiscriminately and make the sorting of waste more difficult. Instead of acquiring the equipment needed,

26 This wage was based on Wage Determination 467 for Unskilled Labour, Certain Areas, 1991. However, this wage determination was cancelled in 2007, and is therefore of no legal effect.

27 Interview with City official, cited by Visser and Theron (2009: 20).

28 It is claimed the average truck utilised by the City's Solid Waste Department is eight years old. See p. 5 of City's 2008 Solid Waste Management Dept Integrated Waste Management and Service Delivery Sector Plan at http://www.capetown.gov.za/en/IDP/Documents/Statutory%20compliance%20plans/I%20Waste%20Plan%20SWM%2017_01_08%20(final).pdf

they argue that it makes more sense to contract out to the private sector. The City lacks expertise to identify and negotiate with the buyers for recyclables. This is better left to private agents. Recycling is, in any event, not a 'core competency' of the Solid Waste Department.[29]

'Core competency' is a term of indeterminate meaning that is routinely advanced to justify outsourcing. However, to argue that recycling is not a core competency in this instance flies in the face of the provisions of the Waste Act,[30] in terms of which waste minimisation will be a local government responsibility.[31] There are also operational arguments as to why the City's recycling strategies are problematic, and as to why the justifications for externalising this function do not hold water.

The recycling rate achieved by the contractor at the City's Material Recovery Facility, for example, has been unimpressive. Although the City has set him the target of salvaging 10–15 per cent of recyclables from the mixed waste delivered to the Centre, the contractor has only managed to salvage about 5 per cent.[32] It is also not correct that specialised machinery is required to sort the bulk of recyclable material currently directed to landfill sites. Elsewhere in the developing world, informal collectors have been able to achieve much higher recycling rates than the formal private sector without 'developed world' technology (Iskandar 2005, Wilson et al. 2009).[33]

The City also does not have to search far to find buyers for recyclables. Glass recycling, for example, is dominated by a single large buyer, the paper recycling industry by two dominant players, with only the plastics recycling sector operating under highly competitive and dynamic free market principles (Lowitt 2008: 9). The City would also have considerable negotiating power with recyclers. Its negotiating power would of course be enhanced if it were directly responsible for the entire process of collecting and sorting of recyclable material.

The reason the aforementioned possibility cannot be contemplated, more clearly in the case of recycling than in the case of waste collection, also has to do with the kind of enterprises that the City is promoting, which in turn determines the kind of employment opportunities it wishes to create. The effect of the pilot scheme to separate waste 'at source', we have suggested, was to limit to eliminate opportunities for the self-employed who make a living from separating recyclables. This is because it would, if successful, cut off their access to a comparatively

29 City official, cited by Visser and Theron (2009: 20).

30 No. 59 of 2008: National Environmental Management: Waste Act, 2008.

31 No. 39 of 2007.

32 Interview with City official, cited by Visser and Theron (2009: 16).

33 Wilson et al. (2009) have found that the informal sector manage to retrieve between 20 per cent to 50 per cent of recyclable material from mixed waste. In Cairo, the Zabbaleen community was reported to recover between 80–85 per cent of recyclables due their intensive manual sorting and expertise (Iskandar 2005). In spite of this, the municipality of Cairo contracted multi-national corporations to take over the waste management system.

lucrative waste stream. In this regard, it must be noted that middle-class areas are regarded as generating far more recyclable waste than poor or working class areas.

A scheme that created opportunities for the self-employed would thus assign them a central role in the separation of waste 'at source.' As it happened, the pilot project – 'Yellow Bag System' – failed initially, because the contractors did not deem it profitable enough. The City's response was not to question whether it should be reliant on private contractors, but rather to introduce a subsidy for the contractors involved.[34] In terms of this subsidy, contractors are paid both by the recycler for material delivered and by the City.[35]

What the City pay contractors, according to one such contractor interviewed, was much more than he received from the recyclers. He reported that his business had grown five-fold.[36] This is also not the only instances in which the City subsidises contractors engaged in recycling.[37] It also seems that contractors who provide waste collection services are generously remunerated. One contractor interviewed estimated that the City paid him three times more than he was paid for an equivalent service rendered to another contractor to whom he was sub-contracted.

In summary, it is perhaps not surprising that there is a class dimension in how waste is managed in the City. This is evident in the different waste management strategies the City utilises, and perhaps even the fact that different divisions in the City are responsible for implementing these strategies.[38] The apparent zeal with which it is promoting black-owned enterprises can also be seen as a way of changing the racial profile of employers as a class. However, the enterprises these employers operate are satellites of the City, dependent on its largesse. Their viability also depends on their exclusion from the wage regime applicable to the City, namely the bargaining council agreement. Accordingly the outcome is the

---

34 The pilot, referred to as the 'Yellow Bag System', was launched at Marina da Gama in the Southern Peninsula in 2002.

35 Interview with City official, cited in Visser and Theron (2009: 16). The City pays the contractor a set price for each kilogram of recyclables sold to the recycler.

36 Interview with city official, cited by Visser and Theron (2009: 21).

37 Contractors at drop-off sites are subsidised in that the Department pays them a set fee for each skip of green waste that is sold for composting. The drop-off centres directly managed by the City do not compete with them, in that no chipping or composting or sorting of recyclable material takes place there (Interview with City official, cited by Visser and Theron 2009). Also see: http://www.capetown.gov.za/en/solidwaste/Pages/Dropofffacilities.aspx.

38 Waste collection in informal areas is the responsibility of an Area Cleansing Division whereas the compactor trucks used in formal areas is the responsibility of the Collections Division. The operational rationale for this division is that the compactor trucks cannot access the narrow, unpaved streets in these areas.

establishment of a hierarchy, in which those that are directly employed can be characterised as insiders, and those that are not directly employed are not.[39]

At the bottom of this hierarchy are, of course, the self-employed who do not enjoy the benefit of any of the protective provisions of labour legislation because they are not regarded as employees. At the same time, we have argued that employment security is critical for workers to be able to associate and organise. It can be argued that the self-employed enjoy greater employment security than workers employed by contractors. Adding force to this argument, there are more indications of organisation amongst the self-employed than workers employed by contractors. The latter are, in any event, only able to derive a benefit from labour legislation for the limited period they are employed. Most, as already pointed out, are on one-year contracts. It is in this context that the possibility of accommodating the self-employed in the City's waste management strategies must be considered.

Section 4: Extending the Notion of the Workplace

Lifting the contractual veil lend substance to an argument as to why the City should be held accountable for the conditions under which all municipal workers work. However, the demand this argument gives rise to is that the City should directly employ all municipal workers. This is typically a trade union demand. Alternatively, the legal logic of such an argument would be that the City is in fact the employer, or should be regarded as the employer in law, based on some notion of co-employment or joint and several liability.

However, a demand to directly employ workers is only likely to succeed in respect of that section of workers that are already partially protected by labour legislation, namely the workers employed by contractors. Even then, it is only likely to succeed to a limited extent, particularly if workers employed by contractors are to be appointed on the same terms and conditions as those who are directly employed. The budgetary consequences of directly employing the number of workers involved would be massive. Such an approach would also not take cognisance of the situation of the self-employed engaged in municipal work. Similarly, it would not overcome inequality.

Reliance on legal notions of co-employment or joint and several liabilities would be similarly misplaced. It is not that there is no merit in the argument, but the legal consequence would be far-reaching, to say the least. Moreover the City has a plausible counter: it prescribes the conditions on which contractors employ workers not because it is itself the employer, but because it is accountable to the residents for the services it provides, and a break-down in labour relations may

39 The establishment and character of the hierarchy being established in the workplace as a consequence of externalisation is explored more fully in Theron (2009: 1210).

result in a breakdown in service, as the 2009 strike demonstrated.[40] To expect the law to achieve such a far-reaching consequence in the absence of organisation, we would argue, is unrealistic. Organisation is essential both to achieve progress in ameliorating inequality, and enabling all municipal workers to exercise their rights.

In fact, existing patterns of organisation largely reinforce the hierarchy we have described: insiders are unionised and outsiders are not. This relates to the way in which the workplace is conceived. In South African labour legislation, the workplace is the place or places where the employees of an employer work.[41] Thus, although workplace is necessarily a spatial concept, the definition assumes there is a separate and distinct workplace for each employer. To this extent it is the status of the employer rather than the physical space where he or she actually operates that is determinative. However, this legal definition is increasingly at odds with the way in which employment is in fact structured, because of externalisation. Outsiders and insiders in fact work in the same physical spaces.

One legal consequence of a definition that is at odds with reality has already been noted in the previous section. It is difficult for a trade union to establish that it is sufficiently representative in the workplace, to qualify for organisational rights. A no less important consequence is to render inequality in the physical space where workers actually work invisible, or to disregard it. Put differently, as long as workers accept a definition of the workplace in which the status of the employer trumps space, there can be no question of solidarity between the different categories of workers.

If, however, the concept of a workplace can be extended to encompass all categories of workers engaged in municipal work (as defined in the introductory section of this chapter), lifting the corporate veil provides a basis for engaging with the City regarding the nature of the subsidies it provides to certain enterprises. It also provides an opportunity to interrogate its waste management policies in terms of who benefits from these policies. Such a process of engagement could indeed address the situation of the self-employed who are or may be disadvantaged by the City's policies.

The concept of a workplace proposed here, therefore, is a defined physical space where workers, whether employed by one or more employers or self-employed, are engaged in a common economic activity, or in different aspects of the same economic activity. In accommodating the self-employed within the same work place, and specifically their right to associate, trade unions may also not be the appropriate organisation. At the same time whatever form of organisation was

40 In August 2009, the two largest unions representing municipal workers directly employed by local authorities, including the City of Cape Town, were on strike. The strike resulted in the trashing of refuse in the streets, which was the subject of some controversy.

41 Where the employer has more than one operation, as in the case of the City, it is all the places where employees work. Section 213, Labour Relations Act, 1995. This definition is subject to certain qualifications that are not relevant in this context.

adopted, trade union recognition of the self-employed as being part of the same workplace, and support for their demands, could play a critical role in ensuring its sustainability. In this regard, it is useful to consider the experience of a community initiative in one of the more affluent suburbs of the City, established at one of the City's drop-off centres.

This drop-off centre was managed by a private contractor. Residents of the suburb became irate when they realised that the recyclables they delivered were not being sorted and sold to the recycler, but simply directed to a landfill site. Following discussions with the City and the contractor, community members were eventually given access to the site, and allowed to sort and sell the recyclables themselves, without pay or subsidy from either the contractor or the City. The contractor, however, continues to be paid by the City to manage the drop-off centre. He also charges for the transportation of sorted recyclables to the recyclers.

The City justifies its refusal to pay the community representatives on the ground that it already paid the contractor to fulfil this service.[42] At the same time, it has been slow to take any practical steps to support them. After repeated requests over some 18 months, the community have secured two chemical toilets and a promise of a solid structure where the workers who sort the waste, most of whom reside in an informal settlement in the nearby township, would have some protection from the elements. These workers have now decided to for a cooperative, and in October 2008 were invited to tender for the management of the drop-off site.

The only income the cooperative generates is through the sale of recyclables. After paying their expenses, the proceeds of the sales are divided among the ten members. Each earns an average of about R1,500 per month. Some would argue this is not a living wage. Yet with more supportive policies on the part of the City, the income of the cooperative would surely improve. More importantly, what members earn from a cooperative is not comparable to wages earned from an employer. The value of having one's own enterprise cannot be quantified. This, we would argue, is the kind of empowerment government should be promoting, rather than the enrichment of a few individuals.

Conclusion

The question raised in the introductory section of this essay related to how one could practically extend rights to workers in the informal economy. In the case of waste management in the City of Cape Town, workers in the informal economy include workers employed by satellite enterprises providing cleaning and recycling services. In externalising these functions, the City has done what other local authorities in South Africa have done, albeit to varying degrees. Waste management is only one of various kinds of municipal work that has been

42 Interview with City official, cited by Visser and Theron (2009: 31).

externalised. At the time of writing, the City was embroiled in a dispute involving another, the parking attendants that patrol the City's parking meters.[43]

The other category of informal worker considered here is the self-employed. The self-employed, the workers employed by contractors and those directly employed by the municipality all operate in the same physical spaces, performing the same kind of work. There is no realistic prospect, we have argued, of all the workers being directly employed. Therefore, the demands of these different categories will probably be different: in the case of some, they may be the demand for labour rights, in the case of others they may be a demand for recognition and support as an enterprise. However, this should not affect their status as workers, or preclude them from supporting one another, and especially the most vulnerable amongst them.

The case of the recycling cooperative provides as example of the kind of support a trade union could give. This support could not only assist the cooperative in achieving recognition, and becoming sustainable: it could also help establish a model for the inclusion of the self-employed.

The workplace must always be the basis for organising workers. An extended notion of the workplace that corresponds to the place(s) workers actually work is therefore a starting point for building organisation that overcomes the differences between them. Without autonomous organisations, it is difficult to see how any bid to extend rights to workers can have any meaningful impact.

References

Ahmed, S.A. and Ali, M. 2004. Partnerships for solid waste management in developing countries: linking theories to realities. *Habitat International*, 28, 467–79.

Bonner, C. 2008. Waste pickers without frontiers. *South African Labour Bulletin*, 32(4), 7–9.

Coad, A. 2003. *Solid Waste Collection that Benefits the Urban Poor.* Workshop Report, Collaborative Working Group on Solid Waste Management in Low- and Middle Income Countries, Dar es Salaam, Tanzania, 9–14 March 2003, Available at http://www.skat.ch/publications/prarticle.2005-09-29.7288084326/prarticle.2005-11-25.5820482302/skatpublication.2005-12-02.0331566765

Ferrara, C., Gutierrez, A., Markel, E. and Slater, Y. 2008. *Opportunities in Waste: From Cape Town to Ruiru.* Working Draft, Economic and Political Development Final Workshop Report School of International and Public Affairs, Columbia University, New York, 2008.

43 Whereas formerly this function was fulfilled by employees of the City's traffic department, this function is now fulfilled by a private contractor. The award of tenders has been the subject of protracted litigation that is ongoing.

Iskandar, L. 2005. *Urban Waste Managers in Cairo: Waste Collectors, Traders and Recyclers: Proceedings of the Tenth International Waste Management and Landfill Symposium* (Sardinia, Italy, 3–7 October 2005).

ILRIG (International Labour Research Group), 2001. *PPPS: A Questionable Strategy for Service Delivery.* Unpublished paper, ILRIG, Cape Town.

Kihato, C. and Schmitz, T. 2002. *Enhancing Policy Implementation: Lessons from the Water Sector*, Centre for Policy Studies, Research Report No. 95, Social Policy Series, October 2002. Available at: http://www.cps.org.za/cps%20pdf/RR95.pdf

Miraftab, F. 2004. Neoliberalism and casualisation of public sector services: the case of waste collection services in Cape Town, South Africa. *International Journal of Urban and Regional Research*, 28(4), 874–92.

Lowitt, S. 2008. *A preliminary analysis of the plastics, paper and glass recycling database: an introduction to the nature and dynamics of the industry*, Centre for Poverty, Employment and Growth, HSRC. Electronically received.

Medina, M. 2005. *Waste Picker Cooperatives in Developing Countries*, WIEGO/Cornell/SEWA Conference on Membership-based Organizations of the Poor. Ahmedabad, India, Available at: http://wiego.org/ahmedabad/papers/final/Medina_MBOP.doc

Mitchell-Weaver, C. and Manning, B. 1991. Public-private partnerships in third world development: a conceptual overview. *Studies in Comparative International Development*, Winter 26(4), 45–67.

Qotole, M. and Xali, M. 2001. *Selling Privatization to the Poor: The Billy Hattingh Community-based Refuse Removal Scheme in Khayelitsha* in Qotole, M., Xali, M. and Barchiesi, F. (eds). The Commercialization of Waste Management in South Africa, Occasional Papers Series No. 3, Municipal Services Project, Available at: http://www.queensu.ca/msp/pages/Project_Publications/Series/3.htm

Samson, M. 2004. *Organizing in the informal economy: a case study of the municipal waste management industry in South Africa.* SEED Working Paper No. 66, ILO, Geneva, Available at: http://www.ilo.org/dyn/infoecon/docs/319/F1093633110/319_en.pdf

Standing, G. 2000. Modes of Control: A Labour-status Approach to Decent Work. ILO, Geneva, Available at: http://www.ilo.org/public/english/protection/ses/download/docs/modes_of_control.pdf

Sustainability Institute. 2007. *Integrated Analysis Solid Waste Baseline Report.* UNDP Project No. 00038512, Available at: http://sustainableneighbourhoods.co.za/index.php?option=com_docman&task=doc_view&gid=66&Itemid=6

Tejani, S. 2003. *Scrap-collectors fight for and win a new legitimacy.* InfoChange News & Features, April 2003. InfoChange News & Features [Online, April 2003] Available at: http://infochangeindia.org/20030406326/Livelihoods/Features/Scrap-collectors-fight-for-and-win-a-new-legitimacy.html

Theron, J. 2005. Employment is Not What it Used to Be, in *Beyond the Apartheid Workplace: Studies in Transition*, edited by E. Webster and K. Von Holdt. Scottsville: University of Kwazulu Natal, 293–316.

Theron, J. 2009. Plus ça Change: Re-inventing Inequality in the Post Apartheid Workplace in *Equality in the Workplace: Reflections from South Africa and Beyond*, edited by O. Dupper and C. Garbers. Cape Town: Juta, 121–36.

Visser, M. and Theron, J. 2009. *Waste Not: Externalisation and the Management of Waste in Cape Town*, PLAAS Working Paper 12. Working on the Margins. Conference, Rondebosch, Cape Town, 26–27 March, Available at: http://www.plaas.org.za/publications/wp/wp12

Wilson, D.C., Velis, C. and Cheeseman, C. 2006. The role of informal sector recycling in waste management in developing countries. *Habitat International*, 30, 797–808.

Chapter 5
Formalising Trading Spaces and Places: An Analysis of the Informal Sector in Lusaka, Zambia

Wilma Sichombo Nchito

Introduction

Urban planning authorities exist in order to create 'picture perfect' cities and towns. In the African context, this often means towns without bustling markets, bus stops and streets. The informal sector, which dominates most cities on the continent, is an amorphous combination of both the positive and negative aspects of city life in Africa. And there is considerable literature available on the various contributions that this sector makes to the continued existence and growth of cities. At the micro level, individuals and households are sustained while at the macro level, industries are sustained through the distribution of goods facilitated by various low cost informal networks. Even though the informal sector is in many cases undesirable, it nonetheless remains vibrant and continues to thrive in urban settings.

While those under whose jurisdiction it falls often ignore the informal sector, it is nevertheless made up of activities that cannot be ignored due to their highly interactive nature. Informal activity may take the form of one or two women strategically located at a roadside corner, plying their wares or hundreds of traders lining streets in the inner city. There are also various levels of interaction and communication within this sector with corresponding informal rules of engagement. These in turn pose several interesting questions. What is the business or social dynamic that makes a street trader select a position next to someone selling exactly the same goods and not next to someone selling something totally different? And what do traders have to do to keep their position at particular intersections year in and year out even though they have no legal right to be there? Moreover, is it these unwritten rules that make traders defy the law and stay on the streets even when new infrastructure is been developed for their use? In an attempt to improve trading spaces and to rid the city of Lusaka of street traders, government, private developers and development agencies have helped build new structures over the past ten years. Unfortunately, this has not solved the problem as Lusaka now has more vendors than ever before. This chapter therefore discusses the various aspects of the provision of modern market infrastructure in Lusaka and analyses the factors leading to the increasing number of street traders in the city. The focus is on three trading areas within the city, the City Centre, the Lusaka City and New Soweto markets.

The issue of space allocation and creation within the city has two main actors. On the one hand, local authorities claim success when a modern market infrastructure is built and this is then used to justify the removal of street vendors. On the other hand, one finds the informal sector, which has to deal with a new structure over which it has limited or no control. For some informal traders, this new infrastructure also means that they have limited access and cannot utilise newly created spaces. The informal traders who are excluded from utilising the new structures feel justified to stay on the streets. Meanwhile a new set of traders, who claim to be a part of those excluded, join the street trade thereby exacerbating the situation and causing the contest for urban space to continue even after a new structure has been built. Urban public space is thus rapidly being modified, but are the expected outcomes being achieved?

The issue is interesting for four broad sets of reasons. First, it highlights the potential of the informal sector to organise itself in informal trading places, which later become sites for modern markets. Second, it reveals the alternative spaces selected by those who are eliminated from their original trading places and shows that there is limited legal redress for those who are excluded. Third, it shows that whereas it is hard for the informal sector to join the formal sector, it is easy for the formal sector to become part of the informal sector. Fourth, it reveals the nature of political forces at play and their impact on the informal sector. This discourse provides a supplement to the limited literature that exists on the exclusion of traders from the new markets that have been built in Zambia in the past decade or so. The construction of a modern market is positive, although in the long run it ends up causing the exclusion of traders who may not be allocated stalls in the new market. New market infrastructures are more visible to politicians who may seek to use them to their own advantage. By analysing the events that have unfolded within the informal trading sphere in Lusaka, this chapter explores possible solutions for the co-existence of various types of activities within the city.

The Informal Sector in Zambia

The informal sector plays a major role in the Zambian economy and accounts for 88 per cent of the total labour force (CSO 2005: 47). Within urban areas, 65 per cent of all employees are employed in this sector. A larger proportion of women are involved than men and the sector is dominated by those with at least primary school education (53.7 per cent).[1] Mitullah (2004) found a similar situation in

1 Only 0.02 per cent of females in a 2005 survey stated that they had no education, while none of the males did so. However, 18.8 per cent did not respond to the question and it is possible that a large percentage of those without education fall within this category (CSO 2005).

Uganda, Ghana and Kenya where there has been a notable rise in the levels of education of vendors. Most informal sector workers are self employed (53.5 per cent), while 40.7 per cent are unpaid family workers and only 4.7 per cent are paid employees (CSO 2005: 47). The sector is dominated by trading, followed by manufacturing and social and personal services and men earn almost two and a half times more than their female counterparts. In general, the characteristics of the informal sector in Zambia are a replica of those found globally and therefore the country does not represent a special case. Nonetheless, the Zambian experience is interesting to focus on because of the increase in the number of new markets within its cities as well as the continued conflict between cities and vendors.

The informal sector has both direct and indirect linkages with the formal sector. In some cases, traders in the informal sector (e.g. street vendors) are employed by retailers or wholesalers who supply vendors with goods and pay them a commission after the goods are sold. Sometimes informal sector traders acquire goods on credit from the formal sector and clients are from both the informal and informal sectors, although due to increasing levels of pedestrian and vehicular congestion in the inner city and within urban markets, clients from the formal sector are finding informal goods increasingly inaccessible. Visiting markets in some parts of town is seen as unsafe and cumbersome for people who own a car, although it is easier for pedestrians and those who use public transport.

Brief Background

From the time of Zambia's political independence in 1964 to the early 1970s, street vending was highly regulated and barely visible in the country's urban centres. Moreover, the government of the time was heavy handed and there was a general adherence to municipal by-laws. The earliest vending activity involved the selling of cigarettes and sweets and later women began selling vegetables. In Hansen's (2004) overview of the development of street vending in Lusaka the effects of political influence are also highlighted. Although during this early period vendors were often chased away from public spaces, it is during this very period that vendors entrenched themselves as part of the urban landscape.

Major changes took place in the late 1970s and the 1980s when, due to the economic downturn, the country experienced shortages of major essential commodities such as sugar, soap and cooking oil. These shortages proved to be a boost for vendors who were able to bring such commodities, most often illegally, from neighbouring countries such as Zimbabwe and Malawi. Because of its illegal undertones street trade during this period was sometimes referred to as the 'black market' (Hansen 2004: 63). The general situation of a shortage of essential commodities made traders realise that almost anything could be sold, and apart from selling small items like newspapers, magazines, cigarettes, handkerchiefs, razor blades and sweets, vending took a new dimension. Supplies of an assortment of goods such as clothes, footwear, cell phones and accessories, children's toys, books, fresh fruit and vegetables, pets and various other accessories found their way to the street. At the same time liberal policies which promoted free market practices saw the closure of state-owned manufacturing and service industries due to Structural Adjustment Programmes (SAPs). The increase in the number of people in the informal sector can therefore be linked to the liberal economic policies of the 1990s.

Vending as an activity assumed greater prominence in 1993 – after vendors had clashed with the police – when President Frederick Chiluba created a so-called 'vendors desk' at State House. This move created a feeling of legitimacy among vendors who started referring to themselves as belonging to the 'Office of the President' (ibid: 65). Indeed, acknowledgment from the highest authority in the land made vendors feel 'untouchable' and secure in their trade. This 'security', even though transient, encouraged a growing number of people to find trading spaces within the inner city. Shop owners could only watch hopelessly as the shop corridors filled with agents of the 'Office of the President' and many also left designated markets around the city and headed for the inner city streets. The legitimacy provided by the Presidential initiative to establish the 'vendor's desk', however, abruptly came to an end in 1997 when vendors were forcefully removed from the streets and their shacks burnt down one early morning. Hansen (2004) notes that coincidentally the Lusaka City market was opened a day after vendors were removed from the streets. For a while sanity returned to the streets, but two years later the situation had deteriorated and a forceful removal was carried out again in 1999. The issue of vendors in the inner city continues to remain contentious, and the local authority sees their forced removal as the only solution. Further, since formal employment continues to elude a large portion of the urban population, the informal sector often is the only real option for many in the country's capital.

Lusaka, the capital city, is characterised by a high population density, and therefore became attractive to vendors who needed high volumes of sales. Currently, vendors have become accustomed to taking over streets and any open spaces within designated markets, thus increasing congestion in the central business district (CBD). Vending is illegal and the city council's efforts to remove vendors from the city streets have met with limited success. The informal sector is also found within markets which are the designated trading areas recognised by the council. Due to immense pressure from the large number of unemployed people who opt to start trading, these markets have been filled to capacity and have often become hazardous with numerous fires breaking out.[2] Over the years traders usually make improvements to their trading spaces and build permanent structures and, in some markets, develop their own management system through market associations. Such markets basically have low operational standards, little

2 In September 2006, Lusaka's city centre market was gutted in the early hours of the morning and the New Kamwala market had the same experience in April 2008. The cause of market fires is always left to speculation as investigations never come up with any results ('Lusaka Town Centre Market Stalls Gutted', *Times of Zambia*, Monday, 25 September 2006; 'New Kamwala Market Gutted', *Times of Zambia*, Monday, 14 April 2008).

regulation, low business costs, low or no rent and perceived or actual multiple ownership of the whole space. These markets also consist of traders who operate from the outside, for instance on the edges of the market boundaries. Such traders are often former vendors who were chased off the streets and who subsequently surround and suffocate the existing 'formal' market. Further, this group of traders are constantly in conflict with the law and with traders with stalls inside the markets who feel disadvantaged by their presence. Councils, on the other hand, collect revenue and provide few or no services. Traders often complain about not having ablution and garbage collection facilities even though they are levied on a daily basis. Insecurity is another problem faced in such markets and goods are often pilfered. Over time these spaces become less attractive and in some cases even become a health hazard and attract intervention from government and cooperating partners like the European Union (EU) who come in to upgrade or build totally new markets. Eventually, when the construction of a modern market facility takes place, the local authority goes on to claim ownership.

When the new modern structure is finally opened, traders find themselves excluded from the space they had previously occupied. Such exclusion results from the inability to pay, discrimination based on political sympathies, gender and social status. Moreover, such forms of exclusion result in loss of trading space and loss of income for a group of people who are already in the low income bracket. In some cases, exclusion is partially caused by newcomers who may have political or financial influence which enables them use the informal sector spaces at the expense of those who have always been there. These newcomers are government employees (civil servants), party officials and business persons from the formal sector who manage to obtain stalls. Meanwhile excluded traders continue to occupy temporary sites where they are joined by new traders. Some of the temporary sites are the streets in Lusaka's CBD and the inhabitants of these sites often refuse to move to other locations, arguing that they were excluded from their old trading spaces in the first place. Since their right to a new trading place has been taken away, they feel they have a 'reciprocal right' to stay in a place illegally. The temporary location therefore gradually becomes permanent and the processes of creating new spaces for street traders starts all over again.

Demand for space in the legal markets is high and traders often occupy spaces outside the markets. There is also the infilling of spaces within the markets, making them unattractive and overcrowded. Two separate entities are concerned with trading spaces, the first being the informal sector whose solution is to trade wherever there is space. Secondly, the local authorities who try to build custom made user friendly trading areas. They also provide undeveloped trading spaces in designated places in an attempt to solve the problem. When funding is available, modern trading places are developed and traders who had settled in the spaces are often excluded either through planned elimination or by the fact that the new market spaces are too expensive for them to rent. At this point the market spaces become attractive to those who were not trading in the original places or not even part of the informal sector. There is also a high level of political interference as was seen in the allocation of stalls in the most recently modernised market. The result is that traders remain in the temporary locations and base their argument on the grounds that they were disenfranchised having been part of the original market. This situation weakens the local authority's basis for chasing traders from the streets and other illegal places.

The Empirical Focus of this Study

A part of the problem is within the CBD of Lusaka where trading spaces are inadequate and where local authorities are trying to improve market infrastructure. Lusaka being the largest city in the country has the biggest problem with street vending. The main markets in the city are the Luburma (Kamwala) market, the City Centre market, the Lusaka City and New Soweto market complex and the Common Market for Eastern and Southern Africa (COMESA) flea market. Construction of new market infrastructure has influenced the location of street traders in certain parts of the city with the main city centre being the most affected space. The location of street traders within a city ultimately has implications on its accessibility. Places and spaces are limited and traders often improvise by finding space within the city legally or illegally. The other part of the problem is the drastic reduction of employment opportunities in the formal sector. Informality becomes the only option, and as a result people end up trading in places and space that are illegal. These are not condoned or recognised by local authorities, who do, however, often turn a blind eye due to the magnitude of the problem. The government may also occasionally find it politically expedient to ignore the problem if the ruling party feels it can garner support from the street traders on crucial national issues or during elections. Indeed, the political divisions at the national level in Zambia are currently replicated within the informal sector. Thus certain markets and bus stops are controlled either by the ruling party or by the opposition. Clashes between the party supporters are common and the general fear is that a move to force vendors off the street will be met with a violent resistance and so the situation is allowed to worsen. Ultimatum upon ultimatum has been given with no tangible results. And the creation of new spaces, which could potentially solve the problem, has not been possible precisely because of the above mentioned political scenario.

Within the structuralist approach,[3] the informal sector is viewed as part of capitalism because it helps to suppress labour costs (Pratt 2006). Structuralists consider the informal sector to be exploitative – a view with which I do not necessarily agree. The implication is that formal sector employees enjoy security of employment in comparison with their informal sector counterparts. This is not true in Zambia where a vast majority of formal sector employees are employed on a

3 Structuralists argue that capitalism aims at maximising profits and therefore aim at reducing the cost of labour by creating economic conditions which favour informalisation or casualisation. It is argued that downsizing and restructuring of formal economic activity promotes informal activities.

'part time' or 'contractual' basis. The country has very high levels of 'casualisation' of labour, although there are no exact figures. Only 17 per cent of all employed persons in the country are employees, while 43 per cent are self employed, 38 per cent are unpaid family workers, and only 1 per cent are employers. A total of 72.4 per cent of employees are classified as part-time workers, i.e. those who work for less than 40 hours a week. The percentage of part-time workers in urban areas is around 42 per cent (CSO 2005: 34). The 'informalisation' of informal labour seems to be taking place as informal sector employees are no longer assured of a job from one day to the next. This therefore questions the structuralist notion of the informal sector being exploitative since the formal sector is proving to be just as uncertain in terms of job security.

A Theoretical Overview

Literature on the informal sector abounds and it is generally agreed that different labels have been given to the sector which is now commonly called the informal economy. The term 'informal sector' covers a wider range of activities which are globally ubiquitous and dominant in urban centres of developing nations. It is agreed by scholars that it is difficult to define and measure the informal sector (Brown 2006). Generally it refers to economic activities that are not regulated and do not fall within national and local legislative contexts (Brown 2006; De Soto 2008). De Soto's argument that the sector arises as a response to 'inappropriate regulation' is often true as many by-laws have been regurgitated from the colonial era (Brown 2006; Royall 2009). Licensing is also wrought with so much paper work and rules and regulations which are never translated into local languages which can be understood by all. De Soto also argues that the sector would thrive in an environment with low levels of regulation (Royall 2009; De Soto 2008).

There has been a shift in perceptions and the informal sector has in recent times been considered more positively due to global transformations. The sector is viewed as a source of growth and flexibility rather than parasitic and inefficient (Brown 2006). This positive view considers the sector as capable and productive within local economies (Lindell 2010). The idea is that there is much to be learned from informal contracts and transactions which can be replicated within the formal sector.

The creation of markets falls within the spatial dimensions of the informal economy and within the context of urban public space. Informal activities take place within the domain of urban public space which is perceived as being either civic or edge space (Brown 2006). The perception and use of space are influenced by social and cultural factors (Pellow 2002). On the other hand urban spaces are produced within social-political and historical contexts which should be included in any analysis of urban space (Low 2002). Urban public space can be defined as physical space and an understanding of the social relations that determine that space (Brown 2006). Urban public space includes all space that is not delineated or accepted as private and where there is at least a degree of legitimate public or community use. These definitions do not give, however, an indication of who owns the space and thus public space can be owned publicly/communally, privately or by government. Urban public space is also viewed as a resource that is not static but has changing boundaries due to the social negotiations that exist over its usage (ibid.).

There is also the concept that urban space is shaped by culture. Modern urban culture is contrived by the exclusion and inclusion of certain groupings in urban society from urban public space. Within the formal sector certain people are excluded from certain locations because of their wealth, race or power (Gregory 2002). For instance a certain level of business person will have no desire to conduct business on the streets whereas those at lower levels have no problems with being on the streets and would not want to do business in an enclosed formal space.

It is not clear whether traders on the street are there out of defiance for authority or whether it is an acknowledgement of their rights to space. One cannot tell whether they are led to the street by their immediate needs for survival or by their desire to express their right to the use of public spaces. It could be argued that what originates from an economic pursuit for space ends up as a contest for user rights through defiance. In the end, this defiance may be misconstrued as law breaking and the regulating authorities are required to define their position on the informal activity. Within the cultural context the fact that most Zambian still have links with rural areas where communal ownership is the norm it is not difficult to perceive these rural conceptualisations of space being reproduced in urban areas.

It is indeed difficult to quantify the informal sector within Lusaka and it is expressed in so many varied forms. Vendors are not registered by the local authority and do not belong to any organisation unlike their counterparts in markets, or cross border traders. Their extralegal status gives them the freedom not to have to pay levies where as those in markets are expected to pay daily levies. This lack of registration can also be seen as a factor which encourages traders to go to the streets where they become invisible to the authorities in terms of some sort of taxation. On the other hand, registration of vendors is complex because of the highly mobile activity and ease of changing trading places. Since the informal sector is flexible and can easily adapt to any situation it easily permeates urban centres until it becomes undesirable to other users and authorities resulting in removals.

Regulators who seek to increase their control over the sector encourage the development of new structures. This results in disruption of businesses as traders have to find and acclimatise to new trading places. In the end, when the new structure is built, some traders are permanently displaced meaning that even the rough stall they had is taken away from them and this can be a major economic setback for traders. Some could have even invested in semi-permanent structures and the development of new regulated infrastructure means that their investment is totally lost with little or no compensation. Since issues of tenure are often ambiguous in informal markets, traders with structures have a sense of ownership and can even rent out or sell the structures they have built. Within the regulated markets it is very clear who owns the stalls and traders feel insecure since there is no guarantee that they will always have a stall within the market.

It is because of this shift in perception that the EU and other similar agencies have been able to facilitate programmes and projects within the informal sector. In Zambia, the EU has been funding infrastructure development in major cities (Nchito 2002). There is no doubt that the informal sector is a fundamental component of the urban labour market and it contributes greatly to local economies. The concept of a 'trading continuum' is applicable since markets flow out onto the streets and link up with the formal shopping areas. In this case, the outward flow is encouraged by displacement caused by the refurbishing or construction of markets. Brown (2006) acknowledges that markets and home based enterprises which operate from the street are included under street trade and therefore even when a modern structure is built the activity contained in it is still part of the informal sector.

The Political Nature of Urban Spaces

Urban space is also affected by politics which have historically played a big role in Zambian markets. Partisan politics have caused conflicts over the control of urban public space in the cities as party cadres fight for the control of revenue from bus stops and markets. Urban culture in Zambia has undergone politically influenced changes over the years. There was, during the colonial era, strict control of urban public space by the colonialists. Urban space was intended for the utilisation of a few and the masses were excluded (Pellow 2002). The post independence period brought about freedom of movement. Barriers and restrictions were removed and urban society was seemingly inclusive but control of urban space utilisation was still very evident. The third republic which came with multi-party politics in 1991, liberalised the economy and with it the utilisation of urban public spaces. The informal sector seems to have been rightly and wrongly interpreted liberalisation to mean the liberty to do any type of business anywhere. Access to urban public space was open to all who had the ability to utilise it. Thus vendors argue that they are also Zambians just like everyone else and have every right to make a living and should be left alone. This perception was encouraged when in the third republic the president created the vendors desk at state house. This was manned by a cabinet minister whose sole responsibility was vendors (Hansen 2004).

Politically, Lusaka has also experienced 'detachment' from government as the parliamentary and local government positions have, since 2001, been won by the opposition. Since independence the liberalisation of movement within the urban space has not been matched with design processes which remain guided by laws from the era when access was for a few. The Town and Country Planning Act Cap 385 of 1995, which is currently being revised, was taken from the British Town Planning legislation of 1971. The views and needs of all users are not considered and the rights of all user groups are not protected, in other words urban design processes are not democratic. There has been a consistent failure to connect economic events with the needs of the people displayed by the way urban space is used. An example is the failure to provide land for low income housing within the city and yet the urban poor cannot afford to purchase land in the new housing developments that are springing up on the edges of the city.

Design has the ability to negatively affect culture and it is possible for communality to diminish when markets are privatised and sanitised. Market traders no longer stand together as they fight individually to get a stall in the new markets. This can cause a break down in the informal linkages through which informal traders channel mutual assistance and other reciprocal services. Within the urban sphere it is the culture of the rich and powerful which has become dominant and not the indigenous culture or the culture of the poorer groups (Brown 2006). The culture of the rich on the other hand is becoming more and more synonymous with western cultures of consumption which are unsustainable.

Designers of urban space are aware of the ability of spatial arrangements to destroy or sanitise what they deem as the unruly public. The built environment does not determine how people are going to interact with each other but it is capable of increasing the constraints of the amount and range of interaction which in the end can be used to exclude certain groups. Market infrastructure can be used as a tool of exclusion. It can also be used to control street traders by confining them to a regulated place. Police often clash with traders and it is thought that authorities try to facilitate policing by placing traders in a regulated space. Herbert (1998, cited in Brown 2006) argues that 'Policing can never achieve total street sovereignty because control of social dynamics, race and class which affect street life elude them' (McDonogh 2002; Low 2002). It has been argued that it is possible to promote commercial success within controlled environments, which may or may not be true.

It is clear that infrastructure development can cause exclusion. This normally happens when new shopping malls are built to create pleasant urban spaces. The literature has not really considered the situation when the new infrastructure is meant for the informal sector. Exclusion from urban space is generally considered to come about as a result of gender and poverty. Brown (2006) highlights a common design thesis which states that good design has the ability to transform public space but this is of limited significance in the absence of an understanding of the underlying reasons for management and control. For instance if the sole purpose for local authorities engaging in infrastructure development is for aesthetically motivated purposes then the issues of accessibility are ignored. The result is that there will be beautiful markets which are inaccessible by the very people they are intended for. If on the other hand the authorities want to create space for those on the street then the designs will be geared towards space creation and there will be transparency in the distribution of these spaces. As Brown (2006: 27) correctly states it is 'only when the needs of excluded groups are recognised and addressed, will real transformation of space be achieved'.

On the other hand, proponents like Hernando De Soto (2008) have argued that informality has emerged in response to bureaucratic obstacles. In other words the poor have been forced into this sector because of the prohibitive costs associated with regulated activity. To this one can ask the age old question, 'which came first'? It would appear that historically informality preceded formality within the trade sector. Is it possible that the powerful formal sector created this bureaucracy to deliberately stifle its competition? Examples from colonised Africa indicate that the laws created were hostile to the way of life of indigenous people. So although De Soto's argument may be true for today's informal sector it would appear historically that the laws were introduced in order to contain a sector which initially preceded modern retailing and trade. The major constraints to the sector are infrastructure, resource, economic and other issues. The ensuing sections of this chapter deals mainly with infrastructure issues and considers the other issues in this light.

The New Market Infrastructure in Lusaka

Lusaka has 57 designated markets which are acknowledged by the city council (Nchito 2006). The CBD initially had three designated markets but now has five of which four have undergone some alteration. The fifth market is owned and managed by the Cross Border Traders Association (CBTA) which has had plans to put up a new structure. Market infrastructure has historically been allowed to develop haphazardly as traders have built their own stalls within around original markets. Within Lusaka's CBD, the first one to undergo a change was the Lusaka City Market which opened in 1997. Israeli consultants were used and the actual construction was done by the Zambia Army (Hansen 2004). The second market, Luburma or Kamwala market was completed in 2002 by United Engineering Group (UEG) a Lebanese firm which managed to obtain a 30 year lease instead of the legal 15 year lease. There were also complaints about Chinese traders owning most of the shops in this market (Kreglund 2008). The third, City Centre market in the heart of the CBD has been built in phases with the first phase starting in 1999 when over 2,000 vendors were removed from the market. The market was finally reopened in 2007. Construction of New Soweto market, the fourth, began in 2005 and the structure was completed in January, 2009. The market is yet to be officially opened but has since been partially occupied. Some traders (approximately 600) were given keys to the stalls but the allocation process was abruptly halted. These have not given the keys back to the issuing authority and are trading in the market whilst others have set up in the open spaces within the market where the stalls are not being used.

Enter Lusaka City Market, Exit Old Soweto

Construction of markets within the city often appears as a straightforward endeavour where a structure is created and upon completion is occupied. This is not the case within the market sector. The first problem is that the urban space intended for construction is often already being occupied and utilised by the informal sector. Developers have to contend with traders who are not willing to move and often the process has to be started forcefully. Demolition exercises that precede the construction of new markets have been indicating that traders do not leave willingly (Hansen 2004; Ngwenya 2009). Such actions increase hostility between the traders and the authorities. The second problem developers contend with is re-location of displaced traders. Traders have always resisted relocation to areas far from the market they have previously occupied complaining of loss of business. The construction of the New City Market pushed the traders onto the space that came to be known as New Soweto market (constructed on the site of Old Soweto market). While New Soweto already had traders, the new construction saw an increase of numbers with traders placing themselves under high voltage electricity pylons much to the chagrin of the authorities. Traders were often moved from under the pylons but they religiously returned to the site claiming that they had nowhere else to go (Hansen 2004). Some traders claimed to have been trading under the pylons for over twenty years, which was not possible and was obviously refuted by authorities (Zambia Daily Mail 2009). Street trade increased rapidly during this phase and although it can be argued that the situation was made worse by the elevation of the informal sector to 'Office of the President' through the creation of a Vendors desk at State House. When the New City market was finally completed and opened in 1997 a cleanup of vendors eventually followed in 1999. Street vendors were told to leave the streets and occupy the new market which had been built for them. The new market filled up and new Soweto served as an overflow. The success of this cleanup like many others before and after was short lived because in the same year the construction of City centre market began and once again traders were removed to make space for construction.

New City Centre Market

The City Centre market evictions resulted in traders laying their wares on the streets surrounding the market causing extreme levels of congestion as the City Centre market is right in the heart of the CBD. Traders took over one lane of Freedom Way which fortunately was a dual lane thoroughfare in the CBD. One interesting observation is that with time other adjacent streets such as Freedom way, Cha Cha Cha and Lumumba slowly began to fill up with traders who displayed their goods in the corridors and on the sidewalks and streets. The resounding cry at any attempt of removal was that traders were waiting for stalls to be built in the new market. What is surprising is that the authorities should have known the exact number of 'displaced' traders and could have easily realised that many were simply 'imposters' who were taking advantage of the unusual and chaotic situation. There are no records indicating how many traders from city centre relocated to the new City market although Hansen (2004) notes increased infilling in that market during this period. The city centre market was built in phases with the final one completed in 2007 at which point one would have expected the street traders to disappear but this did not happen. The design of the new City Centre market meant that a large number of traders were excluded since they could not afford the large shops which were built. There is also no room for traders to put their wares on the sidewalks although a number have positioned themselves at the corners of the market or on the 'island' where display their goods.

The 'Real' New Soweto Market

As earlier outlined the New Soweto market grew exponentially while the Lusaka City market was being constructed. The site filled up makeshift kiosks locally called '*tunthembas*' or semi-permanent stalls around the edges and numerous trading spaces on the ground. Once again, many traders who ended up at the site claimed to have been left out of the allocation of stalls in Lusaka City market. During the rains the site would become water logged and unpleasant. Traders made numerous self help attempt to improve the site but were unable to make a marked improvement. The site, although a major wholesale market for farm produce, did not attract government assistance and instead there were frequent conflicts over unsafe trading space under power lines. The electricity company was eventually advised to cordon off the unsafe zone. In 2005, talks with the European Union were underway and a possibility of modern infrastructure at the site was slowly becoming a reality. Construction commenced and the market was ready for re-opening in January 2009 after a number of delays caused by heavy rains and cement shortages among other things (*Lusaka Times* 2008). The total funding is said to have been seven million Euros. Displaced traders spilled onto the nearest roads (Los Angeles and Lumumba), as per tradition. As with the other two situations, the number of traders on the streets has far exceeded the number of traders who were previously using the old market and a repetition of previous scenarios is for seen. The main street leading from the new market is teaming with traders while the markets capacity is estimated at only 3,500 although the official figures range between 2,000 and 4,000. Events which have followed the completion of the market are a clear indication that the informal sector, administrators and politicians have taken advantage of poor administrative practices for their own benefit.

According to media reports 2,527 traders were on the initial list of those who had occupied the site originally but somehow the list had expanded to an alarming 15,000 names (Zambia Daily Mail, 2009). Allocation of stalls was being handled by the Soweto Market Development Committee (SMDC) which was accused of allocating multiple stalls to individuals, by the minister of Local Government and Housing who proceeded to disband the SMDC. This was after people suspected to be cadres of the ruling Movement for Multi-party Democracy (MMD) had beaten up two city council employees who had been posted at the new market. A new 'allocation committee' was thereafter set up by the minister who also nullified all the previous allocations of stalls. It was revealed that 600 persons had already received keys to their stalls while another 1,200 had received offer letters which were promptly recalled by the minister (Zambia Daily Mail 2009). Considering previous events it is surprising that the local authority did not see the need to keep track of the numbers of traders displaced to stop 'impostors' from joining them. One wonders why no mention of the original list was made by the minister or other administrators; indeed, the only people who spoke about the original list were the vendors. The minister instead spoke of people making new applications and being interviewed for the stalls. Could the administrative lapse be deliberate in order to fail to account for those who end up being omitted? Without the original list those who have power will be able to manipulate the 'list' while people who were not part of the original list will be able to find their way on it. There were media reports that some traders had paid as much as K60 million (approximately US$ 11, 000) for a single stall. It is highly unlikely that ordinary vendors who had previously been displaying their goods on the ground could afford to pay such large amounts giving credence to the theory that new entrants to the sector are either employees in the formal sector who have access to credit or are already established business men or foreign nationals looking to expand their businesses. The confusion and lack of transparency surrounding the pending stall allocation at New Soweto market indicates it is highly likely that some traders will be excluded. In the case of Lusaka City market there was an adjacent site which absorbed a large portion of the displaced traders whereas the traders from the New Soweto market have had no choice but to move to the street. Hence, the question arises whether they will be allowed to stay there. It is obvious that there is a specific pattern involved. The trend has been that whenever there is a new structure some residual traders will remain in the edge spaces which were considered as temporary.

Politics and the Informal Sector

The completion of City Centre market in 2007 was followed by a major cleanup of the streets with policemen literary camping on the streets and arresting and fining 'offenders'. At the time the cleanup was seen as successful but as the earlier reference to Herbert (1998, cited in Brown 2006) states, it is not possible for the police to have total authority over the streets, so the vendors slowly trickled back. By early 2008 the situation in the city centre had worsened causing the minister of local government at the time to issue an ultimatum. At this point an opposition ward councillor successfully filed an injunction preventing the local authorities from forcefully removing the street vendors until alternative trading places were found (*Lusaka Times* 2009a). The trickle turned into a flood with the death of the president in August, 2008 and the consequent presidential elections. Informal traders took advantage of the political uncertainty and quickly reverted to the streets. They were viewed as supporters of a particular opposition party and therefore their removal could cost the ruling party votes. The plan was to move them after the elections which were held in November 2008. In 2009 there have been a number of pronouncements made by the new Minister of Local Government and Housing who had stated that by 10 June, 2009, street vending 'will be history in Lusaka'.

The injunction was obtained in mid-2008 meanwhile, a year later in mid-2009 the Lusaka city council paid the Ministry of Home Affairs two billion kwacha (USD 370,000) so that the police could remove the vendors and continue to man the streets for three months (Muvi TV News 2009). A political representative tried to use the law to protect the rights of the informal sector, whereas the local authority sought the services of the nation's law enforcement agent, the police, to deal with the informal sector. It is not clear which party will succeed but currently there appears to be a standoff since the injunction is still in place. The local authority has not contested the injunction neither has found an appropriate alternative space for the vendors. Use of litigation is being seen as an alternative in the fight for the rights of the informal sector although there are still very few instances.

Processes of Exclusion

In normal circumstance once a new structure is put up the local authority should be able to ask traders to leave the streets but this is not happening. Once the informal spaces are 'formalised' to an extent they become attractive to a wider sector. Unlike the creation of Malls where entry is more costly and complicated, entry into the urban market sector is easier and cheaper. In fact ordinary vendors often find themselves 'out of their league' when it comes to affording some of the new shops in the new markets. They no longer have to compete only with traders like themselves but the new markets attract workers in the formal sector, larger retailers and even trade cartels in some instances. It has been documented how people who are formally employed venture into the informal sector in order to supplement their incomes or support relatives. This group has a steady income which they can use to borrow either formally or informally thus they will have a stronger starting point in bidding for trading space in the new markets. Some are civil servants who may have links and connections enabling them to acquire trading space. New markets also attract non-Zambians and an example is the Luburma Market which has numerous Chinese shops. It is unrealistic to expect a market trader who previously had a makeshift stall to suddenly manage to afford a USD 200 per week for a shop (Traders at Luburma took their landlord to court for charging high rents). In some cases traders will be allocated a stall but realise that they will not be able to pay the expected rents and therefore sublet their stalls although local authorities continuously warn against such practices (*Lusaka Times* 2009b). Some will even turn into employees of more financially able bidders for the stall. Although places are improved the new spaces created are no longer universally attainable and some traders will inadvertently remain on the streets.

When formal replaces informal in the market sector traders face increased costs, regulation and management, single owner (council) and loss of tenure.

Increased costs can be through a placement of economical rents on trading spaces and or an increased level of revenue collection. Revenue will be collected more vigorously in order to prove viability of the project or in order to recover costs in the case of Luburma market. When urban public space undergoes a transformation of this manner ownership ceases to be ambiguous. Within the market made up of individually built structure traders felt a level of ownership. Whereas some could previously argue that they owned the stall the traded from, they cannot with the new structures. Traders do not only lose revenue, but lose investments and with it a level of tenure. In some cases – like the New Soweto Market – this publicly owned entity evolved from informality. The market started without intervention from the local authority and because of its weak position at the time the council could not stop its growth. Even in instances where markets were established by the local authority, very little oversight was given and markets were allowed to expand inwardly and outwardly with little or no objections.

Conclusion

Informal space utilisation must not be allowed to evolve on its own because of its amorphous nature. Urban spaces are by nature organised and this is why informality results in a level of discordance. A level of regulation is required whether at an extralegal level or formally. This is because other urban citizens also have rights to urban public spaces, but their voices are often not heard as they seek alternatives and try to avoid the city centre which is over run by informality. In this chapter, I have shown that even though the other users could have expressed what they thought of regarding the presence of illegal vendors, it was actually the voices of these vendors that were heard the most thanks to a vocal Zambian media. However, in order to achieve equitable space utilisation, other urban citizens should also be part of the negotiations for the use of such space. A process incorporating everyone's view requires a level of appropriate regulation of the informal sector.

The analysis so far has highlighted the ineffectiveness of policing and the need for lasting solutions. Such solutions will, however, require a reform of the inherited laws, which appear to be rigid and unaccommodating for the city in its current state. There is also a need, as Mitullah (2004) has argued, for the formulation of regulated multiple uses of public urban spaces and an integration of vending into the mainstream economy. Moreover, a more practical – and less elitist – approach to the informal sector will allow the authorities to become more accommodating while at the same time implementing necessary regulation. For example, De Soto's (2008) 'extralegal' informal regulation can be used by the legal regulators to bring order to the sector. It is hence unlikely (as some critics have alleged) that a high level of regulation will stop the sector from thriving. Creation of markets is one way of regulating a part of this trade although it is prone to political interference. While De Soto (2008) takes the stance that people involved in informality need standardisation and legality, this may not always be the case. Some may, however, find the freedoms and uncertainties present in the sector to be attractive. Thus, belonging to an organised group or signing documents may represent having an identity which may render the informal trader vulnerable when it comes to the law. Whereas De Soto's view may be applicable in a country like Tanzania – where there is a higher level of literacy in a single local language (Swahili) – the same cannot be said for Zambia (where there is no indigenous national language) where it is mainly the cross border informal traders (with a higher level of sophistication) who can enter the type of extralegal transaction that De Soto emphasises.

In the modern market, exclusion of traders takes place based on, among other things, the inability to pay, discrimination, political inclinations, gender, and social status. This results in a loss of trading space, the effects of which have not been covered in this chapter but have been adequately dealt with by numerous scholars. This exclusion in turn leads to a continuation of illegality as traders refuse to leave spaces located temporarily. It is clear that the local authority in Lusaka is currently reluctant to deal with the issue of street vending; therefore even when the new Soweto market eventually opens it is unlikely that the traders will leave the streets. It is also clear that the informal sector uses displacements to its own advantage as scores of traders join those awaiting relocation on the streets. This chapter has shown how the local authority does not seem to have the desire to adequately track those who are genuinely displaced and I have examined why this is the case. It would appear that when uncertainty surrounds the authenticity of claims and counter claims of being on lists, it becomes possible to allow non-traders into the new structure. Disputes over who should and should not be allocated stalls have always arisen when markets are opening with aggrieved traders protesting, sometimes violently. The most recent case was a protest over the planned allocation of the New Soweto stalls. Political interference was implied in media reports as accusations of illegal adjustments were made. The result was mob justice as two officials were beaten and paraded in front of television cameras for the whole nation to see. In an attempt to solve the problem, the minister of local government announced the 'he' would allocate stalls!

Apart from attracting the attention of politicians, new structures also attract newcomers, in that agents of the formal sector enter the informal sector. These actors can bring positive development to the sector as they have new ideas and more money. Government employees, party officials and foreigners manage to obtain stalls while the original occupants are left to fend for themselves within the urban sphere. This places them in conflict with urban laws, which insist on maintaining order. By seeking to produce spaces where government can exert its control, the authorities are actually creating an atmosphere for resistance by the informal sector which feels it has every right to remain on the streets. This in turn fuels feelings of exclusion which for some verifies the belief that if you are poor no one cares about you. This notion is aptly reflected in the following statement by a displaced trader: 'Sibangationeko ife, ndise bandani bamene sitiziba chizungu? Batenga chabe bamene bakamba mchizungu, so tizankhala mwamene muno ngati sibazatipasa malo mu market ya nyowani'. [They can't consider us, who are we, who don't even know how to speak English? They just take those who speak English, so we will stay here if they don't give us space in the new market] (*Lusaka Times* 2009b).

The current situation proves that public space is a reflection and mechanism of reproduction of power relations which exist in society. The powerful control the decisions to put up new structures and in the end act as gate keepers controlling access to the newly created spaces. The social imbalances continue to be reproduced at the expense of the socially and economically weak within society. Politics also plays a role when social differences are manipulated for political expedience. The party in power seeks to exclude those deemed to be in the opposition while the opposition tries to maintain its hold over the poor and oppressed. Accusations and counter accusations abound with the opposition accusing the ruling party of failing to deal with the street vending problem while the ruling party accuses the opposition of encouraging public nuisance by legally blocking the removal of vendors. Looking at the numbers of applicants for trading places in the new Soweto market one can ask where will they all go once the market is opened and they are 'left out'. Levels of congestion in the CBD are becoming unsustainable whilst the political tension is also mounting. It is not clear what actions the local authority will take when the market is finally opened. Even the police who have been paid to take action are seemingly reluctant to do so.

Lessons should be learnt from this and transparency should be sought whenever there is displacement. It is not possible for the local authority to successfully achieve this transparency alone and therefore the local authority should work closely with the informal sector. Top-down solutions seem to cause more problems than they solve. Currently the council is planning to reduce vending by introducing a weekend street market in the CBD. Local authorities can also take a leaf from the CBTA which is planning a three storey market in order to cater for all the traders who participated in purchasing the piece of land on which the market is located. This highlights the importance of providing security through tenure to the informal sector. The local authority should not only provide guidance on building plans and standards, but also allow traders to finance their own structures. Whereas local authorities do not hesitate to sell land for residential and formal business activities, it seems they are reluctant to do the same for the informal sector. New shopping centres and malls owned by individuals or consortiums are springing up within the city but local authorities still feel they need to provide infrastructure for the informal sector and retain control for the dominant class and planning elite.

It is true that the authorities want to make the public urban space in the city pleasant and accessible to all but this paper has shown that unless they consider the needs and rights of the excluded groups it will not be possible to transform this space. Traders from Luburma have encroached land along the railway line whilst those from the City centre and city markets have encroached spaces within the inner city where the sector thrives. The sector is quick to seek and find opportunities and will utilise space which is under-utilised in their view. Who is to say otherwise? What is culturally acceptable in the city? Should it include beautiful spaces of no value to a certain type of user or should there be some co-existence? There is an urgent need to rationalise street trade and agree on space utilisation by all stakeholders within the city before the city becomes totally inaccessible for the common man.

References

Central Statistical Office, 2005. Labourforce Survey Report. Ministry of Labour and Social Security, Lusaka, Labour Statistics Branch, CSO.

Daily Mail, 2009. Soweto Market Stall Mess: Which Way? 8 June, 8.

De Soto, H. 2008. Are Africans Culturally Unsuited to Property Rights and the Rule of Law? Some Reflections Based on the Tanzanian Case, in *Rights and Legal Empowerment in Eradicating Poverty*, edited by D. Banik. Farnham: Ashgate, pp. 155–74.

Brown, A. (ed.), 2006. *Contested Space: Street Trading, Public Space, and Livelihoods in Developing Cities.* Cardiff: Intermediate Technology Publication.

Gregory, S. 2002. The Changing Significance of Race and Class in an African American Community, in *Theorizing the City: The New Urban Anthropology Reader*, edited by S. Low. New Brunswick: Rutgers University Press, pp. 37–66.

Hansen, K.T. 2004. Who Rules the Streets: The Politics of Vending Space in Lusaka, in *Reconsidering Informality: Perspectives from Urban Africa*, edited by M. Vaa and K.T. Hansen. Stockholm: Nordic Africa Institute, pp. 62–80.

Herbert, S. 1998. Policing contested space: On patrol at Smiley and Hauser, in *Images of the Street: Planning, Control and Identity in Public Space*, edited by N. Fyfe. London: Routledge, pp. 567–82.

Kreglund, P. 2008. Knocking on a Wide Open Door: Chinese Investment in Africa, Mine Watch Zambia Conference, Lusaka, Zambia, 19–20 September 2008, Available at: http://www.zambia.co.zm/president/index.php [accessed: 7 September, 2009].

Lindell, I. 2010. Introduction, in *Africa's Informal Workers: Collective Agencies and Transnational Organizing in Urban Africa*, edited by I. Lindell. ZED Books, London, pp. 1–32.

Low, S.M. 2002. Spatialising Culture: The Social Production and Social Construction of Public Space in Costa Rica, in *Theorizing the City: The New Urban Anthropology Reader*, edited by S. Low. New Brunswick: Rutgers University Press, pp. 111–37.

Lusaka Times, 2009a. It's PF Preventing Government from Moving Street Vendors-Teta [Online, 21 July] Available at: http://lusakatimes.com/?p=14577 [accessed: 8, September, 2009].

Lusaka Times, 2009b. Government will continue Empowering Zambians, Says Mangani [Online, January] Available at: http://lusakatimes.com/?p=7309 [accessed: 8, September, 2009].

Lusaka Times, 2008, March. Rains Delay Construction of New Soweto Market [Online, March] Available at: http://lusakatimes.com/?p=2395 [accessed: 8 September 2009].

McDonogh, G. 2002. Discourses of the City: Policy and Response in Post Transitional Barcelona, in *Theorizing the City: The New Urban Anthropology Reader*, Edited by S. Low. New Brunswick: Rutgers University Press: 342–76.

Mitullah, W.V. 2004. Stree*t Vending in Africa*, review Commissioned by Women in Informal Employment Globalising and Organising (WIEGO), Kennedy School of Government, Harvard University.

Muvi TV News. A Showdown is Looming between Police and Street Vendors. [Online 2 July] Available at: http://www.muvitv.com/newsindepth.php?id322 [accessed: 8 September 2009].

Nchito, W. 2006. *A City of Divided Shopping: An Analysis of the Location of Markets in Lusaka, Zambia*, 42nd ISOCaRP Congress, Istanbul.

Nchito, W.S. 2002. *New Markets, New Practices: A Study of Management Practices in the New Markets of Lusaka, Zambia.* Unpublished paper presented at the workshop on Urban Governance, Gender and Markets, *Nordic Africa Institute, Bamako, Mali*, 8–12 September 2002.

Ngwenya, W. 2009. *Demolishing Soweto Market by Lusaka City Council* [Online, 12 March] Available at: http://www.lusakatimes.com. [accessed: 8, September, 2009].

Pellow, D. 2002. The Power of Space in the Evolution of an Accra Zongo, in *Theorizing the City: The New Urban Anthropology Reader*, edited by S. Low. New Brunswick: Rutgers University Press, pp. 277–314.

Pratt, N. 2006. Informal Enterprise and Street Trading: A Civil Society and Urban management Perspective, in, *Contested Space: Street Trading, Public Space, and Livelihoods in Developing Cities*, edited by A. Brown. Cardiff: Intermediate Technology Publications.

Royall, E. 2009. Hernando de Soto. [Online] Available at: http://www.vonmisesinstitute-europe.org/pdf/de%20soto%20paper%20Elizabeth.pdf [accessed: 7, September, 2009].

Simone, A. 2002. The Dilemmas of Informality for African Urban Governance, in *Democratising Local Government: The South African Experiment*, edited by S. Parnell, E. Pieterse, M. Swilling and D. Wooldridge. Cape Town: University of Cape Town Press, pp. 295–304.

The Town and Country Planning Act 1995 (c. 385) Lusaka: Government of the Republic of Zambia.

Times of Zambia, 2006. Lusaka Town Centre Market Stalls Gutted, 25 September, 5.

Times of Zambia, 2008. New Kamwala Market Gutted, 14 April.

Chapter 6

The Complexities and Paradoxes of Governing the Informal Sector in Malawi: The Case of Street Vending in Zomba and Blantyre

Blessings Chinsinga and Happy Kayuni

Introduction

It is widely argued that employment is a sustainable means for poverty reduction since it is the greatest asset of the poor. There is a caveat, however. It is not any other type of employment that leads to sustainable poverty reduction such that 'an employment goal which does not distinguish between different forms of work is clearly not sufficient' (Rodgers 2008: 64). For employment to lead to sustainable poverty reduction, it must serve as a means to ensure that income opportunities are widely distributed, contribute to the effective use of society's human potential and provide avenues for participation in both social and economic life.

The global goal to fight poverty under the auspices of the Millennium Development Goals (MDGs) has pushed the question of informal sector employment to the centre stage of the contemporary development debate. It is estimated that about 4 billion people around the world scrape livelihoods in the informal sector which provides society with vital services yet they experience hazardous and dirty work conditions for very low incomes. According to a recent UNDP (2008: 2) report, '... most poor people do not live under the shelter of the law, but far from the law's protection and the opportunities it affords'. The situation is compounded by the fact that most development initiatives tend to focus on the official economy, the formal legal system, and institutions at the national rather than the local level. The rapid growth of the informal economy in recent years is attributed to several factors such as economic and financial crises and deregulation and structural adjustment policies imposed by the International Monetary Fund (IMF) and World Bank, which have been further exacerbated by the forces of globalisation (Horn 2006 and Street Net 2006). In Malawi, it is projected that about 88 per cent of the population earn their livelihoods in the informal sector and the proportion of the same in the Southern Africa Development Community (SADC) region staggers at 90 per cent.

This chapter examines the complexities and paradoxes of governing the informal sector through the lens of street vending in the cities of Blantyre and Zomba in southern Malawi. These cities have populations of approximately 64,000 and 87,000, respectively.[1] The discernible growth of the informal sector in general and street vending in particular coincided with the advent of political liberalisation in early 1990s which saw the United Democratic Front (UDF) replace the Malawi Congress Party (MCP) at the helm of government. By the end of the 1990s, street vending had become a subject of contentious and unending public debate. The general feeling was that the proliferation of street vendors had led to the dramatic deterioration of the aesthetic beauty of cities, and increased congestion, crime and violence. At the centre of this discontent were formal traders, city planners, politicians and the general public. Formal sector traders complained that the vendors were blocking their customers, city officials cited loss of revenue, politicians wanted to demonstrate control over the sector for some political mileage, and the general public complained of regular incidents of indecent assaults and petty crime.

There was therefore considerable pressure to do something about street vending. However, the efforts of the UDF government were not very successful as the street vendors wielded considerable political clout as an important constituency of support for the government through the reign of terror on dissenting voices. The UDF party relied on the vendors to counter its fierce critics. The vendors in turn were a dominant constituency in the UDF's Young Democrats that were unleashed on real or perceived critics of the government. The vendors' political stamina was further strengthened by former President Muluzi's public pronouncements that he was the chief patron of vendors. The political backing of the vendors at the highest possible political level created a culture of open defiance of authority. And this, to a very large extent, accounted for the rather dismal performance of city authorities in enforcing the rules and regulation governing vending in the cities of Zomba and Blantyre.

The agenda was on the table to regulate and legalise the sector by confining the activities of street vendors to purpose-built flea markets. This agenda was, however, implemented with zeal by the Democratic Progressive Party (DPP) government which came to power in 2005. The street vendors were forcibly relocated to flea markets which had been completed at the beginning of the decade but they had previously successfully resisted moving into them. The justification for moving the vendors was that since they would be operating in a regulated place, they were going to be formally and legally recognised through a registration process. This would provide a framework for distinguishing between genuine vendors and those masquerading as vendors when they are actually criminals.

This chapter examines the feasibility of formalising street vending through the creation of designated markets including the extent to which this initiative has led to legal empowerment and protection of the rights of vendors as championed by the International Labour Organization's (ILO) decent work agenda. This

1 2008 Population and Housing Census (PHC) preliminary results. National Statistical Office (NSO), Zomba, Malawi.

is carried out using the human rights-based approach (HRBA) which seeks to empower people to exercise their voice and influence decisions that affect their lives. The overriding objective is to give people their power, capacities and the access needed to improve their own lives and their communities and influence their participation in social, economic, political and cultural life. The HRBA is complemented by an institutional approach in which institutions are defined as essential structural properties of societies which are constituted by the rules that constrain some forms of behaviour and interaction between people and groups and enable others in social, economic and political domains (Leftwich 2007). The institutional approach pays particular attention to the interface between formal and informal institutions through the prism of a scheme of interaction developed by Helmke and Letivisky (2004).

The study on which this chapter is based adopted an entirely qualitative approach which focused on the reactions and comments of stakeholders rather than quantification in the collection and analysis of data.[2] This approach is concerned with understanding the meanings which people attach to actions, decisions, beliefs and values within their social world and understanding the mental mapping process that respondents use to make sense and interpret the world around them (Bryman 2001 and Campbell 2002). It thus provides the means of acquiring an in-depth understanding of human behaviour since it provides the opportunity to explore phenomena and answer questions. The main tools for data collection were key informant interviews and focus group discussions. A total of 35 key informant interviews were held with top city officials, trade union officials, officials of the Consumer Association of Malawi (CAMA), city market officers and chairpersons of vendor associations in the cities of Zomba and Blantyre. In addition, 14 focus group discussions (FGDs), seven in each of these cities, were held with groups of 8–10 vendors chosen from various trades such as groceries, second-hand clothes, electronics, motor vehicle spare parts, basic foodstuffs and general miscellaneous items. An attempt was made to ensure gender balance in the composition of the FGDs but this was not always successful since the vending community is clearly dominated by males.

Understanding the Informal Sector: Theories and Debates

This section examines the theoretical frameworks for understanding the informal sector and the existing debates about how to govern and regulate it so that it has positive impact on the livelihoods of the vast majority of people around the world. It also briefly sketches the magnitude of the informal sector in Malawi in a regional comparative perspective.

2 This study was undertaken in the cities of Zomba and Blantyre between 25 March and 26 May 2009.

The Human Rights-Based Approach (HRBA)

The basic premise of the HRBA is that development needs rights and rights need development (Wheeler and Pettit 2004). It looks at development primarily as the achievement of human rights and describes situations not simply in terms of human needs or development but in terms of society's obligations to respond to the inalienable rights of individuals (Ljungman 2004). The HRBA conceptualises poverty as multifaceted; it is not just about low income but also about vulnerability, insecurity and the inability to make oneself heard. Poverty is thus more than lack of resources but perhaps more critically the manifestation of exclusion and powerlessness (Cornwall and Gaventa 2002).

The HRBA focuses on empowering people to exercise their voice and influence decisions that affect their lives; helping state and non-state actors to realise their responsibilities toward citizens in terms of respecting, protecting, promoting or fulfilling rights; helping donors identify how pro-poor political change can be best supported; and translating human rights principles into reality. The HRBA is different from the other approaches because it does not only focus on the technical nature of the political processes but also 'underscores the fact that politically related governance processes frequently determine the success of development initiatives' (Moser and Norton 2001: 3). Development is thus not merely about providing welfare to passive recipients but is about facilitating the securing of their basic entitlement as right holders. This entails supporting impoverished and marginalised women and men in their processes of self-identification as rights holders and strengthening their voice and influence (DCA, undated). The HRBA therefore offers possibilities for increased sustainability of actions by acting on structural causes to impoverishment and marginalisation, addressing those with responsibility and power to make the necessary changes.

The ultimate goal of the HRBA is not development *per se* but rather the broad-based goals of social justice, access to economic resources, political change and empowerment. It confronts political realities and power structures so as to deal with structural factors that produce and perpetuate conditions of chronic poverty and extreme inequalities. In short, the HRBA provides strategic entry points for addressing a broad range of issues of power and authority as the basis for tackling deeper structures of inequality and confronting these at the legal and political as well as social, cultural and economic levels.

The Institutional Approach

This approach focuses on both formal and informal framework of rules which define and govern the relationship between stakeholders in a system (North 1990). Widely understood as rules of the game, institutions give direction to – as well as describe, explain and legitimise – behavioural codes. They thus empower and constrain actors differently and make them more or less capable of acting according to behavioural codes (March and Olsen 2006).

However, the processes of institutional formation, maintenance and change are often subjects of heavy contestation because the ultimate outcomes distribute advantage and disadvantage to different groups and interests in different and often new ways (Leftwich and Hogg 2007). This is the case because any new institutional arrangement brings with it winners and losers. While winners are motivated to support changes, losers are often determined to maintain the status quo. This suggests that processes of institutional change are not politically neutral; they are in fact deeply imbued political processes.

The process of establishing new institutions is further challenged by the interface between formal and informal institutions. The latter are defined as rules and procedures which are created, communicated and enforced through channels widely accepted as official whereas informal institutions are socially shared rules, usually unwritten, created, communicated and enforced outside officially sanctioned channels. The interface between formal and informal institutions can take four different forms. The interface can be accommodating, complimentary, competitive and substitutive altogether (Helmke and Levistiky 2004). The form of formal and informal institutional interface which obtains has significant implications on whether the process of establishing new institutions is a success or not. The competitive and substitutive modes of interface between formal and informal institutions are a cause of concern because they render formal institutions more or less redundant. In the substitutive interface, it means that formal institutions are quite weak: they exist only on paper as authorities are unable to enforce them. Consequently informal institutions emerge to fill the void created by the non-enforcement of the formal institutional arrangements. The situation is different in competitive interface. The use of informal institutional arrangements means violating formal institutional arrangements at any cost and vice versa. The prominence of informal institutional arrangements also means that formal institutional arrangements are completely trampled upon. The outcomes intended by formal and those that are actually produced by informal institutions are completely divergent (ibid.).

The HRBA and institutional approaches are quite complementary in understanding the informal sector in a broader perspective. While the institutional approach provides the lens for understanding the dynamics of changes taking place in the informal sector, the HRBA points to how the changes ought to be implemented in order to achieve outcomes that would work for the vast majority of the people that earn their livelihoods in the informal sector. It is against this background that the UNDP is currently championing 'legal empowerment' as a development strategy broadly construed as 'a process of systematic change through which the poor and excluded became able to use the law, the legal system, and legal services to protect and advance their rights and interests as citizens and economic actors [whether in the formal or informal sectors]' (UNDP 2008: 3).

Legal Empowerment and the Informal Sector

The basic premise of legal empowerment is that laws, institutions and policies governing economic, social and political affairs deny a large part of society the chance to participate and compete on equal terms. It is estimated that about four billion people eke their livelihoods outside the purview of the formal sector world-wide. These people are poor because they lack recognised rights, they are vulnerable to abuse by authorities that discriminate, seek bribes, or take the side of power interests who may wish to prevent the poor from competing economically or seek to evict them from their land. Therefore 'it is not the absence of assets or lack of work that holds [the poor] back, but the fact that their assets and work are insecure, unprotected, and far less productive than might be' (ibid: 2).

The predicament of the vast majority of the working population around the world has, *inter alia*, prompted the International Labour Organization (ILO) to champion the 'decent work' agenda. The underlying idea of the decent work agenda is to promote opportunities for men and women to obtain work in conditions of freedom, equity, security and human dignity. It is hence seen as central to efforts to reduce poverty as well as a means for achieving equitable, inclusive and sustainable development (Horn 2006 and Rodgers 2008). The main challenge is that workers in the informal sector, which hosts almost four fifth of the total global population, are not regarded as real workers as 'no employer–employee relationship cannot be established' (Street Net 2006: 8).

The reluctance to recognise the people who earn their livelihoods in the informal sector as workers has triggered debate on how best to deal with the informal sector in the quest to improve the conditions of work. The suggestions have ranged from formalising the informal sector to promoting collective bargaining strategies to improve the voices of the stakeholders in the sector (Horn 2006 and UNDP 2008). It is, for instance, argued that governing and regulating the informal sector generates the following advantages:

- Documentation of informal sector widens the tax-base which increases revenue for national development.
- Economic gains expand local markets and increase financial activity at all levels.
- The predatory networks that exploit vulnerable participants in the informal economy begin to unravel.
- More and more people develop a stake in the reduction of crime and maintenance of a peaceful social order.

The track record of these initiatives is, however, less impressive. Street vendors are often relocated to confined spaces where they endure quite high levies but without corresponding infrastructure or services from city or municipal authorities. The process of governing and regulating the informal sector usually fails to respect the human rights of vendors to earn a living especially since this is often done without policy guidelines in place. These initiatives are, in most cases, carried out under the cloak of street beautification, street restoration and development. The experiences of Zambia, Ghana, South Africa and Mozambique show that vendors are 'often dumped in isolated areas without any facilities and [with quite limited space for potential growth of enterprises]' (Street Net 2006: 8). In some cases, attempts to formalise the informal sector lead to further promotion of layers of informality. In São Paulo, Brazil, for example, city regulation of street vendors led to 'black market' regulation of public space. A spot in a public space costs 10 times more than private space and is 30 times more than the annual license paid to the municipality (Street Net 2006).

The informal sector workers also face serious challenges with regard to organising because 'trade unions have not always been open to informal and precarious workers to assist them in the exercise of their rights' (Horn 2006: 2). While trade unions have by and large embraced informal sector workers, the success has been somewhat limited. This is attributed to lack of innovativeness on the part of trade unions in dealing with informal sector workers. The major challenge is that unions are still organising their members primarily as workers rather than as community members or consumers. The point is that union strategies need to be customised to the workplace of workers in the informal economy (streets, markets, homes, etc.) (Horn 2006; Street Net 2006). Collective bargaining is further constrained by the tendency of formal sectors to hijack the cause of informal sector employees for their own selfish motives. Formal sector workers often regard their counterparts in the informal sector as passive and less knowledgeable to the extent that they want to do things on behalf of the informal sector workers instead of organising for them to represent themselves and set their own agenda.

The Informal Sector in Malawi

Systematic studies that exclusively focus on the informal sector in Malawi are extremely few and consequently it is difficult to analyse any emerging trends with precision. This is not only true for Malawi but also in other African countries. Taking into consideration that Malawi is not highly urbanised, the informal sector plays a critical role in the livelihoods of the people. Specifically, only 12 per cent of Malawi's labour force is actually in the formal sector (War on Want 2006: 24). The informal sector and smallholder agriculture absorbs the remainder. Although the periods of study are not similar, the Malawi findings are not very different from other African countries such as Mozambique and Zambia. For Mozambique in 1999/2000, about 65 per cent of the urban workers were operating in the informal economy while a survey conducted in 2004 in Zambia, revealed that 83 per cent of the employed were in the informal sector (ibid.).

As Kayuni and Tambulasi (2009) point out, during the one party era (1964–1993), the MCP led government discouraged the informal sector business but promoted rural agriculture instead. After the multiparty elections of 1994, ruling UDF opened up the informal sector through provision of the World Bank funded small and medium business loans. One of the most notable sectors of the informal sector that flourished was urban area street vending. As Jimu (2005) observes, the sector became one of the most contested business sector in the country with several arguments for or against the sector being raised. In order to show how Malawians took business activities seriously (thus including the informal sector), the BBC-commissioned urban areas survey gives some insights. Between May and April 2004, the BBC commissioned a field survey of 10 countries from the East to the West of the continent (Kenya, Tanzania, Malawi, Rwanda, Zambia, Mozambique, Ghana, Nigeria, Cameroon, and Ivory Coast) involving 750 interviews per country in the urban areas.

Specifically, the survey's purpose was to get a better understanding of how Africans see themselves. According to this survey, people living in Malawi (per cent) were leading Africa 'in their desire to make money, closely followed by Tanzanians (86 per cent)' (BBC 2004). Although Kayuni and Tambulasi (2007) argue that street vending has been wiped out through the government's *Operation Dongosolo*,[3] recent revelations indicate to the contrary. Through Operation Dongosolo, it is estimated that up to 30,000 vendors were evicted from the streets into purpose built flea markets but without any facilities across the country. The resilience of street vending despite serious state suppression underlies the fact that those involved have no alternatives and are desperate for survival to the extent that they are not afraid of the state machinery.

The Challenges and Paradoxes of Governing Informal Sector

Our study finds a mixed picture regarding the welfare of the vendors following their forcible move to flea markets. This is, *inter alia*, attributed to the following: limited space for potential growth of enterprises; corrupt practices by city officials; politicisation of leadership of vendor groups; exploitative class formations among vendors; capture of emerging union and associations by elites ejected from the formal sector as a source of rent; and the absence of supportive environment policy and legislative framework. The first part of this section will hence address the origins, processes and the implementation of relocation of street vendors to flea markets.

3 Operation Dongosolo refers to the campaign mounted by the Democratic Progressive Party led government in April 2006 to drive vendors from the streets into purpose built flea markets.

The Flea Market Idea

The decision to establish flea markets came about through the then ruling party, the UDF. The UDF-led government sourced K123 million (about $12m) from a public entity – Press Group of Companies – to construct flea markets in the cities of Blantyre, Lilongwe and Zomba. Through this construction, the government claimed that it wanted to promote the interest of vendors. Based on almost all local media coverage at that time, it was observed that when the government came up with this idea, there was some semblance of consensus amongst all key stakeholders about the desirability of constructing flea markets. The problem, however, emerged from the implementation process itself. According to a group of vendors, the government initially showed a higher level of commitment towards participation and consultation. For example, the government took the Blantyre chairperson, treasurer and secretary of the vendors on a tour of Zimbabwe, South Africa and Tanzania, in order to show how these countries have modelled their flea markets. The vendors' representatives were supposed to choose the best model for Malawi after learning from the countries they visited. However, they were later surprised to learn that the government decided to construct the type of market which was different from the one that they had chosen. According to the vendors, the government felt that the model the vendors had chosen was too expensive. Some vendors have even dismissed the whole process as not fully compliant to *bona fide* consultation. Accordingly, those who were chosen to visit these countries were mainly the youth wing of the then ruling party; consequently they could not freely express the views of the vendors. As one Blantyre city official commented, 'The previous regime tried to pursue an appeasement policy in its quest to contain the vendors by incorporating some of them into the ruling party youth wing [which was popularly known as the Young Democrats] but this strategy failed; they continued to be a nuisance to the city'. Another extreme view is that those who were representing the vendors were 'bribed' by the government. Thus one vendor in Blantyre observed, 'they just picked a few vendors, booked them a hotel and promised them some loans so as to conform to the authorities; you cannot call that consultation'. And two Blantyre city officials agreed with the vendors that proper consultations were not undertaken, noting that 'consultation was there, but it was at a superficial level' as the government did not have the time to consult. According to these officials, the problem associated with street vending had reached a crisis point and in such a situation it was not possible to engage in an effective consultation process. Furthermore, the government and city officials regarded the vendors as unfit to be accorded such a privilege. In this regard, some vendors that were interviewed pointed out that officials 'regard all street vendors as useless and thieves' and consequently they were seen as unable to provide credible alternatives that officials could adopt.

The Implementation Process: From Streets to the Flea Markets

When the construction of the flea markets was over, the vendors, through their representatives, were asked to register their names pending relocation to these markets. Most vendors were reluctant to register their names as they did not want to occupy these markets. According to city officials, those who registered were allocated space and those who did not were not assigned one. However, most vendors claim that although they were aware of the order to occupy the markets, it did not have a specific date or deadline. A few occupied the market immediately but when they discovered that most of their colleagues were still operating from the streets, they went back. The vendors thus technically defied the government order to move from the streets and occupy the said markets.

The new government led by Bingu wa Mutharika issued a fresh warning to vendors that they should immediately occupy the flea markets. When this order was not complied with, the President mobilised the police and the army in April 2006 in what was termed Operation *Dongosolo* ('order') and the vendors were ultimately forced out of the streets at gun point. Subsequently, the vendors tried to organise demonstrations but these were immediately thwarted through police action, arrests, beatings and use of tear gas. Vendors in Blantyre claimed that despite the government's new order to move, the situation still remained the same and that no date had been fixed as there were discussions underway between city officials and the vendors. To this effect, most of them were surprised when they heard over the radio one evening that they had been 'moved' from the streets to the new premises. Officials argued that a specific date had been set and the vendors were consulted, but according to the market fee collector for Zomba, 'they were used to the tendency of the previous regime which could issue threats without acting, hence they thought that the current regime would also practice appeasement politics and they were surprised to see that the government was serious'.

Almost all vendors pointed out that without the use of force, they would not have occupied the markets. Indeed, they fail to understand why the government was quick to use force when it could easily have achieved the same objective by taking on board their concerns such as modification of the market to suit their interests. The vendors felt that it was not possible to fight against the government, and complying with the order was therefore the only alternative available. Some attributed the government's urgency in the relocation process as purely motivated by domestic political concerns. According to this view, the ruling party wanted to appear before the public as doing something to establish security in the country in line with their promises after a spate of robberies and street thefts that had taken place in many urban areas of the country. As one vendor in Blantyre observed, 'if the government was serious with security of the city as it claims, it could have employed more policemen and bought them enough cars to capably patrol the streets … this [relocation] is just politics'.

The Aftermath of the Implementation Process

Officials have largely considered the process of relocating vendors to be a success story. They claimed that daily market fee collections have improved greatly, so much so that they are now able to meet the amount targeted for collection per day. For example, in Blantyre, at the time of interview their target was K61, 570.00 (US$ 500) per day and this figure had already been reached.[4] This success, officials maintained, is mainly due to the fact that vendors are currently operating in one place. As the Zomba market fee collector noted, 'formerly, they were so scattered, and this made it so difficult to collect ticket fees'. Other officials further claimed that the goods of vendors are now protected from both the rains and thieves as vendors now have a place of their own they can call 'home'. The Zomba market fee collector also observed that some vendors were now making more money than in the past 'although they do not admit it'. He went on to claim that, 'I have personally seen some of these vendors buying cars, owning plots and building good houses in Chikanda [a residential areas in Zomba city] while they had nothing when we were moving them in that flea market'. However, despite the above noted positive developments, we found a number of problems that emerged from this forced implementation of the relocation policy.

Three years after the forced relocation, vendors are still against the original decision to forcibly move them. Interestingly, one official in Blantyre supported the vendors by pointing out that 'this policy has honestly worked to the disadvantage of the vendors in a number of ways'. Some of these disadvantages are discussed below.

Poor Patronage by Customers

Vendors argued that the markets, including those in Blantyre and Zomba, are located in areas that are not frequently used by their customers. They further argued that if the government had adequately involved them in the planning phase, such mistakes could have been avoided. Most potential customers feel it is difficult for them to walk long distances to reach them when in the past they were conveniently located. It was pointed out by some city officials as well as vendors themselves that when the vendors plied their trade in the streets, they gained a lot from their business because they were easily noticed by buyers, and also had an opportunity to influence/market their items to the customers.

Poor Market Design

Vendors also argued that it is difficult to display their wares in the flea markets. The design of the market is not the one that they had earlier advised government to construct. For example, there were no provisions for properly advertising goods

4 Currently, the said target per day still stands.

and it was more of a place where vendors could gather and chat but not necessarily sell their items. The point made here was that the way in which the market was constructed provides no room for the proper display of their wares so as to attract customers. The vendors display their wares on tables rather than on special display shelves. More importantly, the flea market design impedes on their marketing flexibility as all of them, despite the diversity of goods being sold, have to follow a uniform pattern in displaying their wares. In this regard, there is no possibility of enhancing marketing innovation and competition, and hence their marketing skills are not put into full use. Another disadvantage, the vendors argued, concerned the storage of their products. As one vendor in Blantyre observed, 'there are no rooms for storing our goods and we lose a lot of money to the *Ganyu boys* (porters) everyday'. In this case, the vendors had to take their wares out of the market every evening and bring them back again the following day. Apart from the shortage of adequate storage facilities, they also complained that the lack of security in the markets resulted in numerous thefts. Thus a simple matter, such as the regular repair and maintenance of security lights, could have made a major difference if the authorities had heeded the advice of the users. More importantly, the market did not have adequate facilities for basics necessities such as drinking water and sanitary facilities.

A major setback related to the space provided to the vendors to conduct their business – each vendor was allocated one metre square space, an area most considered to be highly inadequate. In a study conducted in 2007, one lady complained that 'outside, I had a lot of space, but here I was only given one square metre … what viable business can you undertake with such limited space? Being a street vendor does not mean that you lack innovation for growth' (Kayuni and Tambulasi 2007). The current Blantyre flea market is also, according to the vendors, too small to accommodate them all. The Chairperson of the Blantyre Vendors Association indicated that there are over 2,000 vendors who are unable to get access into the market.[5] The authorities are aware of this problem and are partly solving it by placing more vendors in the market. Currently, the market has 500 vendors instead of the required capacity of 400.[6] However, the director of administration of the Blantyre City Assembly argued that the market is enough to accommodate all vendors but the problem is that some vendors are selfish and hence occupy more than two spaces while they are allowed only one[7]. This points to the existence of 'black market' regulation of the spaces in the flea markets, where the most powerful vendors receive more than twice as much space while others do not have any place at all. What happens is that some vendors connive with the immediate market authorities and they are allocated more than one space. In the process, the vendor with more spaces offers them for rent to other individuals. Consequently, individuals who are provided space by their

5 'Vendors raid costs business', *The Daily Times*, 26 August 2009.

6 'Smoked out', *The Nation,* 17 August 2009.

7 'The structures were illegal', *Weekend Nation*, 29 August 2009.

fellow vendors pay more than the required official rates. The proceeds from this illicit activity are shared by the vendor who has multiple spaces and the market official. This is clearly a case of informal institutions trampling formal institutions regulating access to market places. The weaknesses in the enforcement of rules of access to spaces in the flea markets have been exploited by the elite vendors and market supervisory officials for their own selfish goals. Instead of empowering the vendors, the flea market policy had had significant disempowering effects on the marginalised sections of the vendors. Actually, some vendors have been driven out of business altogether or they have to pay substantially more than the official premiums for spaces in the markets due to unscrupulous tendencies among some sections of vendors and market officials.

Detachment of Symbiotic Formal and Informal Linkages

Prior to relocation, it was noted by Kayuni and Tambulasi (2007) that the formal sector (mainly shops owned by Malawians of Asian origin), used to benefit substantially from the informal sector. For example, wholesale shop owners received rental fees from some vendors who utilised the open space (often verandas) in front of the shops. Vendors also gained from an informal arrangement with shop owners who provided them with goods to sell on their behalf in other locations. In this case, vendors received a commission for all the items sold. In some cases, the shop owners sold goods in bulk to vendors, and at generally low prices, i.e. products that were close to their expiry dates such as toothpaste, hair lotions, packed foods and other related items. These products were quickly sold out because of their low prices, and hence the vendors benefited from the profits while the shop owners also profited as they were faced with complete loss due to the expiry of the products.

To this effect, one Blantyre market fee collector observed that 'since their removal, all these privileges are no longer there to the extent that some of the vendors have closed down their business due to this harsh environment'. Almost all the respondents pointed out that business interaction between the formal and informal sectors has now disappeared and this has negatively affected both, shop owners and the vendors. However, some vendors were still in contact with the shop owners. And according to one vendor in Blantyre, 'do not be surprised with some of these vendors with bulky goods; those items are not theirs but they sell on behalf of some Indians or some individuals who are preoccupied with other businesses' in the formal sector.

Mushrooming of Non-compliant Vendors

Contrary to the observation made by Kayuni and Tambulasi (2007), street vending has not been completely wiped out. Though small in number, the above study established that 'illegal' street vending is operational and thriving in Malawi.

Illegal street vending is mainly confined to the sale of perishable food items such as buns, *mandasi* (fritters), and biscuits. Such vendors also sell bottled drinks and other items such as necklaces, earrings and finger rings. Normally this group does not operate from a specified place; in most cases, they wander from one corner of the street to the other, hunting for customers and are usually concentrated in the bus terminals. On the other hand, legal street vending is mainly confined to the sale of newspapers and cell phone airtime. The development of illegal street vending was frustrating for other vendors who have complied with the government order and are currently in the designated flea markets.

A critical analysis of these legal vendors shows that they were not doing well in the designated flea markets and in most cases the products they sell are not really relevant to formalised flea markets. The items they sell are more convenient to customers 'in a hurry'; those who do not wish to walk longer distances to purchase their items. This is why they are normally found in the bus terminals, sports centres and other public gatherings. Taking into consideration that they are breaking the city laws, these vendors are most vulnerable to harassment by city officials and the police. During this study it was observed that while selling their products, vendors constantly ensure that city officials are not around. The moment an official is spotted, vendors run away. It is thus not surprising that their items have to be portable so as to necessitate escape from city officials whenever it is necessary.

Taking into consideration that the items that they sell are, by even small business sector standards, very insignificant, it is unlikely that they realise substantial profits – it is merely a sign of desperation for survival in the harsh economic environment. One observer pointed out that some vendors operate in areas where patrols are seldom conducted or they come to the street after 5pm when the city officials have finished their days work.[8] Some even go to the extent of hiding their goods in licensed shops but only carry a few portable items.[9]

Corrupt Practices of City Officials

Although it was claimed that corruption cases have not been officially reported, some Blantyre city market fee collectors stated that 'corruption is inevitable in any transaction that involve money … we must accept that it is there and it is part of life'. They also added that their work needed self control and discipline because there were many temptations to indulge in corrupt practices. The Blantyre city market supervisor mentioned that they have several strategies put in place to check and stop corrupt practices. Some of the strategies include setting targets of the amount to be collected each day by the fee collectors in a specified market. This, according to them, diminishes the incentive to cheat since failure to meet

8 'Smoked out', *The Nation*, 17 August 2009.

9 'Smoked out', *The Nation*, 17 August 2009.

the target attracts penalties (warnings) which may eventually lead to dismissal if they persist.

Despite unavailability of evidence or reported official cases of corrupt practices by the city officials, there was a clear indication that the relocation of vendors had created an opportunity for the same. The lack of officially reported cases does not mean that corruption does not exist. As one market official put it, 'cases of corruption are not done in broad day light but rather in a secret arrangement so it is difficult to say with certainty that the market is free from such malpractices despite having no records of such cases'. A vendor also observed, 'I have a neighbour who works in the same market with the city assembly, I tell you he is building a house which I think he cannot manage to account for if probed by the anti-corruption bureau. What else can explain this other than bribery?' Even vendors who have not complied with the government order that ply their trade outside the market complained against city officials by stating that 'these people are very corrupt, they scare and intimidate us so that we should bribe them'.

More interestingly, the very idea of setting targets may not be highly effective as envisaged. If, on a certain day, business has not gone well, probably due to inadequate number of vendors trading on that day, the amount targeted may not be realised (and the fee collectors may wrongly be deemed as corrupt). Conversely, the fee collectors may, in some cases, mobilise more than the targeted amount and pocket the difference. It is therefore difficult to establish whether the fee collectors honestly execute their duties. Taking into consideration the responses that they gave during interviews, it is clear that corrupt practices are rampant and known but difficult to *officially* establish the scale as the system is flawed hence fails to detect such practices.

Mechanisms for Representation

In relation to representation, it is apparent that the vendors are a very well organised group. They have a committee consisting of a Chairperson, treasurer, secretary and ten committee members. These positions are filled through competitive elections which begin with primaries and for one to stand, they need to fulfil certain conditions such as a clean criminal record, ability to read and write in both English and Chichewa as well as a record of good relations with fellow vendors. The committee represents their colleagues at the city assembly offices and meetings. In order to ensure fairness and significance of these elections, they are facilitated by the city assembly officials, NICE (National Initiative for Civic Education) and other community based organisations such as Bwalo. The positions are held on a two-year basis. Currently there is a lot of interaction among the vendors' committees of Zomba and Blantyre. However, the process of electing vendors top leadership positions is increasingly being affected by party politics. It was, for instance, observed by a vendor in Zomba that:

> At first it was impossible to imagine that, but now the picture has changed because party politics is slowly penetrating the affairs of the vendors. For example, during our elections some individuals were barred from contesting because they were viewed as members of the opposition and they were replaced by those who were perceived to be in good standing with the ruling party.

One critical observation is that the criterion for speaking English significantly excludes other potentially capable candidates. Despite the fact that English is the official language of the country, very few individuals are fluent in the language. There have been several reported complaints that students who completed their Malawi School Certificate of Examination (MSCE) failed to ably express themselves in English. The MSCE is the highest secondary school level qualification and very few vendors have such a qualification – in fact the majority are school drop outs. Taking into consideration this scenario, those who qualify are very few, thus excluding the majority. More importantly, those who may be fluent in English are likely to have had a good education, considerable experience in the formal sector employment and comparatively well positioned in terms of socio-economic status. In other words, they are part of the elite. All this puts into question the effectiveness of the representation being pursued.

Exploitative Class Formations among Vendors

Related to the observation above on mechanisms for representation is the issue of class formation. According to the concerns raised by the Consumer Association of Malawi (CAMA) and Malawi Union of Informal Sector (MUFIS), the main challenge that vendors face is high levels of illiteracy and misconceptions among the vendors regarding their responsibilities. Although vendors want to be viewed as 'one family with a unity of purpose' that 'rejoice together' in good times, 'mourn together' in bad times, and also 'fight their enemies together', this perspective is far from the truth. The reality is that these vendors can be grouped into the literate versus the illiterate and the financially strong versus the financially weak—judging from the goods they sell in the market. The literate easily understand some of the concerns raised by the city officials while the illiterate do not. According to MUFIS officials, this difference makes the vendors disagree even on the simplest of matters. Similarly those who are economically well-to-do, tend to support the status quo while the other group tends to be more militant in their demands for their rights. In this case, the fight for the rights of the vendors is affected by this division.

Control of Emerging Trade Unions and Associations

One innovation towards the effective mobilisation of vendors (and the informal sector, in general) has been union affiliation in the formation of the Malawi Union of Informal Sector (MUFIS). The main objectives of MUFIS are mainly to organise, defend/guard and represent vendors' interest at various forums – be it city assembly or to the NGO sector. They offer training to their members (vendors) in order to make them aware of their rights and responsibilities. They also defend vendors when they encounter what is perceived as unfair treatment from other stakeholders.

Despite this elaborate organisation, the vendors are not effectively being represented because the founder, who is the current President of the union,[10] has strong formal sector union experience and not from the informal sector. In fact, he has never been a vendor himself. Hence, despite the relevant union experience; his lack of informal sector attachment seriously questions his ability to fully appreciate the informal sector phenomenon. In fact, the key official bearers for MUFIS are the retrenched presidents and secretary generals of union affiliates to the Malawi Congress of Trade Unions (MCTU). The view of most vendors is that the leadership of MUFIS is not genuinely interested in promoting the welfare of the vendors but rather use it as a springboard for promoting their own livelihoods. One of the Blantyre-based vendors observed that 'MUFIS officials spend most of the time moving from one seminar to another, both locally and internationally but without putting to use the knowledge gained. They rarely involve genuine vendors; their interest is merely in the per diems and nothing else'.

More importantly, there have been several recent cases of police and city official harassment and brutality against vendors who had defied the order to relocate. Even for vendors who had complied with the order, there are numerous issues that they had been raising but the union (MUFIS) had to some extent not effectively aggregated these interests to effectively present them to policy makers. Specifically, each vendor's market has a committee that represents them. The union (MUFIS) is meant to be an umbrella body for all vendor committees. However vendors themselves recognise their immediate committee members and not the union. In relation to police brutality, the MUFIS official argued that the problem is with the city officials and government's attitude. He pointed out that 'the government views the vendors as troublemakers and agents of the opposition. They attach theft and crime to our members and this negatively affects our relationship with government'. In relation to city officials, the secretary general explained that city officials look at them as a rebellious grouping formed to undermine their authority. Lack of adequate funds, illiteracy of its members, and limited country coverage were some of the additional challenges which the union is encountering.

The Legal and Policy Environment

In relation to legal protection, the situation of the vendors – according to the president of MUFIS – can be likened to 'John the Baptist on the island of Patmos'. He argued that the forced relocation of vendors was 'unjustified', 'unreasonable'

10 At the time of writing this chapter in August 2010, he was still the President of the union.

and against 'democratic principles'. MUFIS argued that the relocation itself was not necessarily a problem but it is the process through which it was done that they feel demonstrated a lack of concern for the rights of the vendors. They pointed out that democratic principles entail that the rights of everyone need to be safeguarded. The Malawian constitution safeguards these rights to each and every individual including the right to demonstrate. When the vendors were planning to demonstrate so as to express their dissatisfaction with the relocation, the government responded by sending the army and armed police. This, according to MUFIS, is against the rights of the vendors. Interestingly, MUFIS officials, who are meant to protect the rights of the vendors, pointed out that they were not aware of any specific law or policy that protects the interests of the vendors let alone the informal sector in general. It emerged that city officials used city assembly by-laws to regulate the activities of the vendors. The officials made mention of Part E of the City by-laws which mention that vendors should pay market fee upon entering the market; not sell their commodities in the streets; observe cleanliness whilst plying their trade especially those engaged in food stuffs.

The application of city by-laws clearly shows that the issue of vendors was (and still is) primarily a local government issue; in this context the city officials. However, the direct involvement of the president who should be concentrating at national matters demonstrates lack of serious commitment and trust in local assemblies to ably enforce their regulation. This 'overstepping' of appropriate and immediate local offices also point to the fact that there are no adequate legal and policy safeguards for street vending in the country.

Implications of the Findings

This study brings into sharper focus two of the most significant factors that are driving and shaping Malawi's political economy in a post democratisation context. First, the transition to democracy has been associated with the increased informalisation of the country's politics which has, in turn, resulted in an incentive framework that privileges the dominance of informal over formal institutional frameworks in policy formulation and implementation. Second, the government's engagement with its various constituents was as paternalistic as was the case during the one party era. Consequently, elites have taken advantage of the massive illiteracy of the ordinary people to exploit the democratic dispensation for their own selfish short-term goals.

The informalisation of the country's politics is a reflection of the collective failure to manage the transition from one party state to a multiparty democratic dispensation underpinned by a gamut of rights and responsibilities. The transition to democracy was wrongly understood as a complete disjuncture with everything associated with one party rule, even it were working – and was in tune – with the new political dispensation (Chirwa 1998; Chinsinga 2007). This more or less created an institutional vacuum in the public sphere to the extent of rendering the entire state machinery ineffective. The formal institutional framework had essentially been supplanted by informal institutional arrangements. Actually, according to Booth et al. (2006), the government's capacity for policy formulation and implementation became thin, and in some cases, virtually non-existent resulting in a complete loss of direction for state business. Moreover, its policymaking capacity quickly declined as a result of total disregard for meritocratic principles in the recruitment of senior public civil servants. Patronage, nepotism and favouritism became the most important determinants for career progression in the civil service.

It is in this context that the vendors progressively wielded tremendous power under the UDF led government, propped up further by the fact that former President Muluzi had actually publicly proclaimed himself as the chief patron of the vending community. The vendors were an important ally of the government in enforcing social order – through the reign of terror in a context of increasing dissent and discontent from both the official opposition and wider public – following the breakdown in the integrity of the civil service as the engine of the state machinery. As a result of rampant favouritism, nepotism and patronage, the civil service and related agencies became highly politicised (Chinsinga 2007). In this environment, the vendors simply became the 'untouchables'. City officials and the law enforcement agencies were virtually powerless. With backing at the highest possible political level, vendors could practically get away with anything as long as it was perceived to in the interest of the regime politically.

This partly explains why it took over six years before the vendors could occupy the purpose built flea markets despite persistent complaints about unregulated vending that prompted the government to embark on the flea market initiative. The UDF led government, however, was not in a position to evict the vendors from the streets because they had become an extremely important political constituent. The government therefore desisted from any actions that could antagonise this critical constituent in fending off dissent from the official opposition and the wider public. Pronouncements were made about vendors to relocate to flea markets on several occasions but neither the city officials nor the government had the stamina to take on the defiant vending community for fear of major political fallout.

The DPP government's swift relocation of the vendors to flea markets should not necessarily be regarded as a sincere commitment on its part. It was purely a function of political exigencies. This was very much a means of building some support for the regime's survival, given the shape and form of political conditions at that particular point in time. The current DPP president was initially elected on the UDF's ticket in the May 2004 elections, which he won with the slimmest of margins at 36 per cent. As if this was not enough, a major political fallout between the current president and his predecessor soon followed. In February, 2005 President Bingu wa Mutharika resigned from UDF and formed his own political party – the DPP – which did not have significant parliamentary support apart from the six MPs who made it in the December 2005 by elections. The major tactic of the DPP government was therefore to generate its own source of legitimacy taking recourse mainly to public sympathy. This was principally achieved by taking decisive actions in areas where the UDF government was deemed to have miserably failed. However, while the DPP government has managed to confine the vendors largely to the flea markets, exploitation of the vendors as a political resource has continued. The DPP political functionaries, most of whom were UDF stalwarts, have ensured that all vendors' committees in both cities are dominated by those sympathetic to the DPP. This has been a relatively easier task because since May 2009 the DPP is a majority party in parliament.

Thus the commitment to participation as an integral part of the evolving democratic dispensation remains highly rhetorical. Given the symbiotic relationship between the vendors and the UDF government, one would have expected that the UDF government would have fully engaged the vendors in the design and construction of the flea markets. However, the vendors that were involved were not representative of the vending community; they were handpicked for the strategic reasons of the decision makers. This is why some vendors felt that their representatives in the flea market project were bribed with foreign trips and monetary rewards to the extent that they failed to speak against the adoption of the flea market design that most vendors did not like. The vendors were thus engaged in the consultative processes merely as a token for some semblance of participation.

Genuine participation is difficult to achieve because of high levels of illiteracy among vendors. Not many vendors have received beyond primary school education. This state of affairs has been exploited by those few vendors that have some kind of relatively advanced education; thus the vendors' committees are dominated by those who are able to read and write English. This is a requirement for holding for office justified as a means of ensuring smooth and productive interaction with the relevant authorities.

The above has had the following implications. First, there has been proliferation of corruption between vendors' committees and the supervisory cadre for the flea markets, particularly in relation to access of spaces in the markets. Some vendors, mostly committee members, have multiple spaces; yet others do not have even one. These vendors, in turn, offer these spaces to desperate colleagues who have to pay substantially more than the official premium. The rents thereof are shared with the market officials. Second, the management of the informal sector unions such as MUFIS has been hijacked by people with relatively higher levels of education. As indicated above, the management of MUFIS at the time of writing this chapter constituted almost entirely of people that did not have any informal sector experience. They were mostly people who had been made redundant in the formal sector. It is therefore not surprising that these people consider their involvement in MUFIS primarily as a source of livelihood and not to articulate the plight, promote, and defend the rights and interests of informal sector workers.

These findings suggest that there is need to examine both internal and external constraints that inhibit the successful retrenchment of the HRBA to development and empowerment processes. Often, the focus tends to be skewed towards external constraints such as political, legal, administrative, socio-cultural economic and environmental factors when these cannot sustain viable pro-poor contexts on their own. We have argued that it is equally important to work on the knowledge, skills and altitudes of the target groups to bolster their capacity, opportunities and interest for claiming their rights.

Conclusion

This chapter has examined the status of street vending in Malawi through the lens of experiences of the cities of Zomba and Blantyre in southern Malawi. The vendors were forcibly removed from the streets to flea markets under the cloak of ensuring that city streets are clean, reduction of cases of theft as most of the thieves used to masquerade as vendors; reduction of congestion in the cities as it was difficult for people to move around; ensuring that vendors are provided with a safe trading environment where they can comfortably display their wares irrespective of weather; enhancing revenue collection by city officials as it was difficult to collect revenue from scattered vendors and there was shortage of parking space in the cities.

However, the project has encountered serious problems mainly due to the manner in which it was implemented and how vendors are perceived by social and political actors. While there were attempts to consult the vendors at the beginning of the project, this spirit was not carried through resulting in the unilateral decision by government to use force to evict vendors without considering their human right to earn a living. The main challenge is that vendors are not seen as stakeholders in their own right with whom government can engage with in a constructive dialogue. This perception has led to arbitrary and unjust actions in the implementation of the relocation of vendors from the streets to the flea markets. The implementation of the project did not take into account the rights of the vendors to earn a living as provided by section 30 of the Malawi constitution. Thus the experiences of vendors in Zomba and Blantyre show that the outcomes of governance – that is, the cumulative effect of policies and institutions on people's lives – will only change if the processes of governance are fundamentally changed (UNDP 2008).

The welfare of the vendors is being further constrained by the incipient influence of politics on the leadership cadres for vendors, lack of effective mechanisms for representation, exploitative class formation among vendors, elite capture of emerging trade unions and associations and lack of enabling and supportive legal and policy environment. The point is that instead of achieving the intended goals and objectives, the relocation of vendors to flea markets has engendered unintended consequences. This is the case because of the project is being implemented without full understanding of the politics of institutional formation, maintenance and change which is mediated by the interface between formal and informal institutions. This is further compounded by the fact that the project is being implemented without policy guidelines in place which has created opportunities for various interests to exploit in accordance with their interests. This has led to a host of unexpected consequences that are adversely affecting the welfare of vendors. The vendors clearly lack capacity to engage with relevant authorities in dialogue to introduce necessary reforms because their emerging unions or associations have been hijacked by elites for their own selfish motives and goals and the authorities do not regard vendors as equal partners in the negotiation processes.

In the current environment, the goal of decent work and legal empowerment of workers in the informal sector in Malawi cannot be achieved. The sector is still marginalised, disorganised and perhaps more importantly demonised as a hot bed of opposition elements. It is therefore treated harshly which makes it very difficult for the vendors to promote effective dialogue with relevant authorities. This, in turn, greatly overlooks the fact that a country with laws and institutions that do not shut out the poor will benefit from the contributions of its entire population and from a legal, social, and economic order in which all segments of society have both a voice and stake.

References

BBC. 2004. *Pulse of Africa*, BBC World Service [Online: BBC World Service]. Available at: http://news.bbc.co.uk/nol/shared/bsp/hi/pdfs/18_10_04_pulse.pdf [accessed: 15 December 2009].

Booth, D., Cammack, D., Harrigan, J., Kanyongolo, E., Mataure, M. and Ngwira, N. 2006. *Drivers of Change and Development in Malawi*, Working Paper No. 261 (London: Overseas Development Institute).

Bryman, A. 2001. *Social Science Research Methods.* Oxford: Oxford University Press.

Campbell, J. 2002. A Critical Appraisal of Participatory Methods in Development Research. *International Journal of Social Science Research Methodology*, 5(1), 19–29.

Chanza, A. 2009. The structures were illegal. *Weekend Nation*, 29 August, 16.

Chavula, J. 2009. Smoked out. *The Nation*, 17 August 2009, 43.

Chinsinga, B. 2007. *Democracy, Decentralization and Development.* Cologne: Ridiger, Koppe, Verlag.

Cornwall, A. and Gaventa, J. 2002. *Bridging the Gap: Citizenship, Participation and Accountability*, PLA Notes No. 40.

Chirwa, W. 1998. 'We Want Change': Transition of Transformation. *Bwalo: A Forum for Development*, 2, 1–23.

DanChurchAid (DCA) (undated) *DCA Programme Policy: Rights Based Commitment* (unpublished).

Helmke, G. and Levitsky, S. 2004. Informal Institutions and Comparative Politics: A Research Agenda. *Perspectives on Politics*, 2 (2), 725–40.

Horn, P. 2006. *Informal Economy Organizations in Southern Africa: Challenges, Achievements and What is Needed from Trade Unions*, A Paper Presented at the FES/LARRI Regional Workshop on Dealing with the Informal Economy:

A Challenge for Trade Unions in Southern Africa, 17–19 October, Windhoek, Namibia.

Jimu, I. 2005. Negotiated Economic Opportunity and Power: Perspectives and Perceptions of Street Vending in Urban Malawi. *Africa Development*, 30(4). 35–51.

Kandiero, C. 2009. Vendors raid costs business. *The Daily Times*, 26 August, 1 (Business Times section).

Kayuni, H. and Tambulasi R. 2007. *Indispensable livelihoods wiped out? The case of street vending in Malawi's urban centre, Zomba.* Conference paper presented at the Vulnerability, Social Exclusion and the State in the Informal Economy, 26–28 March, PLAAS Cape Town, South Africa.

Kayuni, H. and Tambulasi R. 2009. Political Transitions and Vulnerability of Street Vending in Malawi. *Theoretical and Empirical Research in Urban Management*, 3(12), 79–96.

Leftwich, A., and Hogg, H. 2007. *The Case for Leadership and the Primacy of Politics in Building Effective States, Institutions and Governance for Economic Growth and Social Development.* Joint Leadership Programme (Unpublished).

Leftwich, L. 2007. *The Political Approach to Institutional Formation, Maintenance and Change: A Literature Review Essay*, IPPG Discussion Paper Series No. 14, University of Manchester, UK.

Ljungman, C. 2004. *Applying a Rights Based Approach to Development: Concepts and Principles*, A Paper Presented at the Winners and Losers from Rights-Based Approaches to Development, Overseas Development Institute (ODI), November.

March, J. and Olsen, J. 2006. The Logic of Appropriateness, in *The Handbook of Public Policy*, edited by M. Rein et al. Oxford: Oxford University Press, pp. 689–708.

Moser, C. and Norton, A. 2001. *To Claim Our Rights: Livelihood Security, Human Rights and Sustainable Development.* London: Overseas Development Institute (ODI).

North, D. 1990. *Institutions, Institutional Change and Economic Performance.* Cambridge: Cambridge University Press.

NSO (National Statistical Office). 2008. *The 2008 Population and Housing Census – Preliminary Report.* Zomba: National Statistical Office.

Rodgers, G. 2008. The Goal of Decent Work. *IDS Bulletin*, 39(2), 63–8.

Street Net. 2006. *Street Net News No.* 8 September 2006, 8.

UNDP. 2008. *Making the Law Work for Everyone: Report of the Commission on Legal Empowerment of the Poor*. New York: UNDP.

War on Want. 2006. *Forces for Change: Informal Economy Organizations in Africa.* London: The Workers Education Association of Zambia & War on Want.

Wheeler, J. and Pettit, J. 2004. *Whose Reality? Examining the Discourse, Context and Practice of Rights-Based Approaches to Development.* A Paper Presented at the Winners and Losers from Rights-Based Approaches to Development, Overseas Development Institute (ODI), November 2004.

Chapter 7

The Informal Health Industry in East Africa and Implementation of the Legal Empowerment of the Poor Agenda in Developing Countries

Kanakulya Dickson

Introduction

The conception and application of the legal empowerment of the poor (hereafter LEP) approach – particularly as espoused by the 2008 report by the Commission on Legal Empowerment of the Poor (CLEP) – to the informal health industry in Africa can be potentially problematic when examined from the capabilities or development as freedom approaches. A review of the LEP approach undertaken in this chapter indicates some of the challenges of reconciling formal approaches to empowerment with solving problems in the informal sector of the developing world. I will particularly focus on an examination of the avenues of compatibility of CLEP's conception of empowerment of the poor with the capabilities approach (hereafter CA) in relation to the health sector in Uganda. I choose to problematise LEP in the continuum of the capabilities approach because of the current dominance of the former in the development discourse and its growing influence in the empowerment discourse in general (Sengupta 2008). Moreover, the focus on the informal health sector is particularly relevant because good health is a major contributor to empowering an individual; and the majority of the poor in developing countries depend on informal health and medical service providers (Farnsworth et al. 1985: 966).

The study uses a 'diagnostic-critique' in identifying the incompatibility problems between the LEP and capability approaches. This entails identifying the perceptual nuance(s) that are employed in the CLEP Report (2008) and diagnosing conclusions that appear incompatible with the daily realities faced by actors in the informal sector. The diagnosis also aims at identifying possibilities of making the CLEP nuances applicable to policy and practice in the informal health industry. The general case of this chapter is the three East African countries of Kenya, Tanzania and Uganda; but later specific examples are highlighted from Uganda. Examples from Uganda are particularly interesting because the informal sector in the country is growing at a phenomenal rate of 20 per cent per annum (UMI

2005: 1) and hence provide a good indicator of the trends in the informal sector in sub-Saharan Africa. The Ugandan case is examined by focusing on both 'service-rights' and 'labour-rights'; the former aimed to pointing out the risk of rights-abuse that the consumers face whilst the latter concerns the risks faced by the labourers informally employed in the health industry.

The Capabilities Continuum

For the last 25 years, the capabilities approach has established itself as a major theory in political and economic philosophy. It can therefore provide a relevant and up-to-date continuum within which to investigate labour and business rights in the developing world. Even though Thomas Pogge (2003) has attempted a strong critique of the capabilities approach claiming that it cannot produce a public criterion of social justice that rivals the 'resourcist' views (such as Rawls' theory and utilitarianism), his arguments do not appear very persuasive as he pays inadequate attention to Martha Nussbaum's contribution to the theory, which makes the CA approach universally applicable because of the addition of Aristotelianism (Sandrine 2007: 20). Indeed, one of the charges that Pogge brings against the capabilities approach is that Amartya Sen wrongly suggests that traditional theories of political philosophy and normative economics promote normative individualism (Pogge 2003: 6). And Pogge goes on to claim that when it comes to some cases such as communitarian societies, it may not be the case that communitarian positions and normative individualism are mutually exclusive (ibid: 5).

Nonetheless, even as Pogge concedes, Sen's suggestion holds a lot of water because traditional economic theorisation was deeply imbued with extreme notions of individualism. It is this critique of the classical economistic position that made the capabilities approach to inspire the United Nations to create the Human Development Index (HDI); this was a sharp turn away from merely focusing on defining development as economic growth measured in terms on income to a focus on development as quality of human life. The potency of the capabilities approach to direct development paradigm and policy debate towards the quality of human life is what makes it the right continuum within which to discuss questions of empowerment.

There are of course many other theories that have something to contribute to the discourse of development but as Clark observes, other theories, '... have something to offer, but only the CA approach can address all relevant concerns' (Clark 2005: 2). Thus while the Basic Needs Approach (BNA) has raised legitimate concerns regarding the needs of the poor, it originally expressed them in an ad hoc and inflexible manner, which limited its applicability and relevance over a cross-section of avenues. The CA approach solves this challenge by bringing all these concerns into a 'coherent philosophical framework' (ibid: 3), which is more applicable across avenues than the BNA. Clark (ibid: 5) captures the single most important strength of the CA in the following way: 'One of the chief strengths of Sen's framework is that it is flexible and exhibits a considerable degree of internal pluralism, which allows researchers to develop and apply it in many different ways'.

The appeal of the capabilities approach has increased; according to Stanton (2007), one of the areas where the CA has shown tangible influence is the Human Development Index (HDI). This is because it replaced the 'utility' approaches to reporting human development which had dominated earlier development discourse that had mainly been economistic. Subsequent HDIs are getting heavily influenced by the CA. For example, a UNDP Research paper for the 2009 HDR reports on the non-traditional issues of migration and ethics from the perspective of the capabilities approach (Risse 2009). Accordingly, it is argued that the capabilities approach can be presented not only as a theory of development, but also a theory of justice. Indeed Risse characterises the capability approach's concept of functionings to be a form of empowerment (ibid: 15) because it can be successfully applied in the context of immigration whose complexities go beyond 'resourcist' or needs-based approaches (ibid: 17). From my reading of Risse, the CA captures essences; and issues of immigration and ethics are issues of essence, for example the question of the quality of life as a refugee or an immigrant cannot be easily settled by needs-based approaches because mitigating it is not about simply providing needs.

Risse's application of the capabilities approach beyond traditional development concerns such as famine and hunger, to issues of immigration and ethics proves that the approach presents a viable theory within which to discuss empowerment in the informal health industry. The informal health industry is one of the non-traditional concerns of classical development theory. Health, in general, cannot be kept outside empowerment discourse because it goes to the core of human empowerment; without good health it is difficult to achieve true empowerment. However, in many developing countries, the largest health service provider is often the informal health industry; and therefore if health makes an indispensable part of empowerment, then we need to understand the constraints and opportunities that are affordable in this industry.

Health and Empowerment

The World Health Organization (WHO 1948: 2) defines health as the, 'state of complete physical, emotional, and social well-being, not merely the absence of disease or infirmity'.[1] This definition has been modified to include: intellectual, environmental, and spiritual health. Health means wholeness or soundness of being. The admission of the holistic issue of wellbeing into development discourse

1 This has become the standard definition of health having entered into force on 7 April 1948 after being adopted by the International Health Conference on 19–22 June 1946 in New York.

is what connects the conception of empowerment in the capabilities approach (CA) with health care because, '... the CA extends beyond the analysis of poverty and deprivation and often concerns itself with well-being generally' (Clark 2005: 5). Clark thus argues that Sen critiqued classical welfarist theories of development because they conflated well-being with commodity command and desire fulfilment. Sen is therefore concerned with a focus on enhancing human functionings than simply focusing on the reductionist issues of commodities and desires.

As a matter of necessity, health inheres in human functionings; because good health is such a thing that when it is lacking the human person cannot function well, human empowerment cannot be full without promoting good health. It is also obvious that human health cannot simply be reduced to commodities and desires; it goes beyond them because humans have various health preferences. Therefore it is particularly appropriate to capture health as part of human functioning.

There is a rising consensus subscribing to the view that holistic empowerment must of necessity include health care (Israel et al. 1993; Rissel 1994; Ayong 1998; Wallerstein 2002). Perkins and Zimmerman argue that empowerment links individual well-being with the larger issues in the social and political environment (Perkins and Zimmerman 1995: 569). This linkage between individual empowerment and the wider social service provision is what is needed if we are to adequately discuss health care *vis-à-vis* legal empowerment. This approach to health care provision is closely related the social-environmental approach to health which not only focuses on treatment (as the medical approach) but also focuses on personal empowerment and political activism in the interest of health (Pine 1997: 181).

Any conception of empowerment has to grapple with the concept of power. Nanette and Czuba (1999) argue that power exists within the context of a relationship; therefore empowerment must deal with these relations. Power does not exist in a relational vacuum; rather it inheres in the very nature or relations; relations first exist before power is considered, i.e. any consideration of power, especially how to change it, has to start with the ground underneath power, which consists of power relations. Therefore, for effective empowerment to take place, all efforts directed towards achieving it should conceive power in a relational mode. By implication, since power is exists in relations, power itself and power relationships can change (ibid.). Empowerment is thus about changing the dynamics of this relationality in favour of the hitherto disadvantaged or powerless. This is why the socio-environmental approach to health service provision is more applicable to the relational conception of empowerment because social relations play a major role in the social environment in which health services are provided.

Such relations exist in society between, or among, the service providers in formal health systems and the poor whose mode of existence is basically informal. Coming from informal modes of existence, they would easily feel excluded and disempowered by formal health care systems which demand formalisation of every aspect of their lives. The informal mode of existence within which large groups of the poor exist has more to do with the way they perceive existence – life entails accessing as much basics needs and services as possible. The poor in the informal sector pay little or no attention to formal rules of procedure and behaviour; they perceive such rules as posing unnecessary obstacles in their daily lives. It is this relation between the formal and the informal that explains the empowerment challenge that exists today.

These relations, which are responsible for the power dynamics, are normally regulated by both legislative provisions and non-legal formal norms or unwritten formal rules of procedure and behaviour. It is at both these levels that the poor are excluded and disempowered and this negatively affects labour relations and business rights. Empowerment must take place at the relational level since that is where power is determined. However, since a change in a relationship requires a process, so too must the goal of empowerment be viewed as entailing a process or multiple processes. To ensure the possibility of empowerment, i.e. to be able to engage or foster and catalyse this process, it is necessary to correctly conceive the nature of power. This observation *ipso logico* indicates that engaging in the empowerment process requires a conception of power which allows for not only the possibility of change, but also more importantly, expansion. As Nanette and Czuba (1999: 1) observe, 'The possibility of empowerment depends on two things. First, empowerment requires that power can change … Second, the concept of empowerment depends upon the idea that power can expand'.

Gita Sen (1997) argues that there are two mutually exclusive aspects of empowerment – the extrinsic and the intrinsic. She writes,

> … genuine empowerment typically includes both elements i.e. extrinsic and intrinsic and is rarely sustainable without either. A change in access to external resources without a change in consciousness can leave people without the resilience, motivation and awareness to retain and/or build on that control, leaving space open for others to wrest control. Many (especially but not exclusively) government-run development programmes which start with good intentions, degenerate in this way. However, the reverse is also problematic … (Sen 1997: 2)

Extrinsic empowerment is about being enabled to decide one's destiny by way of exogenous means. It may take forms such as giving the poor loans, defending them in courts of law, among others. In this form of empowerment, the powerless or poor are assisted by providing an outer environment which can foster their independence such as the political, economic, and others. However, the challenge is that while it is possible to provide the right outside environment, the powerless may fail to benefit from this due to a lack of inner capabilities. By contrast, intrinsic empowerment involves enabling the powerless to realise, appreciate and apply their inner abilities to get them out of powerlessness and to accept and execute their responsibility as power-bearers. Under this aspect of empowerment we find elements such as inner transformation, self-consciousness, self-motivation, among others (ibid; Chamberlin 1997: 44). Ensuring good health to the people means empowering them (Bryne 2004) and such empowerment can be intrinsic because it deals with the inner aspect of human life. Unfortunately, the formal health sector denies a large majority of the poor a chance to get intrinsically empowered.

The poor people always find refuge in this aspect of empowerment which may not be physically visible and yet provides them with considerable inner energy to keep going on in life despite all the odds stacked against them. Moreover, since the formal health care system is disempowering, the poor look for avenues of health provision where they believe that they can feel, and become, empowered. These are avenues of health provision which they think they can understand and which do not involve formal rules of procedure that they cannot comprehend nor justify.

In formal health care systems, for example, the communication between the health worker and the client is normally literal, which assumes that the client possesses the skill of reading. The clients are given numerous documents or posters that make communication both difficult and impersonal. Besides, the language used by the health workers ensures that the client does not know what is actually going on. This can be frightening and make people feel very uncomfortable. I have personally been witness to several such incidences. Thus, in 1993 – when my father was undergoing treatment in Mulago Hospital in Kampala (Uganda's national referral hospital) – I met an elderly lady who asked for help to read the instructions on the prescription provided to her by the doctor. Unfortunately, even I could not decipher the writing on the piece of paper and hence could not help her. This is an indication of disempowerment and partly explains why the poor often prefer to consult with local traditional healers who speak a language they understand and can easily identify with.

Disempowerment Within Formal Health Systems in East Africa: A Brief Overview

There are challenges in ensuring that health is accessed by all in many developing countries because the burden borne by formal public health care systems is enormous. For example Taryn (2008) claims that the formal health care system is largely plagued by corruption and apart from leading to abuse of persons (e.g. neglect of patients by over-worked staff, use of counterfeit drugs, etc.), corruption also keeps many people away from these formal health care systems. Such challenges are stretching the available resources to the limit (Hursh-César et al. 1994: 4). To demonstrate the great health burden that formal health care systems in East Africa are subjected to, I will, in the ensuing sections, discuss health funding, epidemiological considerations, and regulative provisions.

Table 7.1 Financial Indicators for Health in Kenya, Tanzania and Uganda[a]

Indicator	Kenya	Tanzania	Uganda
Population (in millions) – 2007	36.9	40	28.5
Per capita expenditure on health (US$) – 2007	86	29	135
% of Government budget spent on health care – 2008	8.1	15.1	19
% GDP spent on health – 2003	4.3	–	7.3

Sources: Adapted from UBOS (2010), UNdata,[b] Infoplease,[c] UNAIDS,[d] WHO (2002; 2004), MoH- Kenya (2005), MoH-Tanzania (2003) and MoH-Uganda (2002; 2003), HDR (2007)

Notes: [a] The data in the table has been adapted by the author from various sources. [b] UNdata, Per capita total expenditure on health, http://data.un.org/. [c] See website provided in note 5. [d] http://www.unaids.org/.

Health Funding

Because Kenya is economically better off than its neighbours, trends in its health sector are indicative of the general trend in formal health provision in the sub-region. Kenya's Ministry of Health reported in 2005 that the country's households (the majority of which are poor) bear 51 per cent of health expenditure (MoH-Kenya 2005). According to the WHO, Kenya spent only 16.4 per cent of its total budget in 2001 on health (WHO 2007). Government reports indicate that by the year 2000 only 1.44 per cent of the country's GDP was added to the government's expenditure on health and by 2005, the increase was a mere 1.91 per cent (MoH-Kenya 2007). Kenya thus spends more on debt servicing than health, and it is obvious that its health care system cannot adequately meet the population's health care needs.

The above trends can be seen in other East African countries. Thus, although funding of Uganda's health sector rose from 6 per cent in the 1999–2000 budget to 9 per cent in 2002–2003 (MoH-Uganda 2003), the government still faces an enormous challenge of providing primary health care. Access to health services remains a major challenge and life expectancy at birth decreased from 48 years in 1991 to 46 in 2000 (USAID 2003), and by 2002 it was 43 years (MoH-Uganda 2002). There are 159,071 persons for each Health Center IV[2] and at least 70 per cent of the population lives in rural areas where the highest referral facility is the Health Center IV at county level (Ongodia 2004). Moreover, there are 18,700 persons for every doctor (non-traditional practitioners) and 3,065 persons per each nurse or midwife (MoH-Uganda 2002).

2 Author's analysis of the Ministry of Health Midterm Review Report (2003, especially section on referral facilities and their ownership).

The situation in Tanzania is similar because the formal public health per capita expenditure is USD 4; the government spends just 12 per cent of its overall resources on the health sector (MoH-Tanzania 2003: iv). With a population of 37 million, and a majority of whom are poor, Tanzania faces an uphill task of improving its health care services (Lorenz and Mpemba 2005). The rural population (almost 90 per cent) still relies on local and informal medical service providers. That is why the spending of 12 per cent of government resources on health is questionable; the majority of the population depends on informal traditional healers whose services are not covered under government subsidies. The question to ask is: where does all that 12 per cent go and for whom is it spent? People do not get a lot of support from the state as far as expenditure on health is concerned and that is why they resort to local medicine which is readily available. Table 7.1 provides an overview of the finances that are committed to the health sector in the three countries:

A consideration of the funding available to the health sector in the three countries indicates that the governments have an enormous health burden to bear. The percentage of the official budget that is committed to health care is indeed inadequate to meet the health needs of the populations in these countries. According to the UNDP's Human Development Report 2007,[3] Uganda had a per capita expenditure on health of USD 135, while Kenya and Tanzania followed with USD 86 and USD 29, respectively. But this is meagre expenditure because this region has seen a surge in population growth and increase in disease burden especially with HIV/AIDS and malaria. Other poor countries fare better than this region when placed in comparison; for example Rwanda which has a smaller population has a USD 126 per capita expenditure on health while Zimbabwe which is supposedly has a run-down economy has USD 139.[4]

Of the three countries examined in this chapter, Kenya is economically better off than the rest and yet its health sector is facing huge challenges of adequately providing for its population. At least 40 per cent of the health services in Kenya are provided by church health facilities, which have received no subsidies from the government since 1998 (WHO 2004: 1). Meanwhile, the poverty level in Uganda is 35 per cent while that of Kenya is 56 per cent and in Tanzania the poverty rate was 33.4 by 2007; meaning that there are 12.8 million persons living below the poverty line in Tanzania (Policy Forum 2007: 1).

Epidemiological Considerations

Apart from the challenge of finances, these countries also face a heavy disease burden with both curable and incurable diseases on the rise. Kenya faces a health

3 These figures were from Infoplease-Pearson Education Inc. adapted from the Human Development Report (HDR) 2007, http://www.infoplease.com/ipa/A0934556.html#axzz0ylP5qjy2 [Accessed: 27 August 2010].

4 Norway is the leading spender on health at USD 4763 per capita. Poor countries need to double their spending if they are to achieve better health for their citizens.

Table 7.2 Disease burden and other epidemiological indicators in Kenya, Tanzania and Uganda

Indicator	Kenya	Tanzania	Uganda
Adult prevalence of HIV/AIDS (15–49 yrs) – 2008	8.03%	8.08%	4.01%
Reported Malaria cases – 2003	–	10,712,526	12,343,411
Persons with TB per 100,000	888	479	646
Physicians per 100,000 persons (2004)	13.2	2.3	4.7

Source: Prime Minister's Office-Tanzania, WHO, MoH-Kenya, Globalhealthfacts.org, MoH-Tanzania and MoH-Uganda, WMR-2005

care crisis caused by a rapidly growing population of reproductive age, and an explosive HIV/AIDS epidemic. At the same time, child mortality rates due to preventable diseases such as malaria are beginning to worsen. As one publication notes:

> The health of the people of the three countries of Kenya, Tanzania and Uganda have similar characteristics, for example, with respect to the disease burden (challenges of new diseases such as HIV/AIDS and old endemic diseases like malaria), delivery systems (decentralised health care delivery through Districts, Governmental and NGO providers), constraints imposed by limited budgets, and other health care services have escalated well beyond the capacity of our respective Ministries of Health. (East African Community 2006: iii)

To represent the similarity in the general health problems that are faced by the East African countries, it is helpful to look at some indicators that are shared by them. Table 7.2 provides selected epidemiological indicators and the disease burden faced by the three countries.

It is obvious that when the disease burden is contrasted with the number of doctors in formal health care system in these countries, there appears to be a big deficiency; this simply illustrates further that, if left as it is in its present state, the official or formal health care systems in East Africa cannot provide all the health needs of the people. The formal health industry is stretched to the limit in developing countries. And if it is to take the leading role in providing health services to the poor, then it must be reformed so as to tailor its services to the lifestyle of the poor who constitute the majority in the population. Of course, there is also a need to increase budgetary allocations to the health sector, but that alone cannot ensure that the poor receive more or better services. The regulatory provisions (such as formal rules of procedure and behaviour) in the formal health sector must be revisited and re-thought in the long run if the poor are to benefit more from such schemes.

Regulative Provisions

The relations which determine the power dynamics (that are disempowering to the poor) are normally regulated by both formal legislative provisions and non-legal formal norms or unwritten formal rules of procedure and behaviour. It is these provisions that entrench the disempowerment of the poor in the health sector.

Former president of Tanzania, Benjamin Mkapa, served as a member of the Commission on the Legal Empowerment of the Poor (CLEP). And in his 2008 address to the joint AU and ECA conference of ministers of finance, he pointed out although the poor constitute the majority of the population in Africa, they do not have a legal identity (Mkapa, 2008). Moreover, almost USD 30 billion of the Tanzanian economy is estimated to be in the informal sector and 98 per cent of businesses operate 'extralegally'[5] while 89 per cent of real estate property is held in the same informal extralegal manner (ibid.).

Although Mkapa argues that the poor have little knowledge of the formal law, I think the real issue is that the poor do not like formal law because it disempowers them. Thus the formal legislative provisions that regulate the formal health industry make the poor uncomfortable; they prefer the informal health care providers because they apparently speak a 'language' they can identify with. Take the example of mental illness, which is among the domains where informal medicine is quite popular. Mulumba (2007) argues that the legal provisions that govern this domain are disempowering both to the patients and the service providers. This is because most of the service seekers live in informal settings; but when they come to the formal health facilities that provide mental health services, they do not understand the methods of treatment or the language used. This frequently leads to a conflict between the formal health workers and the relatives of the patient who may to compliment the formal psychiatric services with treatment from informal service providers. In general, the formal legal regulations in the health care industry in most African countries therefore tend to exclude and demonise the informal health care services and this makes the poor who live in informal settings uncomfortable (ibid: 13).

There are also non-legal formal norms or unwritten formal rules that govern behaviour within the formal health industry. For example, the service providers in the formal health industry have a tendency of considering their professions to be of a 'higher' status than others. Traditionally, the informal 'medicine men and women' command considerable respect in the villages and slums, where they easily operate from, and where their services are usually unquestioned. The poor from

5 This term refers to informal entities or businesses that exist and operate as though they were legally registered. Usually, the law enforcement agents 'let them be' because they have gained a legitimate status among the people even though they are not legal entities.

such places generally come with the same attitude to the formal health workers; but as mentioned earlier, they feel disempowered because they cannot understand and/or identify with the practices and procedures of the formal system.

The above challenges indicate that the formal health care industry disempowers the poor and they turn to the informal health industry. The state health care funding is low and epidemiologically these poor countries have enormous burdens such as high disease incidence and an imbalanced physician to patient ratio. Additionally, the formal rules of procedure and behaviour in the formal health systems coupled with higher costs of services in formal medicine contribute to pushing the poor people more towards the informal health industry.

The Informal Health Industry

The term 'informal sector' was first coined by the British economist Keith Hart in a study of economic activities in urban Ghana. The term, which is almost synonymous with 'informal economy', includes 'all economic activities by workers and economic units that are – in law or in practice – not covered or insufficiently covered by formal arrangements', directing both enterprise and work relationships (Larsson 2006: 1). One of the sub-sectors of the informal sector is the informal health industry, which can be divided into two sections: the informal *traditional* medical service providers and the informal *modern* medicine service providers. While the former deals in local and traditional or alternative medicine, the latter deals in modern Western medicine but providing their services informally.

Informal Traditional Medical Service Providers

This informal health sector in developing countries, especially in Africa, is synonymous with traditional or alternative forms of medicine. In *WHO Traditional Medicine Strategy 2002–2005*, the World Health Organization observes that informal medicine is widely used and is a rapidly growing section of the global health system, steadily gaining in economic importance (WHO 2002). In Africa, up to 80 per cent of the population uses traditional medicine to meet their health care needs and the WHO reports that this is the trend in many developing countries. For example, in Uganda and Tanzania reports indicate that traditional medicine is used by 60 per cent of the people. There is also growing use of alternative medicine in the developed countries, with Canada having the highest rate of usage of such medicines among developed nations, with 70 per cent of the population claiming to have accessed such services (ibid: 9–11). The WHO has thus added its voice to other international groups such as the EU that are calling upon their member states to promote official recognition of this type of medicine (ibid: 18).

Bannerman et al. (1983) have argued that informal or traditional medicine can help countries arrive at solutions to the challenge of how they could make health and medical care available to all their citizens. Thus, Bannerman observes that there is a 'reawakening of interest ... [and] ... rediscovery of local traditional systems of health care and the importation of traditional practices from abroad' in many scientifically advanced societies (ibid: 12). In the same book, Koumare (1083: 25) discusses the nature of this type of medicine in the African context and argues that African informal medicine is a distillation of African culture and its character cannot be independently understood without looking at the 'environment and social evolution' within which it emerges.

As for the challenges encountered in traditional informal medicine, Iwu (2002: 3) has identified the need to 'format a strategy that will make traditional medicine available to a wider population while preserving the cultural bases of the healing systems'. He discusses the challenge presented to conventional western medicine of understanding the spiritual healing aspect of traditional medicine and the tension that exists between practitioners of conventional western medicine and traditional medicine. Iwu's advice is, however, that 'Regardless of the preferred form of treatment, a common underlying tenet is that the selection of the therapeutic agent should be based on solid evidence of efficacy and safety' (ibid: 5).

Informal Modern Medical Service Providers

Since there are many poor people who cannot access and/or afford formal medical service, there are always those who are willing to provide the same medicine or services at more reasonable prices. There is thus a big and thriving underground industry of modern medical services and drugs in many parts of Africa. And many of those engaged in this industry are directly linked to government medical stores or NGOs that provide health services. They often engage in the smuggling of these drugs and equipments through backdoor channels and make a lot of money out of it. Some scholars have referred to this as the 'informalisation' of the health care industry (Birungi 1994).

This aspect of the informal health industry exists and is sustained in countries like Uganda because of previous experiences of political and economic collapse (Walt 1996). Between 1980 and 1985, for example, Uganda experienced social and political upheaval when the National Resistance Movement attempted to overthrow the government. This period brought about the total or near collapse of many institutions including the formal health care system. Moreover, due to institutional challenges, the Ugandan government could not adequately plan or monitor long term development of the health sector and this laxity gave way to the proliferation of unlicensed and informal health providers all over the nation. By the mid-1990s, the government started formulating strategies for incorporating both the informal and formal health care providers (Okuonzi and Macrae 1995). It was no longer feasible to ignore the informal health service providers and as the government sought to incorporate them into the mainstream health system, numerous challenges arose. But above all, the biggest challenge was related to transforming those who had been accustomed to working under informal systems, to suddenly accept to operate according to formal rules and procedures.

Table 7.3 Expansion of household informal enterprises in Uganda 1993–2003

	1993–2003		2000/03		% change
Region	**Number**	**%**	**Number**	**%**	**%**
Central	283	22.8	562	31.8	98.8
East	356	28.7	566	32.1	59.0
North	418	33.7	437	24.8	4.5
West	184	14.8	198	11.3	7.6
Total	**1,241**	**100**	**1,763**	**100**	**42.0**

Source: Uganda National Survey (2002/3).

Labour and Business Conditions in the Informal Health Industry

Given that Tanzania's former president Mkapa reports that 89 per cent of real property and 98 per cent of businesses in his country are operated outside the formal legal bracket – and since the WHO also reports that in 2002, up to 80 per cent of the population in Africa was using informal traditional medicine to meet their health care needs – it appears without doubt that the informal sector employs many people. Mkapa further adds that over 50 per cent of rural labour is working in the informal peasant economy; and in urban areas, many are self-employed in activities such as hawking, illegal stalls, informal vending, etc.

The informal economic segment of the economy is generally characterised by several characteristics, including ease of entry, the predominance of self employment, the application of labour intensive production methods, low levels of organisation and low productivity and income (ILO 1972; GoK 1999; Wells 2001). Workers in this sector are always under uncertainty and job insecurity is part of regular life. The sector is also highly flexible, which means that business operators and service providers can easily change their businesses in response to changing market conditions (Mullei and Bokea 1999). All these characteristics make the informal economy largely beyond the reach of formal legal instruments and this presents various and unique conditions of working and doing business in this sector.

Who, according to the Uganda National Survey 2002/2003, are these government care-givers? Most informal enterprises in Uganda are operated mainly at the household level, estimated to be about 1.8 million households which make up almost 36 per cent of the total households in the country (UMI 2005: 3). Table 7.3 shows the expansion of the informal sector by regions in Uganda over a period of 10 years.

Official surveys, however, often misrepresent or distort the actual nature and size of the informal health sector because the informal enterprises that provide health services are officially classified under the categories of 'food processors' or simply 'services' (ILO/UNDP 1996). Thus, according to the report *Health Care in Uganda* (2010, cited in Businge and Okoth 2010: 4) by the Foundation for Human Rights Initiative, the draft bill to regulate informal herbalists and spiritualists who provide health services is still pending because Ugandan legislators are still examining the legal language to apply to them. This distorts the actual state of the informal health sub-sector because almost 80 per cent of the population uses local or informal traditional medical services. Consequently, there must exist numerous traditional or informal health service providers. It is often easy to mistake informal health service providers for 'food processors' because most of the herbal and traditional medicine is packaged or presented as food or food supplements. Hence, there is a thin line between informal health services such as therapies, consultations, etc. and other general informal services. It is therefore possible to miss some pertinent labour and business characteristics in the informal health sector because of this distortion.

Labour Conditions

The labour conditions in the informal sector in East Africa are generally similar. Like anywhere else in this region, the informal sector is the largest employer in Uganda; it is estimated that there are over 800,000 SMEs are currently operating in Uganda and they provide over 1.5 million jobs. The employment potential of Uganda's informal sector is thus estimated to be expanding at a rate of 20 per cent per annum (UMI 2005). This vast labour force is largely hidden from the official records and there is hardly any detailed understanding among government officials or academics regarding the labour conditions that exists in this sector. Our understanding is based mainly on anecdotal information that may appear sporadically in the press or be made available through informal information channels such as talking to friends and relatives who work in this sector.

By 1999, it was reported that the informal sector in Kenya was growing faster than the formal economy; there were over 1.2 million informal enterprises that were contributing 18.4 per cent to the GDP and employing close to 3.7 million people (Mitullah and Wachira 2003: 5). Again Mkapa estimates that for Tanzania,

> … half of the working poor in the informal economy are self-employed, a quarter are employed by informal enterprises of households, and a quarter are informally employed by formal enterprises. Average earnings and working conditions are low and risks are high in the informal economy. (Mkapa, 2008: 2)

The general level of risk in the informal sector is shared by the informal health industry. This risk is not only faced by labourers but also by those who are use such services. The working conditions are dictated by the enterprise owners who are often accused of abusing workers with little or no fear of legal repercussions because the informal sector is generally out of the radar of formal law surveillance and enforcement.

In a specific case of such abuse of workers by a traditional medicine man in Uganda, it was established that the treatment he administered to his workers was dependent on orders from the spirits. And in response to such orders of treatment, the medicine man regularly kept a number of people chained and used them as unpaid labourers in his shrines and farms because he claimed that they were mentally ill (Lukwago 2006). It was further reported that this man had supporters occupying high positions in government and therefore when cases of abuse were reported to the police, nothing much was done.

Since the informal sector is highly flexible, there is an increased likelihood of seasonal unemployment. Unfortunately, there is little or no adequate data to illustrate the extent of this problem. From cursory observation one finds many labourers working on road and trench repairs during the heavy rainy seasons and now that Uganda is experiencing a construction boom, many can be found working on unsafe construction sites. But the predominance of the application of labour-intensive techniques of production presents an avenue of possible massive employment. The average earnings in this sector are minimal and worse still, they are seasonal since most of the activities are done seasonally. Effectively, the labour force in this sector is disempowered.

Business Conditions

One of the main characteristics of this sector is the ease of entry and exit in business. For example in Kampala, there are many informal clinics that being established and disappearing on a daily basis. In my research, I could not come across any study or research or database to establish the number of informal clinics in the Uganda or Kampala for that matter; yet as one moves about in the suburbs of the capital, one cannot miss seeing at least a couple of them on a busy street or area like Bwaise, a Kampala suburb. During a visit I found numerous clinics in operation, some having existed for many years while others had recently been opened. And such clinics are usually established in slum corners where rent is cheap and the clients are primarily slum dwellers.

The above situation is allowed to continue because these health service providers are outside the radar of government. They include providers who are not licensed by government but are appreciated and legitimatised by the communities which they serve (Birungi et al. 2001: 82). These informal private health providers are constantly faced with the threat of closure from government officials; as such they engage in a lot of bribery to continue operating. Even when government considers integrating them into its health policy, there is a high likelihood of not getting government help such as funding or subsidies, because the question of spending public funds on private businesses arises (ibid: 83). With the push for privatisation, there is always a tension when public funds are diverted to private enterprise and governments are often challenged whenever they use public money to bail out or aid private businesses.

The businesses or enterprises in the informal health industry contribute tremendously to the sustaining of the formal industry. This is because they provide not only the raw materials on which the ‘secondary’ formal industry feeds, but they also provide raw knowledge which is of far greater value to the formal industry more than anything else. It is this raw knowledge (sometimes referred to as indigenous knowledge) that the formal health industry processes to develop its own services and products. However, if this value of the informal health sector is not recognised by the legal system, there are many disadvantages that it suffers.

Empowerment and Health: The CLEP Connection

The CLEP recognises that the vast majority of the world's population lives in the informal or extralegal sector and hence one of the foremost aims should be to empower this group in achieving the Millennium Development Goals (MDGs). The CLEP Report (2008) argues that one of the tools that can be used to empower the poor is enabling them to access legal instruments and thus legal empowerment is defined as 'the use of legal services and related development activities to increase disadvantaged populations' control over their lives' (Golub 2003: 25). However, and as the following discussion will highlight, legal empowerment is difficult when people living in poverty are denied access to a good legal system because they will not be able to engage and challenge forces of abuse and manipulation.

Examining CLEP's 'Empowerment' in an Informal Sector

The CLEP defines legal empowerment as, 'the process through which the poor become protected and are enabled to use the law to advance their rights and their interests, vis-à-vis the state and in the market' (CLEP 2008a: 26). However, it cautions that according to its conception, the objective of LEP is not to 'fix' the informal economy which is equivalent to punishing efforts to cope rather than 'supporting' it (ibid.). Accordingly, the 'principal cause of informality is the failure of formal laws, institutions and governance' (ibid). Thus the Report equates legal empowerment with access to justice when it, for example, argues that, 'Access to justice and the rule of law are to be considered the fundamental and enabling framework that supports the realisation of these rights', while at the same time stating that, 'Legal empowerment is thus a comprehensive framework with four pillars, access to justice and the rule of law, property rights, labour rights, and business rights' (ibid: 27).

The conceptual framework advanced by the CLEP thus identifies access to justice as a goal of the empowerment (ibid). While Sengupta (2008: 32) has argued that, 'Empowerment refers to both a process and the resulting outcome', it is in this conception that one may find challenges to the eventual operationalisation of legal empowerment. There seems to be a slight lacuna of conceptual confusion in connecting the two notions of 'legal empowerment' and 'access to justice'. Is it the case that legal empowerment is equitable to access to justice? This question is pertinent because in some instances, the CLEP apparently means that legal empowerment is establishing legal identity for the poor in the informal world

(CLEPb, 2008: 8). If this is the case, does establishing or getting a legal identity mean that the concerned individual or entity will automatically access justice? Does it therefore follow that getting legal identity means getting legally empowered?

There is a latent challenge that comes with granting the poor a legal identity; the practicalities involved in formalising the informal sector present a gap where the possibility of disempowerment may arise. For example the CLEP (2009b: 9) report noted that, 'care must be taken not to grant local elites a monopoly on the provision of formal legal identity'. This reveals a latent knowledge that the very process of granting legal identity to the informal poor can be hijacked by the elites who are versatile with the formal procedures and rules.[6]

Obviously, the assumption here is that the poor in the informal sector suffer abuses because they are existing in the informal mode; we are therefore supposed to understand that this problem can be resolved by granting the legal identity which makes the formal legal system work for the them. This generalisation can be accused of being either distorted or misinformed because not all of those that have legal identity in the formal legal system can in reality access justice. It could actually be the case that most of those that manipulate the formal legal system to their advantage, do so through informal means and an informal culture that lies beneath the manipulation of the formal system. Thus, many local and/or national elites who manipulate the formal legal system to their advantage are members of special interest groups that engage in self-benefiting and clandestine activities that are hidden from the official radar of the formal legal system. This means that beneath the officially recognised formal world of rules and procedures, there exists a world of informality created by the elites who understand how the formal systems work and how to manipulate them. It is this underworld of informality that determines the outer world of formality; indeed, improved analyses are required to understand how the interaction that takes place between the two actually functions.

The outer world of legal systems includes formal legal provisions and rules or procedure and practices. These are formal, and those who engage in the disempowering of the poor manipulate these formal provisions to their advantage. This is what makes the poor feel excluded and they end up disregarding the formal systems. But underneath the outer world are the unseen and out-of-radar informal networks and interest groups. I believe it is far more interesting to examine why the poor prefer to remain informal even as the ranks in the informal sector are increasingly being filled by educated groups, who would normally be found in formal arrangements. Thus, if we agree that there indeed exists the above two worlds that have been described, then we can challenge the following statement by the CLEP, that:

---

6 This observation augurs with the challenge that countries such as Uganda have faced in trying to formalise land ownership. Many poor people who were accustomed to holding land informally have lost their land holding rights due to manipulation of the rules and procedures of formalisation by the elite.

> The principal cause of widespread informality is the failure of formal laws, institutions, and governance. Consequently, many people shy away from the state and public institutions and remain in the traditional, informal economy. (CLEP 2008a: 9)

I believe the above statement is a simplistic causal connection because there are those who prefer to work within informal settings not because of the supposed 'failure' of the formal laws and institutions, but because that is where they maximise their personal advantage. It is invariably the rich and the middle class who manipulate the formal laws to their advantage through informal backdoors. Again the example of the manipulation of the process of the formalisation of the land holding system in Uganda comes to the fore. Okoth-Ogendo (2006: 20–4) presents a compelling argument to this effect; namely that the formalisation of hitherto indigenous property rights claims in Africa does not *ipso facto* lead to economic empowerment.

Hence it is difficult to accept the argument that the rich do so because of the 'failure' of formal laws and institutions; these groups actually perpetuate this failure so that they may benefit in the end. The poor in the informal sector see and know this because stories (both evidential and anecdotal) abound in informal circles of how the elite become very wealthy within a short time, despite being in government service, as they manipulate the rules and make hefty sums of money.

Giving Informal Workers CLEP's Legal Identity vis-à-vis Sen's Functionings

Identity makes up a key pillar of the legal empowerment approach (Banik 2009: 120); but a focus on identity does not necessarily lead to access to justice. By focusing on 'legal identity', the CLEP appears to have veered into legalism instead of justice. The poor prefer the informal way of life because they perceive that the formal justice system disempowers due the complicated rules that they can hardly understand or identify with. Therefore 'legal identity' ought to be followed with 'legal simplification' both in terms of the procedural justice and the language employed. If we are to use Sen's capabilities approach to critique the focus on legal identity, we can arguably conclude that this focus on legal identity simply reverts back to the utility approach which Sen has largely discredited. Sen (1984: 512) argued that there is more to life than simply deriving utility or happiness from something because this represents only a small fraction of human existence. This focus on the utility of legal formalisation (which passes for empowerment according to the CLEP) can easily end up being problematic because of a tendency to be turned into cultural hegemony by the richer countries (Nussbaum 1988: 175).

The poor prefer to live and work in the informal sector because to them, as it were, living in this sector enhances their functionings. This is because they have command over the services and commodities in the informal sector both because they understand the language involved in their production and distribution and they can identify with them. Since they understand and identify with the informal 'technicalities', they can easily modify the services and commodities in the informal sector to suit their environments and limited resource base. This is because a functioning is 'an achievement of a person: what she or he manages to do or be. It reflects, as it were, a part of the "state" of that person' (Sen 1985: 10). It moreover refers to 'the *use* a person makes of the commodities at his or her command' (Clark 2005: 4). The aspect of a functioning that is important here is that of command. The informal sector gives the poor command over the resources and commodities that they use. The challenge in reconciling this aspect with the legal empowerment approach through legal identity is that when the poor are given legal identity there is no guarantee that they will still have command over their resources such as knowledge, skills, property, etc. As I have shown earlier, gaining legal identity places the poor and their resources at the feet of the privileged rich who use informal networks to manipulate the formal legal system to the disadvantage of the poor. This is also why it is sustainable to argue that the poor do not resort to informality because of the failure of formal systems, but because they know that that is how society works. They realise that power flows from the underworld of informality to the outer world of formality. The CLEP's argument that power must submit itself to law in order to be legitimate (CLEP 2008a: 3) would have been true if the reality was in line with it. Unfortunately, the reality is that in many cases, power simply appears to have submitted to the law; in most cases, power manipulates the law to its advantage.

The poor do not simply 'shy away' from the state's formal systems; they actually go about their informal enterprise boldly as a statement of power. And I highly doubt that the push for them to abandon informality will convince them. The poor understand what everyone knows, but is not usually said openly, that 'real' power flows from informal networks or relations. Perhaps Mann (1986: 3–4) came close to stating this when he argued that social power is much more complicated than we may want to concede – 'Societies are much more *messier* than our theories of them'. The 'messed up' informal networks that such modernity seeks to formalise are actually the real sources of power – this is the attitude of the poor who live in informal settings, from my personal observation, and it is not easy to change it. This is particularly the attitude in the informal health sector in most of Africa. The reasons here may be historical, but also logical; the logic flows from the historical facts. Traditional or informal health service providers in Africa consider themselves legitimate because of the argument that they existed before modern formal medicine came to Africa.

Reconciling Informal Workers' Empowerment with 'Marketism' in CLEP Report

'Marketism' here refers to a strong belief that the market can solve development problems anywhere. The CLEP tried hard to ensure that legal empowerment appears 'marketable' i.e. LEP had to fit into the market logic. The Report therefore exhibited a sustained belief in the capacity of the market to help solve the problem of the disempowered poor in the informal sector. According to its conception, legal empowerment is best realised within the market framework as the following indicates:

> A thriving and inclusive market can provide the fiscal space that allows national governments to better fulfil their own responsibilities. The relationship between society, the state and the market is symbiotic. For example, the market not only reflects basic freedoms such as association and movement, but also generates resources to provide, uphold, and enforce the full array of human rights. It is processes such as these, in which the poor realise their rights and reap the benefits of new opportunities, which enable the fruition of citizenship – in short, legal empowerment. (CLEP 2008a: 3)

Tagging meaningful legal empowerment to the market is problematic because the logic of the market has been demonstrated over the years that it does not ultimately favour the poor. One of the key tenets of the 'market logic' has indeed been identified to be the elimination of the concept of 'public good' (Martinez and García 2000). According to the market logic, cutting public expenditure for social services implies reducing the safety-nets for the poor. At the economic level, the market is promoted alongside privatisation of hitherto public assets. At the political level, the state is told to cut expenditure on public social services. While at the legislative level, legislators are encouraged to pass policies of deregulation, i.e. there is complete faith in the ability of the private driven economy to deliver. This appears irreconcilable with legal empowerment of the poor who may not be able to compete in a market system.

Sengupta (2008) has also argued that the CLEP approach suffers a fundamental flaw of reconciling its conception of empowerment with the dominant market system.

> While the report highlights several issues that keep the poor in poverty and the programmes that are needed to move people out of poverty, it nonetheless suffers from a fundamental problem of reconciling its approach of market-based reforms to the realisation of human rights. In a process of market-based reform, the entire emphasis is on efficiency, or securing the maximum value from the use of any input, by removing impediments to the free exchange of legal entitlement to the inputs that are regarded as property by participants in the market. (Sengupta 2008: 31)

In a market system, the so-called rule of law works for the maintenance of the market structures. But from the classical times of Adam Smith's *Invisible Hand*, the underlying logic of the system is self-interest (even though the original conception of self-interest by Smith differs from that of today), which basically boils down to survival of the fittest – the fittest being the rich and skilled at manipulating the market. Even though the labourers in the informal sector face a constant risk of losing their jobs, bringing them into a formal system that is oiled by the for-profit-

or-nothing-else logic, may mean exposing them to a more risky environment than they are working under now.

We have seen this demonstrated time and again – anytime a business owner in a formal market system observes a threat to his/her profits, the first to suffer are the workers who are laid off. But the informal worker-employer relationships that exist are not founded on profit motives but on informal social or communitarian considerations. In these relationships there are no formal contracts which demand that 'either you make me a profit or you are fired'. Such grounds make the risk of losing a job much higher while the considerations for employment in the informal sector give more job security.

Easy Access to Formal Workers Savings by Corrupt Vultures

Based on the discussion above, I argue that the informal sector provides a safety-net for the poor which they have control over. In contrast, the safety-nets that are traditionally available to those in formal employment are increasingly under uncertainty, because they are out of the workers' control. There are various examples of the misuse of supposed safety-nets for those who work in the formal sector, especially in Africa. In Uganda, there various incidences where savings by workers are accessed and misused by corrupt officials using the formal legal system. Thus, for example, it was reported in the media in August 2009 that the Uganda Court of Appeal had 'awarded' a fake construction company 20 billion shillings as reward for a construction contract that had been cancelled. In the report the same court had ruled some months back that the company did not exist.[7] Another example is that of The National Social Security Fund (NSSF) is the formal government managed saving scheme operated by the state which requires by law that everyone in formal employment saves at least 15 per cent of their monthly salary. This would appear to be a good service which those in the informal employment sector (they could join this scheme only if and when they got legal identity through legal empowerment). However, from historical evidence, it appears that this scheme does not substantially benefit the workers since the money has been misused again and again by successive Ugandan governments. Recently, the Monitor Newspaper (2010) interviewed the then acting Managing Director, Isabirye Grace, who admitted that the history of NSSF has been marred by misuse of workers' funds when he openly appealed to the public 'not to judge NSSF by its history' (Business Power 2010: 12). And in their analysis of the social security systems in Uganda, Kasente et al. (2002: 157) observe that the informal social security systems are 'most widespread and effective of all' because the history of the NSSF has left an enduring perception that the formal security system is just a fund for the powerful to abuse.

Legal empowerment would thus require that when the workers in the informal sector get legal identity, they would then subscribe to such a savings scheme to act

7 'NSSF Case: Who will take sh20b award?', *New Vision*, 31 Aug 2009.

as a safety-net in case of old age or accidents. But there are numerous examples of formal workers who have retired only to find that they had nothing to show in terms of savings for the years they worked. Yet, and despite the informality of the arrangements involving informal labour, members of a given informal business community usually have their own arrangements through which they help each other in times of trouble. These 'Munno mu Kabi'[8] (a friend in need) groups are proving to be of greater use to the informally employed than the formal arrangements such as NSSF.

No Distinction between Traditional and Modern Informal Health Sectors

The assumption behind the conception of the nature of the informal is that it is homogenous in the sense that it is characterised as that sector which lies outside the formal arrangements. However, I have mentioned earlier in this chapter that there are also informal health services that are provided within the government's licensed service providers and this employs an unknown number of workers.

When we refer to the informal sector in the health industry, it does not only mean those involved in local or traditional medicine but it should also include those who operate informally even with the formal health system; for example, there are numerous reports of health workers in government hospitals who secretly transfer patients to private clinics that are not formally licensed to operate. It is thus important to take note of this because operationalisation of legal empowerment can encounter numerous challenges if this kind of informality is not factored in. Those who work under these arrangements are usually far away from the official government legal monitoring mechanisms and the conditions of the workers are largely unknown. But apparently this kind of informal service provision was overlooked by the Commission in its conception and definition of the 'informal'; there are many workers who have legal identity and recognised in formal arrangements, and yet they also provide informal services either within the very system under which they work or elsewhere. There is thus a need to demonstrate how legal empowerment could include them and how they would benefit.

8 'Munno mu Kabi' is a Luganda word which is the equivalent of 'A friend in need'. There are many groups in the local Ugandan informal sector where members agree to render help to each other in case of personal loss or disaster. These groups are usually found among market vendors, luggage carriers, motor-cycle taxi ('boda-boda') operators, etc. They pool resources together in cases such as death of a loved one and assist the affected person. This is an example of informal social security and that is why it is more important for the members to treat each other with trust as they may inevitably need help from other members of the group at a later point in time. This arrangement also entails members taking care of the children of a friend who has died of HIV/AIDS; indeed, this is one of the ways in which locals have coped with the impact of the epidemic on children.

Conclusion

In this chapter I have argued that the conception and application of the legal empowerment of the poor approach (particularly as espoused by the CLEP 2008a report), to the informal health industry can be problematic when examined from the capabilities (or freedom as development) approach to development. I have suggested that the way forward is to rework the LEP approach to include, and cater for, the complex nuances that exist within the informal sector. It requires a vigorous re-examination of the conception of legal empowerment as it applies to those in the informal sector to go beyond just legal identity and voice provision.

This chapter has used the informal health sector in East Africa to demonstrate the need for re-examination of the LEP approach in order to not only establish dimensions of its incompatibility within such an important sector, but also to generate solutions that can address this incompatibility challenge. This is necessary because the informal sector contributes tremendously to many economies and livelihoods of large groups of people in the world; and these people need to be empowered.

When applied to the informal sector, there appears to be a fundamental and profound divergence between the LEP and CA approaches. And I have argued that the CA can be flexibly applied to the dynamism of the informal sector while the LEP ultimately seeks inflexibility. Formalisation, in most cases, seeks to make things rigidly predictable and controllable; yet this is what those who live in the informal sector always wish to avoid. Even though they desire to realise and enhance their functioning, they equally desire to maintain their independence from the formal systems, which are considered disempowering. In my view this is where the challenge lies if we are to reconcile or make the two approaches to development compatible. The informal sector will continue to exist alongside formally organised economies. This means that if we are to empower those who prefer or find themselves living in the informal sector, we need flexible and dynamic tools that can be tailored towards that sector.

I have argued that attempts to promote empowerment of the poor should avoid giving the impression that they aim to control the actors in informal sector. If those in the informal sector perceive such attempts at controlling their lives, they will invariably invent newer and more creative ways of existing informally. Rather, strategies to empower the poor in the informal sector ought to focus on making their chosen mode of existence 'more efficient' and 'more enabling' for their functioning. Simply put, efficiency could be taken here to mean competence in performance. From its etymological roots it means being a effectual agent. The agency of the poor who exist in the informal sector needs to be enhanced in such a way that their informal existence will enable them to realise and enhance their functionings, thus making them empowered.

References

Ayong, A.M. 1998. *Empowerment Through Health Education*. Louisiana: Vita Press International.

Banik, D. 2009. Legal empowerment as a conceptual and operational tool in poverty eradication. *Hague Journal of the Rule of Law*, 1, 117–31.

Bannerman, R.H., Burton, J. and Ch'en Wen-Chieh (eds), 1983. *Traditional Medicine and Health Care Coverage: A Reader for Health Administrators and Practitioners*. Geneva: World Health Organization.

Birungi, H. et al. 2001. The policy on public–private mix in the Ugandan health sector: Catching up with reality. *Health Policy and Planning*, 16 (2), 80–87.

Birungi, H. 1994. *The Domestication of Injections: A Study of Social Relations in Health Care in Busoga, Eastern Uganda*. Copenhagen: Institute of Anthropology, University of Copenhagen.

Bryne, D. 2004. *Enabling Health – Empowering Citizens*. Conference of the European Health Management Association, Potsdam, 23 June 2004.

Business Power. 2010. Don't judge us by history-NSSF. *Monitor*, 25 May.

Businge, C. and Okoth, C. 2010. Herbalists treat most Ugandans. *New Vision*, 27 August.

Chamberlin, J. 1997. A Working Definition of Empowerment. *Psychiatric Rehabilitation Journal*, 20(4), 43–6.

Clark, D.A. 2005. The Capability Approach: Its Development, Critique and Recent Advances. *Global Poverty Research Group*. Working Paper Series, GPRG-WPS-032.

CLEP, 2008a. *Making the Law Work for Everyone*. Vol. 1. Geneva: United Nations Development Programme.

CLEP, 2008b, *Making the Law Work for Everyone*. Vol. 2. Geneva: United Nations Development Programme.

East African Community, 2006. *Regional East African Health Policy Initiative* (REACH-Policy). Arusha: EAC Secretariat.

Farnsworth, N.R., Akerele, O., Bingel, A.S., Soejarto, D.D., Guo, Z., 1985. Medicinal Plants in Therapy. *Bulletin of the World Health Organization*, 63, 965–81.

Golub, S. 2003. Beyond Rule of Law Orthodoxy: The Legal Empowerment Alternative. *Carnegie Endowment for International Peace*. Working Paper Series. CEIP-WPS-41. Available at: http://www.carnegieendowment.org/files/wp41.pdf [accessed: 18 August 2008].

Government of Kenya, 1999. *National Micro and Small Enterprise Baseline Survey 1999*, Nairobi: Government of Kenya.

Government of Uganda, 2009. Uganda: A Public Expenditure Review 2008: With focus on affordability of pay reform and health sector. *Public Expenditure Review*, May 2009, 49361-UG. Geneva: World Bank.

Hursh-César, G., et al. 1994. *Summary of Country Studies: Private Providers' Contribution to Public Health in Four African Countries*. Private and

Nongovernmental Providers: Partners for Public Health in Africa, Nairobi, Kenya, 28 November – 1 December 1994.

ILO/UNDP. 1996. *Employment Generation & Poverty Reduction in Uganda.* Addis Ababa: ILO-Eastern Africa Multidisciplinary Advisory Board Mission.

Infoplease. 2008. Per Capita Health Expenditure by Country 2007. [Online: Infoplease-Pearson Education Inc.]. Available at: http://www.infoplease.com/ipa/A0934556.html#axzz0ylP5qjy2 [accessed: 27 August 2010].

International Labour Organization. 1972. *Employment, Incomes and Equality: A Strategy for Increasing Employment in Kenya.* Geneva: ILO.

Israel, B.A., et al. 1993. Health education and community empowerment: Conceptualising and measuring perceptions of individual, organisational and community control. *Program for Conflict Management Alternatives.* Working Paper Series. PCMA-WPS-038.

Iwu, M. 2002. Introduction: Therapeutic Agents from Ethnomedicine, in *Ethnomedicine and Drug Discovery*, edited by M. Iwu and J. Wootton. London: Elsevier.

Kasente, D. et al. 2002. Social Security Systems in Uganda. *Journal of Social Development in Africa*, 17(2), 157–85.

Kimalu, K.P. 2001. *Debt Relief and Health Care in Kenya.* Conference on Debt Relief and Poverty Reduction, Kenya Institute for Public Policy Research and Analysis (KIPPRA), UNU/WIDER, Helsinki, Finland, 17–18 August 2001.

Koumare, M. 1983. Traditional Medicine and Psychiatry in Africa, in *Traditional Medicine and Health Care Coverage: A Reader for Health Administrators and Practitioners*, edited by R.H. Bannerman, J. Burton and Wen-Chieh Ch'en. Geneva: WHO.

Larsson, A. 2006. *Empowerment of the Poor in Informal Employment.* Background Paper for the Commission for the Legal Empowerment of the Poor. Geneva: UNDP.

Lorenz, N. and Mpemba, C. 2005. *Review of the State of Health in Tanzania 2004.* Dar es Salaam: Ministry of Health-PORALG April. Available at: http://www.muhef.or.tz/articles/ref%20116.pdf. [accessed: 14 April 2006].

Lukwago, J. 2006. Poliisi Ezinze Jjajja Ndaula. *Bukedde*, 28 November 2006, 2–3.

Mann, M. 1986. *The Sources of Social Power: A History of Power from the Beginning to A.D 1760.* Cambridge: Cambridge University Press.

Mitullah, W.V. and Wachira, I.N. 2003. Informal labour in the construction industry in Kenya: A case study of Nairobi. ILO Working Paper Series. ILO-WPS-204.

Mkapa, B.W. 2008. *Empowering the Poor.* 1st Joint Annual meeting of the AU conference of Ministers of Economy and Finance and ECA conference of African ministers of Finance, Planning and Economic Development, Addis Ababa, 31 March – 2 April 2008.

MoH-Kenya and Division of Health Care Financing. 2005. *Ministry of Health Expenditures (Gross).* Nairobi: Government of Kenya. Available at: http://www.health.go.ke/. [accessed: 20 March 2007].

MoH-Tanzania. 2003. *National Immunisation Program Financial Sustainability Plan*. Dar es Salaam: Government of Tanzania.

MoH-Kenya. 2005. *Kenya National Health Accounts 2001/2002*. Nairobi: Government of Kenya.

MoH-Uganda. 2002. *Statistical Abstract (Working Paper) 2002*. Kampala: Government of Uganda.

MoH-Uganda. 2003. *The Health Sector PEAP Review Paper*. Kampala: Government of Uganda.

Mullei, A. and Bokea, C. (eds), 1999. *Micro and Small Enterprises in Kenya: Agenda for Improving the Policy Environment*. Budapest: International Centre for Economic Growth.

Mulumba, M. 2007. Analysis of the Uganda Mental Treatment Act from a Human Rights and Public Health Perspective. SSRN, Working Paper Series. SSRN-WPS-23. Available at: http://www.psychrights.org/Countries/Uganda/UgandasMentalHealthLaw.pdf. [accessed: 28 August 2009].

Nanette, P. and Czuba, C.E. 1999. Empowerment: What is it? *Journal of Extension*, 35(5). Available at: http://joe.org/joe/1999october/comm1.html. [accessed: 28 September 2008].

New Vision Reporters. 2009. NSSF case: Who will take sh20b award? *New Vision*, 31 August 2009, 1–2.

Nussbaum, M.C. 1988. Nature, Function and Capability: Aristotle on Political Distribution. *Oxford Studies in Ancient Philosophy*, 1, 145–84.

Nussbaum, M.C. 2000. *Women and Development: The Capabilities Approach*. Cambridge: Cambridge University Press.

Okoth-Ogendo, H.W. 2006. Formalising 'Informal' Property Systems: The Problem of Land Rights Reform in Africa. Available at: http://www.undp.org/legalempowerment/reports/National%20Consultation%20Reports/Country%20Files/15_Kenya/15_4_Property_Rights.pdf. [accessed: 6 September 2010].

Okuonzi, S. and Macrae, J. 1995. Whose policy anyway? International and national influences on health development in Uganda. *Health Policy and Planning*, 10, 122–32.

Ongodia, A.O. 2004. Issues in the Implementation of Sector Policies at Local Level in Uganda: Primary Health Care. *Basic Principles of Decentralisation*. Kampala: GDLC, Uganda Management Institute.

Perkins, D. and Zimmerman, M.A. 1995. Empowerment, theory, research and application. *American Journal of Community Psychology*, 23(5), 569–79.

Pine, C.M. 1997. *Community Oral Health*. Wright: University of Michigan.

Pogge, T.W. 2002. Can the capability approach be justified? *Philosophical Topics*, 30(2), 167–228.

Policy Forum, 2007. Growth in Tanzania. Is it Reducing Poverty? [Online: Policy Forum – Tanzania] Available at: http://uwazi.org/uploads/files/Groth%20in%20Tanzania_Policy%20Forum.pdf. [accessed: 6 September 2010].

Risse, M. 2009. Immigration, Ethics and the Capabilities Approach. UNDP–HDR Research Paper 2009/34. Geneva: UNDP.

Rissel, C. 1994. Empowerment: the holy grail of health promotion. *Health Promotion International*, 9(1), 39–47.

Sandrine, B. 2007. Why the capability approach is justified. *Applied Philosophy*, 24(1), 16–25.

Sen, A.K. 1984. *Resources, Values and Development*. London: Blackwell Publishers.

Sen, A.K. 1985. *Commodities and Capabilities*. London: Elsevier Science Publishers.

Sen, A.K. 1999. *Development as Freedom*. Oxford: Oxford University Press.

Sen, G. 1997. Empowerment as an Approach to Poverty. *Human Development Papers 1997 – Poverty and Human Development, UNDP, New York, 1997*. Available at: http://www.hsph.harvard.edu/hcpds/wpweb/97_07.pdf [accessed: 20 February 2006].

Sengupta, A. 2008. Political Economy of the Legal Empowerment of the Poor. Doctoral course on *Human Rights and Legal Empowerment of the Poor*. Centre for Development and the Environment (SUM), University of Oslo, 2–4 October 2008.

Stanton, E. 2007. The Human Development Index: A History. *Political Economy Research Institute, University of Massachusetts*. Amherst Working Paper Series. PERI-WPS-127.

Taryn, V. 2008. Review of corruption in the health sector: theories, methods and interventions. *Health Policy and Planning*, 23, 83–94.

UBOS. 2010. *Demographic Statistics* [Online]. Available at: http://www.ubos.org/ [accessed: 6 September 2010].

USAID. 2003. *Uganda Demographic and Health Surveys (1988/89–2000/01): Country Health Statistical Report*. Kampala: USAID.

Wallerstein, N. 2002. Empowerment to reduce health disparities. *Scandinavian Journal of Public Health*, 30(3), 72–7.

Walt, G. 1996. Policy analysis: An approach, in *Health Policy and Systems Development*, edited by K. Janosky. Geneva: World Health Organization.

Wells, J. 2001. Construction and capital formation in less developed economies: Unravelling the informal sector in an African City. *Construction Management and Economics*, 19(3), 267–74.

WHO. 1948. *Constitution of the World Health Organization*. Geneva: WHO.

WHO. 2001. *Summary Country Profile for HIV/AIDS Treatment Scale-Up*. [Online: WHO] Available at: http://www.aidshealth.org/images/whouganda.pdf. [accessed: 10 March 2007]

WHO. 2002. *WHO Traditional Medicine Strategy 2002–2005*. Geneva: World Health Organization.

WHO. 2004. *Perspectives and Practice in Antiretroviral Treatment: Mission for Essential Drugs and Supplies, Kenya*. Geneva: World Health Organization.

Chapter 8

Human Rights of the Working Poor in Uganda's Informal Sector

Lilian Keene-Mugerwa

Introduction

The focus of this chapter is on the regulatory and operational challenges in the empowerment of the poor in the informal economy based on research undertaken by the Platform for Labour Action – a civil society organisation[1] that works on issues of social injustice among adult domestic workers and on risks and vulnerabilities to HIV/AIDS in the informal sector in Uganda. The chapter will further explore the strategies for collectively organising informal workers based on the current initiatives in the country. I will further examine how workers within the informal economy can be better protected by new legislation in Uganda without impeding the country's economic growth and business competitiveness. I will therefore cover issues such as implementation and applicability of existing legislation and its enforcement, together with challenges related to minimum wage, privacy, work hours and working conditions, including the relationship between occupational safety, health and freedom of association. Specific case studies on child labour and adult domestic workers will be used as well as information gathered from other informal sector groups such as food and non-food sellers, service providers, soft and hard manufacturers. In this chapter, 'food sellers' refers to women and men selling raw, cooked, semi-processed or fully processed foods within the markets and outside markets, on verandas of shops and markets and on the street. 'Non food sellers' refers to those who sell commodities such as cloth, soap, paraffin, matches, crockery, bags, books and pens, whether in shops or as mobile hawkers. By 'service providers', I mean tailors, touts, barbers, porters, taxi operators and motorcyclists ferrying people. The category 'soft manufacturers' refers to bicycle and garage repair shops, craftsmen, weavers, potters and carpenters while 'hard manufacturers' include hardware welders and those making gates, coffins,

1 Platform for Labour Action (PLA) is a local Ugandan NGO established in 2001 to promote and protect the human rights of vulnerable and marginalised workers, a majority of whom are women children and youth in the country's informal sector. PLA offers free legal services to these categories of workers, undertakes actions to combat child labour, promotes human rights education, HIV/AIDS prevention and impact mitigation campaigns in the informal sector, as well as advocacy, networking and research to inform policy and legal reform.

furniture and other metal works. These are some of the visible forms of work in the informal economy in Uganda.

This essay is contextualised on the understanding that most of the poor live in the informal economy, and there are correlations between poverty and informality. Despite the fact that numerous laws have been enacted in Uganda to ensure the protection of workers' rights, there is still a huge gap in the enforcement of such legislation in the country. Indeed, just as in many other countries in the region, Uganda too faces the 'representational gap', aggravated by the fact that workers within the informal economy are not recognised and/or protected by legislation due to the nature of their work. And most employers within the informal economy are generally unaware of their rights.

The findings of the study indicate that informal sector workers can be organised and are indeed eager to be organised through concerted efforts. Although domestic workers are generally hidden from the public spotlight, they can be reached, organised and made aware of their rights. Informal sector employers and employees can also be supported with legal aid to promote their rights and formalise some of their relationships. The applicability of existing legislation to the informal sector can, moreover, be achieved through the use of community-based monitoring systems to, for example, address child labour and community legal education.

The material for this study is based on secondary data sources acquired mainly through a desk review of the existing literature on the subject and experiences of the author, in addition to research undertaken in the course of her work in running PLA. A major part of the research, on which this chapter is based, was undertaken in 2006 in Lira Municipality in northern Uganda, but I will also draw on an earlier study from Kampala and Wakiso districts carried out in 2003. In the Lira study, around 200 persons were interviewed, with 50 individuals from four markets and selling points in each of the four divisions of Lira municipality. Four focus group discussions were also conducted each with twelve persons. A random selection of respondents was made from amongst food sellers, non-food sellers, service providers and soft and hard manufacturers, with an equal proportion from each of the above-mentioned sectors. The gender-disaggregated data shows that out of the 248 respondents, 44 per cent were females. The Kampala and Wakiso study included 203 respondents – with equal shares of males and females and urban and rural respondents – and six focus group discussions were held with food sellers and service providers. The participants drew two community resources maps of their working places in order to reflect the different sub-sector working locations in the market, location of facilities, pathways, drainage, and possible sites for training.

The chapter is divided into four sections. First, I provide a brief overview of poverty and the informal economy in Uganda and define key concepts used in the study. Second, I discuss the current regulatory frameworks and operational challenges in empowering the poor in the informal economy in Uganda. Third, I explore some of the strategies for collectively organising informal economy workers based on the current initiatives in Uganda. In the final section, I will draw some general conclusions based on the studies from Uganda.

According to the Commission on Legal Empowerment of the Poor (CLEP 2008), a large majority of the poor live in the informal economy, working in small informal businesses, and there are strong correlations between poverty and informality. The informal sector in Uganda, which dates back to the 1970s, gained considerable visibility in the 1980s, and consolidated in the 1990s through growth in the sector and increase in self employment as opposed to other forms of employment. Many factors have contributed to this development, including the economic crises of the 1970s and the 1980s which resulted in the expulsion of enterprising members of the Indian community by the Idi Amin regime, the collapse of the formal economy and political instability (Okumu 1994). What followed were compulsory layoffs of workers in state-owned corporations and government departments, including the armed and policing services. The situation was exacerbated by student drop outs at the upper primary school level, on-going rural-urban migration of unskilled labour and the freezing of public sector recruitment (Ssemogerere 1996). This pushed many unskilled workers into the informal sector in urban areas of the country.

In this chapter, I will adopt the wider definition of the informal economy which incorporates certain types of informal employment that were not included in previous definitions of the concept. Thus, I understand the informal economy to include the whole of informality as it is manifested in industrialised, transition and developing economies, in addition to the real world dynamics in labour markets today, especially the employment arrangements of the working poor. This definition therefore covers those working in unregulated environments and without contracts, including invisible and hidden services such as domestic work. By doing so, I wish to extend the focus from enterprises that are not legally regulated to employment relationships that are not legally regulated or protected. Such a broad understanding of the informal economy thus focuses on the nature of employment in addition to the characteristics of enterprises. These characteristics include the following: self employment; employment without written contracts, benefits or social protection; employment in small unregistered or unincorporated enterprises; unpaid family workers; casual or day labourers; and domestic workers (Chew 2005).

The informal sector in Uganda accounts for almost 80 per cent of the work force and includes agriculture, construction, and the sale of goods and services. Certain sub-sectors of the informal economy have, however, been recently regulated. For example, the informal money transfer market was regulated in order to safeguard private funds, check money laundering and funding of terrorism, and in order to protect the clean image of the financial sector that operates within the parameters of the law. The Foreign Exchange Act (GOU 2004, Section 5) thus currently provides that 'except as permitted by any other law, no person shall engage in the business of dealing in foreign exchange without a licence issued under this Act'. Despite such partial successes, a large majority of the remaining sub- sectors in the country, including domestic work, remain unregulated.

According to Ocici (2006), a relatively recent survey of the informal economy indicated that it was costly and tedious to register a business in Uganda. The occupants of the sector lacked information on the legal requirements such as procedures for registration, obtaining business licenses and taxation. In addition, access to the institutions charged with this responsibility was cumbersome, particularly for the rural and urban poor. Ocici further indicates that the processes of registration was described by the informants of the survey to be time consuming and costly, a situation further exacerbated by corruption.

Other writers also highlight obstacles and barriers faced by actors in the informal economy. These include difficulty in accessing finances due to restrictive legislation amidst high interest rates among available alternatives and competition from cheap imports – especially from China, India, Taiwan and Malaysia, following the removal of trade barriers – which in turn opened the sector to competition from cheap but of high quality (and state subsidised) products from developed countries (World Bank 2005). In addition, workers in the informal sector lack safety net mechanisms in case of job loss, injury, sickness and death. The absence of organised and recognised interest groups, such as unions and associations, to negotiate with government agencies to solve the problems affecting the sector have further exacerbated the lack of voice of informal sector workers in decision making and implementation processes. Inadequate regulatory policies and regulations to address, often unique, problems in the informal sector thus prevail in Uganda in addition to widespread discriminatory attitudes of private sector actors and developed country donors (World Bank 2005). Such a scenario is further worsened by perceptions that services and products from the informal sector cater only to the poor.

Current Regulatory Framework and Operational Challenges

A number of laws regulate business and work and therefore impinge on the urban poor in the informal economy. However, the majority of the poor are not conversant with these laws, including the Public Health Act (Laws of Uganda Chapter 281, Vol. 1, 2000), which requires local authorities to safeguard and promote public health and the Markets Act (Laws of Uganda, Chapter 94, Vol. IV, 2000), which provides for the establishment and management of markets. In addition, the local authorities and their agents are responsible for the provision of services such as urban water and sanitation, roads, housing and related infrastructure, education, health and garbage disposal. However, the reality is quite different and recent studies indicate that the urban poor in the informal economy lack adequate toilet facilities, a place to store their goods, childcare facilities and remain vulnerable to criminal acts (Platform for Labour Action 2010). Moreover, the collection of market dues does not take cognisance of whether a vendor has made any sales or not. And such practices continue to go unchecked as the poor lack voice to demand improved services and extract accountability from the local authorities.

Similarly, the Trade (Licensing) Act (Laws of Uganda, Chapter 101, Vol. IV, 2000) provides for trading and other matters and prescribes the procedures for applying for applying for licences. For example, it requires hawkers and travelling wholesalers to have licences (Sections 1 and 20) and, in addition, those issued with licences are required to keep books of accounts (Section 26). Despite such provisions that are aimed at regulating business, no education efforts have been made to create awareness on these procedures among workers in the informal economy. Moreover, the procedures are often unfavourable to the poor; for example, the procedure for acquiring licences is lengthy, bureaucratic and expensive. In addition, a requirement for complying with other laws – such as the Public Health Act (Sections 84–6) – before licences can be issued, is not realistic for small traders in the informal sector. Consequently, most employers within the informal economy operate from the underground in that they do not follow any legal process to register and operate their businesses.

As described above, the numerous and cumbersome procedures make entry into, and participation in, the formal sector lengthy, complex and expensive. Thus, Uganda has 17 procedures or steps to follow when formally starting a business. According to a World Bank (2006: 157) publication, it took 36 days to start the business and/or fulfil the procedures at a cost of percentage income per capita of 117.8. Moreover, there are 19 procedures for licensing a business and it takes, on average, 155 days to register the business and 861.8 as cost of percentage income per capita (2006: 157). With such complex and burdensome requirements, most people opt not to register their businesses or enterprises and this leads to the further growth and sustainability of the informal economy. Available literature also indicates that recruitment agencies in the country are not regulated by the Ministry of Gender Labour and Social Development (which is responsible for labour-related issues), and are thus allowed to operate without supervision (Namara 2001).

In addition, harassment by city and municipal officials is a common practice. Recent studies have indicated that a relatively large number (49 per cent) of people in the informal sector reported harassment by municipality and market management officials. High and un-regulated taxes, high rent, frequent power cuts (for those who work at night) and a reduction in the number of customers were some of the other insecurities that informal sector workers were faced with (Platform for Labour Action 2010).

Distinguishing the 'Informal' from the 'Formal'

While defining 'workers' and 'employees', neither the Employment Act nor the Occupational Safety and Health Act 2006 (No. 9) differentiate between the formal and the informal economy. Under the Employment Act, an employee is 'Any person who has entered into a contract of service or an apprenticeship contract including without limitation any person who is employed by or for the government of Uganda, including the Uganda Public Service, a local authority or a parastatal organisation but excludes a member of the Uganda Peoples Defence Forces'. Further, the Act stipulates that, 'Except as otherwise provided … this Act applies to employees employed by an employer under a contract of service' (Section 1). It further states, 'This Act does not apply to employers and their dependant relatives when dependant relatives are the only employees in a family undertaking as long as the total number of dependant relatives does not exceed five' (Section 2a). Similarly, according to the Occupational Safety and Health Act (Section 2), a 'Worker means a person who performs work, regularly or temporarily for an employer and includes a public officer'. It therefore implies that all workers are covered by the occupational safety and health legislation. However, while these definitions encompass the informal sector, the majority of workers in the informal sector operate under trust and oral contracts which are difficult to enforce.

Uganda's 1995 Constitution stipulates the economic rights of its populace to include the right to work under safe, satisfactory and healthy conditions and enshrines the principles of equal pay for equal work, the right to rest and reasonable working hours as well as paid holidays (GOU 1995, Articles 40, 1). In addition, the constitution provides for the rights of workers to join trade unions, engage in collective bargaining and representation, withdraw from a labour contract and enjoy adequate protection during pregnancy and after birth (ibid: Article 40, 3). The constitution thus incorporates the principles of the International Covenant on Economic Social and Cultural Rights (1966) which provides for the right to work, the enjoyment by every person to just and favourable conditions of work and the protection of young persons from economic and social exploitation.

Despite the above, Uganda – like many other developing countries – faces a 'representational gap'. Indeed, my studies among informal sector workers in Lira Municipality in northern Uganda reveals that 81.5 per cent of the respondents did not belong to a trade union or work-related organisation, a situation further exacerbated by 90 per cent of self employment as 'own account workers' and unpaid family workers (UBOS 2007).

Domestic Workers

A major category of people in the informal economy that does not enjoy the right to freedom of association are domestic workers. Since the Labour Unions Act 2006 does not explicitly exclude paid domestic workers, it implicitly recognises their right to associate (Platform for Labour Action 2007). The significance of this right cannot, however, be overstated in view of the historical relevance of the industrial action of the 1950s by domestic workers in Uganda and the general vulnerability of domestic workers. Indeed, despite the fact that Barya (2001) confirms that domestic workers can freely join trade unions in Uganda,[2] there is to date no evidence of a union that has mobilised domestic workers to join it. The available evidence also reveals that employers undermine the freedom of movement and association of domestic workers in various ways. Thus, according

2 Until the establishment of the Central Organisation of Free Trade Unions (COFTU), the National Organisations of Trade Unions (NOTU) was the sole umbrella trade union for all workers in Uganda.

to the Platform for Labour Action (2007), employers do not permit freedom of association for domestic worker due to the need to protect the security of the employer's household from external influences. Moreover, a recent ILO (2010) report shows that domestic workers are among the least protected internationally and one of the major abuses they face include severe restrictions of the freedom of movement.

As mentioned above, restrictions on the right of domestic workers to associate makes it difficult for them to join trade unions and hence to participate in collective bargaining, which in turn is a crucial factor for the improvement of conditions of work and enhancement of other rights. Given their employment within a private space, and compounded by isolation, it has been difficult for relevant actors to reach out to domestic workers in different households for purposes of collective bargaining in developing countries (Chew 2003).

Uganda's Employment Act (2006) also provides workers with many rights, including the right to rest, the freedom of association and entitlements to annual and sick leave, including maternity and paternity leaves (Sections 51, 54 and 55). However, the actual circumstances of life in the informal sector render the issue of leave and rest not easily applicable because working for long hours is part of the norm as domestic workers try to survive in an environment characterised by a general lack of alternative employment opportunities. A good number of workers therefore continue to exist in the informal economy simply because they have no other option. Most of them are self employed and as such find it difficult to take leave.

The situation of domestic workers is further exacerbated by their location in the employer's house, which negatively impacts on other issues such as working hours, leave periods and termination notice (Chew 2003). Indeed, the long hours of work, lack of rest and absence of holidays and/or leisure time have been directly attributed to the employer's house being the worker's worksite and venue of accommodation (ibid.). And because of this, the employer gets access to the employee at all times of day and night and makes it difficult (if not impossible) to regulate hours of work. Time off is virtually non-existent for the traditional domestic worker employed in low and middle class families (ibid.), with the standard work day lasting for more than 12 hours, starting from 5–6 a.m. and often continuing until 10 p.m. or midnight (Rukooko 2001). Moreover, work during these hours is full time, often without breaks or rest hours (Namara 2001). Further, the workday may also last for up to 17 hours at a stretch if there is an ailing child or infant in the house (Rukooko 2001). The little time off available to domestic workers are usually brief sessions of rest between chores or when going for prayers on recognised days of worship (mainly Sundays), when their employers are at home (Namara 2001). Ultimately, the domestic worker is denied sufficient rest and the opportunity to consider alternative careers or leisure. In addition, while theoretically every female employee who is pregnant is entitled to 60 working days of leave from work on full wages, of which at least four weeks should follow the child birth or miscarriage, in practice this right is seldom enjoyed by Ugandan women (Employment Act 6 of 2006, Section 56). Thus, despite many legal provisions that can provide domestic workers with many rights and privileges in theory, the very nature of their working environment makes it difficult for them to enjoy such entitlements. And most, in fact, do not ever get to enjoy a holiday (Rukooko 2001; Namara 2001).

Sexual Harassment and Termination of Employment

The Employment Act further provides a wide definition of sexual harassment of an employee by an employer or his/her representative. The definition encompasses not only requests for sexual intercourse but also includes sexual contact, as well as oral or written language, visual material and physical behaviour of a sexual nature.[3] Sexual harassment of an employee by the employer or the employer's representative attracts an order by the labour officer similar to that of unjustified disciplinary penalty or unjustified dismissal (Section 7.2). Unfortunately, this provision disfavours the majority in the informal sector such as domestic worker in the sense that it only obligates employers with more than 25 employees to put in place measures to prevent sexual harassment occurring at the work place (Section 7.4). Employers in the informal sector often employ one or two employees and there is usually a higher incidence of sexual harassment within working conditions in the private arena. Despite this there is no specific requirement for such employers to put in place policies to address sexual harassment.

The Employment Act also provides for notification and hearing before termination of an employee on grounds of poor performance or misconduct. The employer is obliged to explain to an employee the reason for dismissal in a language he/she understands and in the presence of any person of his or her choice (Section 66). It also provides for a clear grievance settlement procedure. Furthermore, an employee or employer has a right to refer a compliant under a contract of employment to a labour officer (Section 12). And the labour officer has powers to investigate the complaint and settle the matter through a wide range of methods, including the use of conciliation, arbitration or adjudication or any other procedure deemed appropriate to the parties but with the involvement of

3 The Employment Act 2006 (Section 7) provides that an employee shall be sexually harassed in his/her employment if an employer or his representative if 'a) directly or indirectly makes a request to an employee for sexual intercourse, sexual contact or any other form of sexual activity that contains an implied or express promise of preferential treatment in employment; an implied or express threat of detrimental treatment in employment; an implied or express threat about the present or future employment status of the employee b) uses language whether written or oral of a sexual nature c) uses visual material of a sexual nature d) shows physical behaviour of a sexual nature; all of which directly or indirectly subjects the employee to behaviour that is unwelcome or offensive to that employee and that either by its nature or through repetition has a detrimental effect on the employee's employment, job performance or job satisfaction'.

any labour union at the place of work of the complainant (Section 12). The labour officer can also call evidence of witnesses, require the production of a document or hold hearings to determine the legal validity of the matter.

However, a labour officer has no jurisdiction to handle torts arising out of an employment relationship. Such claims have to be brought before court; for example, a party aggrieved by a decision of a labour officer can appeal to the Industrial Court (Section 94.1). Although some of the above mentioned provisions may be immediately useful to the informal sector, the labour officers are only located at district and division offices, which are, in reality, distanced from, and not accessible to, the informal sector.

The Labour Disputes (Arbitration and Settlement) Act (2006, Section 2) defines a dispute is defined as 'any dispute or difference between an employer or employers and an employee or employees, or a dispute between employees or between labour unions, connected with employment or non-employment, terms of employment, the conditions of labour of any person or of the economic and social interests of a worker or workers'. It is also noteworthy that the law provides a wide range of informal dispute settlement mechanisms namely voluntary procedures, conciliation, mediation and Industrial Court not to be bound by rules of evidence in its civil proceedings (Section 24). These mechanisms are less technical than traditional formal courts and appear to be more suitable to regulate the working conditions of domestic workers. However, the nature of the employment contracts, which are oral, greatly determines the manner of termination of employment, which is also oral. This therefore impacts on dispute/ grievance handling mechanisms available to the domestic worker (Platform for Labour Action 2007).

Safety and Health in the Workplace

The Occupational Safety and Health Act (2006, Act No. 6) regulates the occupational safety and health of employees and other persons in the work place. A workplace or work environment is described as 'all places of work and all sites and areas where work is carried out including not only the permanent, indoor, stationary places of work, such as factories, offices and shops but also temporary places of work such as civil engineering sites, open air places such as fields, forests, roads, oil refineries and mobile places of work such as cabs of trucks, seats of tractors and excavators, ships, galleys, freight decks of aircraft and without exception; places where workers are found as a consequence of their work (including canteens and living quarters onboard ships)' (Section 2). Both definitions of a 'worker' and 'a work place' thus appear to adequately encompass workers in the informal economy, and to this extent make the law applicable to them. Also implied in the legislation on occupational safety and health is the right of an inspector to enter, inspect and examine during the day or at night any workplace and every part of it where he or she has reasonable cause to believe that any person is employed in it (Sections 3 and 6a). However, the number of inspectors is limited and as such they have not been able to reach out to majority of informal sector sites.

The Workers Compensation Act 2000 (Chapter 225) provides for compensation to workers for injuries suffered and scheduled diseases incurred in the course of their employment. These provisions and apply to all employment in Uganda with the exception of the armed forces (Section 2) and the Act further provides for medical treatment in case of accident, and insurance by employers. However, this law has been described by employers as burdensome, especially since it does not create incentives for firms to make their operations safer (GOU PEAP 2005). In the case of employers in the informal economy, many are unaware of this law and the requirements therein. In addition, those engaged in agricultural activities around the household (such as digging) often suffer insect and snake bites, open wounds and eye irritations and infections, but there is seldom any evidence of such workers being covered by medical insurance. This law has thus remained unenforced in relation to the informal economy. It should, however, be noted that even in the formal sector very few sites are inspected by labour inspectors to assess the extent of adherence to occupational safety issues. The main argument advanced for lack of these inspections is the limited number of inspectors and lack of adequate resources allocated by government towards such activities. The informal nature of the relationship between the employer and employees in the informal economy (such as domestic workers) renders it even more difficult to apply regulations and undertake regular inspections.

In addition to the above, Uganda's minimum wage currently stands at USD three per month and this has been in force for more than two decades. Thus, fixing of minimum wages under the statutory machinery is an important and necessary safeguard for all unskilled workers, especially those who may not be covered by collective bargaining. The absence of a revised minimum wage and policy further exposes workers in the informal economy to exploitation. Since different sub-sectors of the informal economy have the potential to pay different types of minimum wage packages, some trade unionists, employers, parliamentarians and technocrats in government argue that it is difficult to standardise a policy of minimum wages. However, sub-sectors such as construction, water and food vending can easily regulate minimum wages since these are services that can be assessed in the market. The absence of minimum wages for such sub-sectors has therefore meant that these workers continue to be exploited by contractors. For example, informal workers at the construction sites earn approximately USD one dollar a day, working long hours and without access to workers compensation/ insurance in the event of accident during work. Moreover, they lack voice and representation in dispute resolution processes, which makes them vulnerable to exploitation.

Child Labour

Uganda has ratified the United Nations Convention on the Rights of the Child and the African Charter on the Rights and Welfare of the Child, which recognise the right of the child to be protected from economic exploitation. The African

Charter, for example, protects a child from performing any work that is likely to be hazardous, interfere with the child's education or to be harmful to the child's health or physical, mental, spiritual, moral or social development. It also calls for the fixing of the minimum age for admission to employment (OAU Article 32) as well as regulation of hours and conditions of employment, and providing for appropriate penalties for enforcement (OAU Article 32.2 a, b, c). Uganda has also ratified the two key ILO Conventions on child labour. First, the Minimum Age Convention (1973) calls upon member states to pursue a national policy designed to ensure the effective abolition of child labour and to increase progressively the minimum age for admission to employment, or work to a level consistent with the fullest development of young persons. Second, the Worst Forms of Child Labour Convention (1999) prohibits the engagement of children in any forms of slavery; using children for prostitution or pornography, illicit activities such as drug trafficking; or work which, by its nature or the circumstances in which it is carried out, is likely to harm the health, safety or morals of the child. As stated earlier, Uganda's Constitution (1995, Art. 25 and Art. 34.4) also prohibits slavery and the engagement of children in hazardous or dangerous work (Employment Act, Section 55). Pornography is criminalised under the Penal Code Act (1950, Chapter 116, Section 139) and the Constitution specifies an age limit of employment of children in hazardous work at not less than 16 years of age. The Children's Act (1997, Section 8) also prohibits harmful employment of children and empowers Local Councils to safeguard children and promote their welfare within their areas (Section 10). However, the level of enforcement of the above prescriptions remains inadequate and it is estimated that approximately 1.76 million 5–17-year-olds in Uganda are engaged in child labour (UBOS 2008).

The challenge of protecting workers in the informal sector from exploitation and unsafe work environments is recognised by the Government (GOU/SDIP 2003/4). Informal sector workers are some of the main vulnerable groups in Uganda and their vulnerability, according to the government, arises mainly out of their poverty. The fact that a good number of these workers are paid minimal wages, and in cash (GOU/PEAP 2005: 43), makes it difficult for them to have and enjoy formal social security arrangements. In particular, low paid and migrant workers are often exposed to harsh conditions, generally lacking personal security, living in unhygienic conditions and women are highly exposed and vulnerable to sexual harassment (GOU/SDIP 2003/4).

Moreover, the current formal social security arrangements do not cater to the informal sector, particularly self employed and small businesses employing less than five employees. The majority of these workers survive on voluntary assistance from relatives and well wishers during their old age, a mechanism which is also not sustainable. Although there are informal mechanisms for social security such as burial and saving groups among the some informal sector sub- groups, their impact and effectiveness has not been explored by policymakers in terms of documenting the best practices and mechanisms for scaling up such initiatives. Employers of small enterprises are also not in position to meet the legal requirements of a 10 per cent contribution on behalf of their employees to the formal social security scheme, the National Social Security Fund. This is due to limitation in capital bases and the small profit margins of these firms. Consequently, they have not been eager to subscribe to formal systems of social security.

Vulnerability in Uganda has traditionally been mitigated by cultural community mechanisms such as non-formal and kinship-based social security, where the surviving family automatically take over responsibility of orphans through the extended family structures. Similarly, the elderly may be looked after with the help of voluntary assistance from relatives and well wishers. However, such community-based systems are slowly breaking down partly due to the impact of HIV/AIDS and orphan hood. HIV/AIDS attacks the working population in its productive age and due to early deaths, orphans are left to be cared for by older care givers. Thus, an increasing number of elderly are taking on responsibilities of care-giving to orphans amidst high levels of poverty. And a majority of the elderly cannot work to earn a living.

Safety, poor working conditions, abuse of workers' rights, lack of capital, difficulty in getting payments from customers and the lack of proper tools to carry out their work are some of the major challenges facing urban informal sector workers. The working conditions in most urban informal economy sites are appalling and workers work for long hours without rest. They also lack adequate toilet facilities, a place where to store their goods and child care facilities. The Lira study, for example, revealed that poor hygiene among informal sector workers affected women most because a large number of them carried their children to work and in some cases, both the children and the adults suffered from diarrhoea and other related diseases due to the unhygienic work environment. In addition, they were not safe from crime and almost half of the respondents reported harassment by municipality and market management officials. High and un-regulated taxes, high rent, load shedding (for those who work at night) and a reduction in the number of customers were some of the other insecurities that informal sector workers faced on a regular basis.

Strategies for the Collective Organisation of Informal Workers in Uganda

This section presents the strategies and some of the existing initiatives for the mobilisation of workers in the informal economy for collective action. A number of international human rights instruments, such as the Universal Declaration of Human Rights, the International Covenant on Civil and Political Rights together with Uganda's Constitution provides for the freedom of association and assembly as well as participation in development. Despite these provisions, workers in the informal economy spend most of their time struggling to work hard for survival. Consequently, they are not given an opportunity to participate objectively in politics of development and decision making processes, and hence continue to lack voice. Rukooko (2001) describes denial of the right to movement and association as 'oppressive and nearly creates an image of a prisoner', while Namara (2001) considers the refusal of movement of domestic worker as 'tantamount to imprisonment within the home'.

Although still at a stage of infancy, the current work of the Platform for Labour Action confirms that informal sector workers can be mobilised.

A study among domestic workers in four district of Uganda – Iganga, Lira, Mbarara and Kampala – found that although only 4.7 per cent belonged to some form of association, 78.7 per cent were willing to join such groups if an opportunity arose. In this study, only 21.3 per cent of the respondents, who did not belong to any association, had reservations about joining such organised groups (Platform for Labour Action 2007). Factors prohibiting domestic workers to belong to associations groups include lack of time, prohibition by employer and general lack of interest (Ibid.). Thus, although domestic workers may appear hidden, they can be reached by NGOs, researchers and local leaders. It should, however, be noted that reaching out to domestic workers is a challenge and involves several protocols such as seeking permission from local leaders and soliciting their support, talking to employers to allow outsiders to have access to their households, negotiating for free time and ensuring that the association does not negatively affect the job security of the domestic worker. Nonetheless, the civil society experience so far is that promoting accessibility to organisations and helping individuals become more visible is an important first step towards freedom of association for domestic workers.

Another study – conducted among food and non-food sellers, soft and hard manufacturers and services providers – focused on whether informal sector workers possessed any bargaining power to show case their problems to relevant authorities and raise their concerns on the policy agenda (Platform for Labour Action 2010). Around 82 per cent of the respondents indicated that they did not belong to a trade union or organisation related to the work. Only 16 per cent answered that they were members of a work-related organisation, and mentioned the following: women's groups, loan schemes, microfinance schemes, fresh foods association, bicycle repairs, special taxi hire associations. These findings show that there is some level of group organising and association of informal sector workers based at the workplace.

Despite the existence of such groups, however, our focus group discussions in the Lira study indicated that the informal sector workers did not have a stronghold for advocacy because they lacked a cohesive voice or body that could push their concerns, and demand accountability from different actors. Hence, a key finding is the need to establish a network of informal sector workers who can aggressively campaign for their rights since they are generally treated unfairly by market and municipal authorities. Indeed, according to focus group discussions, the rights of informal sector workers were often abused and the relationship between them and local authorities was one of mistrust and counter accusations. This, according to the workers, stemmed from the fact that taxes were charged unfairly and at arbitrary rates, irrespective of the nature and type of work. Workers generally also expressed limited awareness of their rights and attributed this to their failure to boldly take further steps to overcome such oppression.

The fact that the respondents were demanding an effective voice also shows that a key strategy for protection of the poor in the informal economy involves mobilisation and group formation. This could involve, for example, groups that are able to voice grievances and engage in a dialogue with local authorities on taxes and with market officials on services provided. Uganda has recently witnessed a growth in the number of informal sector associations operating within its territory. Hence, a number of markets currently have unions and associations, as well as networks such as the Kampala City Traders' Association, which currently lobbies, advocates and influences the creation of sustainable business partnerships and linkages between and among the local business community and other foreign corporate business companies. However, this association is city-based and does not address the needs of other towns and municipality-based businesses. Nonetheless, the emergency of such groups cannot be delinked from the current support by donor governments to private sector development. Moreover, market associations and unions have been on the increase due to HIV/AIDS-related programmes by donors, which support access to HIV/AIDS services in the markets.

NGOs and trade unions also have a crucial role to play in mobilising workers in the informal economy. For example, the Platform for Labour Action has, following the studies it has undertaken in the informal sector, mobilised workers – mainly women and youth in the informal economy – to form community-based groups. And thus far, the organisation has established nine such groups spread over four districts – Kampala, Wakiso, Iganga and Lira. Most of these groups are involved in HIV/AIDS behavioural campaigns and the welfare of informal sector women and youth in the development process. Moreover, these groups also engage in demanding transparency and accountability from local leaders and improvement in general services. Evidence emerging from the Lira municipality study confirms that issue-based collective bargaining is possible. The municipality has, for example, provided water facilities to markets and the police have strengthened security in dark places where the informal sector workers were facing insecurity after work due to frequent robberies. Thus civil society interventions has helped informal sector workers, particularly women and youth, to identify relevant issues and facilitated, through various forums, meetings with relevant officials where workers have been able to present their problems to law and order officials, and even the Mayor. The issues ranged from taxation and licensing on the one hand, to the lack of access to water and adequate security on the other. Further, and following such meetings, the officers have taken action following meetings with these categories of workers, for example by streamlining the amount of dues that should be paid when dealing in produce and also provided tapped water to the markets.

The above discussion shows that collective organising in the informal economy is plausible and has to be issue-based. This could, for example, include demands for better toilet facilities, cleaner water in the market, day-care facilities and the need to address threats of eviction following re-allocation of sites to industrial developers. According to Navin Chandra,[4] any movement advocating the legal empowerment of the poor must consider the characteristics of poverty in the informal sector, including low wages, long working hours, and insecurity of employment, and what he categorises as forms of deficits in income, health care, educational, housing and voice. Chandra further argues that the poor acquire their power from control of production, and as such their legal empowerment should encompass legal protection in the context of being productive, in addition to social security. Moreover, the ability to market their goods without exploitation and having social security tools that are relevant and affordable are important issues in this context. Such benefits cannot accrue to informal sector workers without a critical mass of individuals that can effectively create a demand; hence the need for the formation of groups and associations.

Informal sector employers and employees can also be supported with legal aid to promote their rights and formalise some of their relationships. The process of registering and licensing a business is lengthy and thus the need to have accessible legal aid services to advise actors in the informal economy and also demystify the registration process are crucial steps that can be undertaken in a country like Uganda. Laws, in most cases, are used against informal sector workers – such as cases relating to individuals being idle and/or disorderly and hence risking arbitrary arrest – and thus there is a further need for mechanisms for such individuals to defend themselves against such allegations.

On the issue of child labour, the applicability of existing legislation can be achieved through the use of community-based monitoring systems to address child labour, and awareness rising in general. The training of law enforcement agencies on the rights of the informal sector occupiers and the manner in which the informal economy works can also reduce levels of harassment.

Conclusion

In this chapter, I have discussed both the theory and reality of legislation on workers' rights in Uganda. There are indeed several legislative documents in the country that direct local authorities and agents to provide services in markets where also a good number of operators in the informal economy are based. Despite this provision, the services provided are highly adequate. Thus, operators in the informal economy must be mobilised into associations or unions as a forum for demanding and pressurising the local government and market officials to provide better and targeted services. The licensing legislation also requires traders to have licences and books of accounts; however, with low literacy levels, the majority of informal operators have not taken steps to upgrade their businesses

4 'Labour Rights and the Working Poor', http://www.undp.org/LegalEmpowerment/reports/National%20Consultation%20Reports/Country%20Files/12_India/12_5_Labor_Rights.pdf (Accessed: 02 September 2009).

and further lack awareness of the procedures to be followed. I have also argued that the occupational safety legislation can be progressively interpreted to cover the informal economy, but for this to take place, additional and properly trained labour inspectors must be appointed. These individuals must also undertake regular inspections of workplaces, paying particular attention to health hazards. It can thus be inferred that despite the existence of legislation that would protect all workers including those in the informal economy, its enforcement in general, and with regarding to the informal sector in particular, remains abysmal.

However, there is also some positive news. The empirical evidence discussed in this chapter shows clearly that there is potential for the informal sector to get organised in order to address specific issues such as demanding for services from the local and national governments and better accountability for taxes collected. Collective mobilisation, therefore, should be the starting point for these operators to realise the right to freedom of association, a right guaranteed by the Uganda Constitution. To realise this potential, we must make workers and operators in the informal economy aware of their rights, and specifically the benefits of freedom of association. This should then be followed by actual mobilisation and formation of groups initially based on issues at hand, until the groups mature to take up more complex issues. In relation to domestic workers, there is need to educate employers, local leaders and domestic workers themselves, on the benefits of freedom of association and this could commence by the formation of peer support groups.

Moreover, the central government needs to revisit its policies and regulations in order to understand how these appear unsuited to tackling challenges in the informal economy. Any new regulation aimed at this sector must include the voices of workers and address their specific needs. Thus, for example, the government could start by revising its policies that require hawkers to apply for licences. The focus here should be on making the process efficient, quick and as cheap as possible. Attention must also be provided to combat corruption by officials involved in the licensing process.

Mobilising the informal sector is not, however, an easy task and organisations involved in this field face numerous challenges. Workers in the informal sector are, in most cases, struggling for survival and thus taking time off to attend rights awareness or problem analysis sessions can be difficult. And workers may demand compensation for the time lost when attending training sessions. The informal sector is also 'mobile' in nature, especially in urban informal settlements. This requires ongoing mobilisation and training new teams of volunteers to replace those who have moved on to newer areas. And civil society organisations must constantly adjust their programmes, which can be resource draining. Moreover, mobilised groups of workers may also not survive for long if the parent civil society organisation does not continuously monitor or support such groups by regularly providing resources. This is partly because the idea of group formation may not necessarily have been that of the informal sector groups themselves. Thus, a major challenge for organisations working in this field is to make workers in the informal sector aware of the advantages of taking the initiative to form groups on their own before larger organisations can be invited to further build capacity among the workers.

References

Chandra, N. (unknown), Labour Rights and the Working Poor, Available at: http://www.undp.org/LegalEmpowerment/reports/National%20Consultation%20Reports/Country%20Files/12_India/12_5_Labor_Rights.pdf [accessed: 14 September 2010].

Chew, L. 2003. *Programme Consultation Meeting on the Protection of Domestic Workers against the Threat of Forced Labour and Trafficking.* Discussion Paper prepared for Anti-Slavery International in co-operation with ILOs Special Programme to Combat Forced Labour. http://www.antislavery.org/includes/documents/cm_docs/2009/a/antislavery_domestic_workers_discussion_paper_0203.pdf [Accessed: 14 September 2010].

GOU/PEAP, 2005. Uganda Poverty Status Report: Progress in Implementing the Poverty Eradication Action Plan (PEAP). Government of Uganda, Ministry of Finance and Economic Development.

GOU/Ministry of Finance Planning and Economic Development, 2005. Poverty Eradication Action Plan, 2004/05–07/08.

GOU/Ministry of Gender, Labour and Social Development, 2006. Social Development Sector Investment Plan.

ILO, 2010. *International Labour Conference, 99th Session Proceeding Report*, Geneva, ILO. Available at: http://www.ilo.org/public/english/protection/condtrav/pdf/dw_eng.pdf [Accessed 14 September 2010].

Katabira, S. 1995. A study of various informal sector activities: A case study of Katwe. Master's thesis, Makerere University, Kampala.

Martha, A.C. 2005. Rethinking the Informal Economy Linkages with the Formal Regulatory Environment Research Paper, No. 2005/10.

Namara, A. 2001, The Invisible Workers: Paid Domestic Work in Kampala City, Uganda, *CBR Working Paper No. 74, Centre for Basic Research, Kampala, Uganda.*

Ocici, C.A. 2006. Working Paper on Entrepreneurship presented at National Consultation Conference: Legal Empowerment of the Poor, Speke Resort Munyonyo 24–25 November 2006, Available at http://www.undp.org/legalempowerment/reports/National%20Consultation%20Reports/Country%20Files/25_Uganda/25_5_Entrepreneurship.pdf [Accessed 14 September 2010].

Okumu, R.R. 1994. *The experience of the youth in the informal sector: A study of traders in Gulu Municipality*. Kampala: Makerere University.

Platform for Labour Action, 2007. *Adult Domestic Workers in Uganda: An Analysis of Human Rights and Social Injustice.* Kampala, Fountain Publishers.

Platform for Labour Action, 2010. *Risks and Vulnerabilities of HIV/AIDS in the Informal Sector. Case Study of Lira and Iganga Districts in Uganda.* Kampala, Fountain Publishers.

Rukooko, B.A. 2001. *Gender and Labour: Understanding the Status of the Paid Domestic Worker in Urban Areas of Bushenyi and Kampala*', CBR Working Paper No. 74, Centre for Basic Research, Kampala, Uganda.

Ssemogerere, G. 1996. Uganda's Experience of Employment and Labour Markets during Adjustment, Employment and Training Department, Geneva, ILO. Available at: http://www.ilo.org/wcmsp5/groups/public/---ed_emp/documents/publication/wcms_125395.pdf [Accessed: 14 September 2010].

UBOS, 2007. *Labour Market Conditions Report Based on Analysis of 2005/06 Uganda National Households Survey*. Uganda Bureau of Statistics.

UBOS, 2008. *Understanding Children's Work in Uganda Based on Analysis of 2005/06 Uganda National Households Survey*. Uganda Bureau of Statistics.

World Bank, 2005. *Urban Informal Sector in Uganda*, Available at: http://info.worldbank.org/etools/docs/library/211247/Uganda_Urban%20Informal%20Sector.pdf [Accessed: 14 September 2010].

World Bank, 2006. *Doing Business in 2006: Creating Jobs*. Washington, DC: World Bank. Available at: http://www.doingbusiness.org/documents/DoingBusiness2006_fullreport.pdf [Accessed: 14 September 2010].

International Human Rights Instruments

Office of the United Nations High Commissioner of Human Rights, 1966. *International Covenant on Civil and Political Rights.*

Office of the United Nations High Commissioner of Human Rights, 1966. *International Covenant on Economic, Social and Cultural Rights.*

Office of the United Nations High Commissioner of Human Rights, 1989. *United Nations Convention on the Rights of the Child.*

Organisation of African Unity, 1990. *African Charter on the Rights and Welfare of the Child.*

National Legislation – Uganda

Constitution of the Republic of Uganda (1995), (Vol. 1 2000), p. cxxvi.

Employment Act (2006), Act No. 6

Foreign Exchange Act (2004) Act No. 5.

Labour Disputes (Arbitration and Settlement) Act (2006), Act No. 8.

Laws of Uganda Public Health Act, Cap. 281 (Vol. 11 2000), p. 6084.

Laws of Uganda Markets Act Cap 94 (Vol. 4 2000), p. 1808.

Laws of Uganda Trade (Licensing) Act, Cap 101 (Vol. 4 2000), p. 5487.

Laws of Uganda Workers Compensation Act Cap 225 (Vol. 9 2000), pp. 4929.

Occupational Safety and Health Act (2006), Act No. 9.

Chapter 9
Informal Labour and the Ethic of Care: Legal Protection of Care-givers in Malawi

Ngeyi Ruth Kanyongolo

Introduction

Care work is part of the informal labour which remains undervalued, neglected and poorly regulated in Malawi. In a country with increasing levels of HIV/AIDS and growing demands for family and community based care for the sick, the importance of unpaid care work cannot be overemphasised. In most communities in Malawi this is commonly performed by volunteer care-givers, mainly women. This chapter is about care-giving, care work and the legal protection of care-givers. It draws on the theory of an ethic of care in order to show how care-giving in Malawi is a poorly regulated form of labour.

The ethic of care is premised on fully relational subjects who exist in complex webs of interdependence with others (Robinson 2006: 322).[1] Thus, Sevenhuijsen (2000: 29)[2] argues, 'the conception of people as working and caring citizens is better attuned to the needs of … all persons living in networks of care and responsibility than is achieved if the starting point is that of equal rights-holders'. Using the ethic of care perspective, the results of my study show that volunteer care work in Malawi is undervalued and care-givers are vulnerable to exploitation and infections and therefore in need of legal protection.

Despite its growing importance, labour regulation in Malawi focuses on and favours paid labour and the formal labour market. It neglects unpaid care labour, which is mostly performed in the informal sector. Volunteer care-givers work for long periods of time mostly during the day. They lack protective materials such as gloves and disinfectants and are therefore at risk of contracting diseases. Moreover, they do not receive any form of psycho-social support amongst other needs. This chapter therefore argues for legal protection of care-givers through policies and specific legislation that reflect and addresses the special needs of unpaid care-givers.

This study is based on research on care-givers which I conducted in Zomba and Lilongwe districts in Malawi from June to July 2009. Several studies (including Action Aid Malawi 2000; Umoyo Network 2000a: Umoyo Network 2000b), have

1 For further details, see Tronto (1993) and Daly (2002).

2 Cited in Robinson (2006: 321, 322)

focused on home-based care and on people living with HIV/AIDS in Malawi. However, while most of these studies focus on the sick and the 'care-receivers' and how they can best be served, limited attention has been paid to the people who actually provide care for the sick and on how responsibility for such care is regulated and shared among various actors. Noting this gap, my research set out to investigate the nature of care work, the characteristics of care-givers, the challenges they face and the responses to such challenges.

This study involved desk research, individual interviews, focus group discussions and observation. A number of materials such as previous research reports, policies and statutes were sourced, collected and reviewed. Individual interviews were conducted with a total of thirty individuals that included officials that run care-giving organisations, care-givers, care-receivers and government officials.

Focus group discussions were held with a group of officials from civil society involved in care work and a group of care-givers. Each group had six members. In both individual and focus group discussions, a standard guide was used to investigate the above issues. Although standardised, the guide was flexibly used and modified where necessary. Observations were carried out through a field visit to a local community where one of the care-givers provides care. Care-givers were observed at work and later interviewed on their experiences. The care-receiver was also interviewed. The findings were qualitatively analysed. The research methodology was therefore grounded and explored the lived realities of volunteer care-givers from a selected sample of care-givers.

Hiv/Aids and Care-giving

There are increasing numbers of people in need of care due to HIV/AIDS in Malawi. There are also an equally increasing number of children orphaned through HIV/AIDS-related deaths and in need of care. In a population of about eleven million, the adult HIV prevalence rate is estimated at 14 per cent with 760,000 adults living with HIV/AIDS (National Aids Commission 2007). HIV/AIDS prevalence among people aged 15–49 is 12 per cent as per 2007 surveillance report (Malawi Government 2008). This is down from 14.4 per cent in 2003. And as of 2007, HIV prevalence among pregnant women was at 12.3 per cent. There are 70,000 HIV positive children under the age of 15 and HIV prevalence is particularly high in urban areas at 25 per cent when compared to 13 per cent in rural areas (National Aids Commission 2007). The challenge posed by HIV/AIDS provides an interesting context for understanding the importance of care work and the role played by various actors especially care-givers.

Although Malawi has a free public health care service, the same has come under great strain in view of increasing health care demands, some of which are HIV/AIDS-related (National Economic Council 2000). In this context, local communities have been instrumental in providing supplementary and often the only form of care. Various actors, from primary care-givers such as family members to secondary care-givers such as community volunteers, have complemented government efforts in providing care to the sick, children and the aged (Centre for Social Research 1996). Care and care-giving have in this regard become critical to the survival of people living with HIV/AIDS among others in need of care. A conceptual understanding of care is therefore crucial to the analysis of the various roles, demands and responses of the different players and actors.

Care relates to both paid and unpaid work involving the nurturance of necessarily dependent others, children, the sick, the elderly, as well as non-relational social reproduction work that is necessary to ensure the daily maintenance and ongoing reproduction of the labour force (Robinson 2006: 322). Such an understanding therefore removes the boundaries between paid and unpaid work, the public and private, and formal and informal, and can create new forms of social solidarity at different levels (Lewis 2002: 348).

Caring is usually seen as natural, unskilled and a feminine activity and is consequently devalued in society (Cancian and Oliker 2000: 9). Indeed, societal recognition of care-giving as an important form of labour, challenges the legitimacy of the existing inequitable distribution of power, resources and privilege (Tronto 1993: 112). Such recognition of care is therefore not enough without *legitimating* care, which combines recognition with distribution of costs and responsibilities of care across actors and sectors (Daly 2002: 263).

Tronto (1993: 105–7) highlights four types of care. First, 'caring about' is related to recognition that care is necessary to meet a noted need. Second, 'taking care of' which involves assuming responsibility for the identified need and determining how to respond to it. Third, 'care-giving' relates to the direct meeting of the needs for care. Fourth, 'care-receiving' focuses on how the subject of care responds to the care received. Tronto's analysis hence highlights the importance of care and requires the following: recognition of the care needs; identification of the responses to the need and the need of actual care-givers; and whether those receiving care acknowledge that their needs are being met. My study focused on care-giving as a form of labour and in this chapter I will critically analyse the responses, especially the regulatory response to the needs of care-givers as workers. In discussing the nature and challenges faced by care-givers, I will discuss the extent to which various actors are taking up responsibility for meeting the different needs of those in need of care, especially with regard to the administrative and legislative regulation of care work.

Informal Labour, Care Work and Care-giving

The livelihood of a majority of the people in Malawi is dependent on a mixture of mainly cash crop agriculture and wage labour. Participation in paid work by the poor is, however, limited, especially for women. In 2002, only 4.8 per cent of women were employed in the formal sector, a figure that increased to 5.1 per cent in 2005 (Malawi Government 2005). The majority of these women, however, is in low-level employment and segregated into care-related jobs. For example, 90 per cent of women are engaged in domestic work compared to 24 per cent of men (Malawi Government 2005: 58). Domestic work includes care work and is normally categorised as informal labour. In my study, the majority of informants defined care work as including 'any activity such as taking care of the sick who are unable to work on their own. It also includes taking care of orphans and the elderly who cannot work earn an income'.[3]

In almost all cases, the emphasis among care-givers was on the provision of care and caring for others especially those in need and unable to take care of themselves on their own. This was identified as a form of labour and categorised in terms of paid and unpaid labour although the later was dominant.

The primary responsibility of caring for those in need of care – such as the sick, and children – falls on family members, mostly women, and hence these are the *primary care-givers*. However, primary care-givers have been overwhelmed by the increasing demands for care, and in the process, the role of *secondary care-givers* in the country has increased. The formation of community-based groups and organisations has proliferated in the context of HIV/AIDS. Historically, and in times of need, women formed community-based groups to assist each other in care work. Today, most secondary care-givers are community-based and belong to religious and other civil society organisations, mostly referred to as Community-Based Organisations (CBOs).

The nature of care work in Malawi today remains gendered, with the majority of those involved in care-giving being women, mostly those who are not a part of the formal labour market economy. This was highlighted in one focus group discussion as follows: 'There is inadequate involvement of men in care work. Men tend to associate such work with females and therefore feel uncomfortable to be part of the work. Men also feel that attending to care work actually deprives them of the time they would be involved in gainful employment or economic activity'.[4] Most women care-givers feel overburdened by care work (VSO-RAISA 2007). Although some justified this on the traditional division of labour, most bemoaned the low number of men that volunteer.

The following constitute key players involved in care work: volunteers in community-based organisations (CBOs) composed of men, women, and youth who are actually doing the care work on the ground; church leaders and traditional authorities; community leaders who coordinate the work of the volunteers; government care officers and support project officers, such as District Health Office (DHO) staff who are supposed to provide home-based care training and medical kits, and agricultural officers who provide nutrition and livelihood training and local NGO representatives such as those from the National Association of People

3 Focus Group Discussion 1 Zomba, Home-Based Care Organisations.

4 Focus Group Discussion 2 Care-givers, Zomba.

living with HIV/AIDS in Malawi (NAPHAM), Youth Net Community Organisation (YONECO), World Vision International (WVI) and Immanuel International.

The majority of the volunteer care-givers are nominated by community members on the request of religious or other charitable groups. Others volunteer on their own to care for the sick. In both cases, they take the responsibility to respond to some of the needs of those that are in need of care. However, the majority of participants argued that the bulk of the responsibility should be shouldered by the government which, they claimed, has a duty to provide health care to the needy and support those that provide such care. Further, a number of NGOs and religious organisations have assumed responsibility over care work by working with community volunteer care-givers. Most care-givers provide direct care to the chronically ill and people living with HIV/AIDS by doing household chores such as bathing the patient and cooking food for them. In the following section, I will discuss some of the challenges that care-givers face in their work.

Challenges and Needs of Care-givers

Care-givers identified a number of concerns related to their work. These included the lack of training, lack of adequate resources to provide adequate support to the sick, limited or non-existing psycho-social support, lack of recognition of their efforts from government officials and lack of remuneration. I will discuss each of these issues in detail below.

Lack of Training

Most care-givers were concerned that they were not trained or not adequately trained to care for people with HIV/AIDS. This poses a risk of inappropriately providing care, and of cross infections. The importance of training was ranked high in all discussions. Most of the funding proposals that have been sent to potential donors by most CBOs were related to the provision of proper training. However, the training programmes have been very limited in both quality and quantity. One informant in a focus group discussion noted the following:

> Not all care-givers have been trained, and for our group called Togetherness, only two care-givers were trained; the remaining twenty-five people are not trained in care-giving. In many CBOs that I know, only two or three care-givers are trained; the rest are not. The expectation is that those of us who are trained should also train others at CBO level, which does not happen due to financial constraints. We cannot start training others when we don't have any funds for doing such an activity. In most cases we are provided with limited information

> due to lack of time. Training programmes are run for 2 to 3 days, which is inadequate to cover all the materials.[5]

Despite this training and probably in view of its limitation, care work is not seriously considered a profession especially in relation to the many volunteers that are involved in care-giving. There are very few professional care workers that have undergone professional training. As another informant observed, 'We would like the government and the public to view care work as a profession because the time and energy that we use could be used for other personal activities, but we dedicate it to care work. This is contributing to poverty in our families as we spend most of our time doing unpaid work'.[6]

Lack of Resources to Support the Sick

Most primary care-givers cannot afford medication and are failing to meet nutritional demands of people living with HIV/AIDS. In cases where medication is provided for free, the major challenge is lack of transport to and from the clinic. This problem increases frustration on the part of care-givers and creates tension between care-givers and patients as the expectations of the latter are not adequately met. The lack of adequate material support in the form of gloves, medication, bicycles and other care-related equipment was identified as a key issue of concern for most secondary care-givers as well. Thus, the lack of hand gloves when cleaning patients forces some care-givers to resort to improvising, using plastic bags meant for sugar as gloves, which in turn increases the risk of infection. Moreover, care-givers need bicycles to transport the sick to hospitals and drugs to administer to the sick during visitations.

Limited Psycho-social Support

The other challenge that care-givers face is the lack of psycho-social support. Home-based care volunteers are affected because some ridicule them for doing work that does not provide a salary. As a result, the volunteers feel they are not adequately valued by the community which negatively affects them psychologically. Most care-givers are hence under stress due to high expectations on the part of patients and low resources available to meet the expectation. They are also affected by deaths of people they care for. Interestingly enough, psycho-social support did not feature highly among the concerns of care-givers. Most were worried about the physical dangers of their work in the form of infection rather than mental wellbeing. When raised as a possible issue, most of them agreed that it was an important issue which they do not take seriously probably because they are usually more worried about the welfare of those that they care for than

5 Focus Group Discussion 1 Zomba.

6 Focus Group Discussion 2 Zomba.

they are about themselves. But those that worked with care-givers (e.g. NGOs and government officials) acknowledged psycho-social-related problems as a major issue of concern that needs to be responded to urgently. They felt that the government should provide counselling and other related services to care-givers.

Lack of Pay

Most of the care-givers that were interviewed considered themselves as volunteers in the first instance. The issue of pay for their work therefore did not seem to be a priority on their agenda for action. It was only during or after a critical analysis of the burden of care work and its personal impact on them, that almost inevitably they would all raise the issue of remuneration. Almost all care-givers interviewed argued that they would benefit a lot from remuneration for their work. It was also claimed that if care work was paid, most men would be involved, partly easing the burden on women (although one may argue here whether this could in turn lead to less opportunities for women). According to government officials, the major challenge with regard to remuneration of care-givers is, however, the lack of public resources. Related to this fact is that care workers have not made serious demands for pay. One care-giver observed: ‘Government has failed to provide to us basics materials such as gloves. It would be unrealistic to start demanding remuneration’.[7]

Further, primary care-givers considered it their moral duty to provide care to members of their family and community. The issue of remuneration therefore did not arise. Secondary care-givers too considered themselves as volunteers doing charity work and therefore the issue of remuneration was not on their agenda either. Care work therefore remains an important form of unpaid informal labour that nevertheless has serious challenges that require attention. And care-givers indicated that although they continuously raise their concerns with those that they feel have the responsibility to address their concerns – especially the government – there have been limited responses to such demands.

Responses to the Needs of Care-givers

Both government and NGOs endeavour to respond to the various needs of care-givers in varying degrees. Government officials interviewed acknowledged the existence of, and the important role played by, care-givers in families and communities. They also seemed to appreciate the extent to which this care subsidises and/or complements government delivery of health services. Direct government responses to some of the concerns of care-givers include limited provision of financial resources through the National Aids Commission. The government also provides funding for training and other resources to some community-based care

7 Interview, Togetherness Community-Based Organisation.

organisations such as medical kits, including gloves, and other first aid materials which are on high demand among care-givers. Community-based organisations specialising in care work register with their local social welfare offices, which in turn offer them operational certificates. Such registration, it was argued by officials, makes it easy for the government to monitor the organisations and further helps CBOs to access donor funding.

In relation to lack of pay, the government does not seem to have prioritised the provision of remuneration to existing care-givers. This was attributed to lack of resources and donor policies. One official indicated that ideally community care-givers should be paid. Another official noted that:

> There is actually a proposed policy in the pipeline, which envisages employing at least 8,000 community care-givers to work for pay. The government intends to recruit, train and deploy community workers who will be appropriately hired by local government and will be paid for the work. However, donors who fund a large part of government programmes are not fully supportive of the proposal, arguing that this is not sustainable. This is likely to affect the final approval and implementation of the policy to pay care-givers.

It is doubtful whether the government will have the capacity to employ enough care-givers to meet the demand. The shortfall will continue to be filled by volunteers who will now have the burden of comparing themselves against the salaried care-givers, thus further exacerbating the psychological strain of doing extremely demanding voluntary work.

NGO responses to remuneration of care-givers are also minimal and most organisations indicated that the issue is not really on their agendas. One NGO representative mentioned that they had worked with most care-givers as volunteers and – apart from training, providing them with materials and occasional seminar allowances – the issue of their welfare has not been seriously considered. And another NGO informant noted, ‘In most cases, the focus is on care-receivers and how the care-givers are responding to the latter’s needs’.

The major support that has been provided by the government to care-givers is training, despite the view that this is inadequate for failing to cover the majority of care-givers. Some of the care-givers interviewed indicated that they had been trained by government or were awaiting such training. Government, through the National Aids Commission, disbursed funding to individual CBOs involved in care work for purposes of training. A standardised training manual focusing on nature of HIV/AIDS, treatment and care among other topics was produced by government and is used by most trainers (Ministry of Health 2005a; National Aids Commission 2006).

There are also non-official responses to the training needs of care-givers and both international and local NGOs play an important role in complementing government provision of training (Anderson 2008). While most care-givers continue to use government provided training manuals, YONECO (Youth Net

Community Organisation) is one institution that has provided support from a medical perspective to build capacity of care-givers on medical issues such as use of dispensing drugs and dressing wounds. The organisation has also focused on providing psycho-social support through training in counselling for people living with HIV/AIDS and education covering areas such as environment health and infection prevention. World Vision International (Zomba) is another organisation that has provided a different type of training, for example in group dynamics, financial management and care of orphan and vulnerable children.

According to my care-giver informants, material support from the government included provision of home-based care kits, gloves, training in dispensing simple medication and provision of food supplements. The government appears to recognise the importance of material support but what it provides is very limited in size and scope. Indeed, a radical increase in resources is required to meet the high demand. Most care-givers further suggested additional and more sustainable fund building activities through the provision of seed money for income generating purposes.

Psycho-social support was equally identified as an important area of concern for government in most of the policies. However, the actual response on the ground is decimal. The response is varied too. For nurses and other health paid workers, there are programmes which provide psycho-social support. The same is not available to community-based volunteer care-givers. One of the major challenges in providing psycho-social support was identified as inadequate expertise to provide the necessary services, especially in rural areas. It is also a challenge, as noted earlier, that most care-givers do not give much thought to, or actually downplay, their mental wellbeing.

Lessons can thus be drawn from psycho-social programmes that focus on nurses and other paid health workers to broaden the provision to community care-givers, including volunteers. Care-givers need to be trained in caring for their own mental wellbeing. Moreover, HIV/AIDS programmes should include a component that provides for psycho-social services.

Overall, the study shows a failure by institutions to fully recognise the care needs of people living with HIV/AIDS, which in turn means that there is a low assumption of responsibility to determine how to respond to the needs, and a devaluation of care work in general. A part of the explanation on the devaluation of care work and care-giving lies in legal discourses around gender and care work, which is the focus of the next section.

Gender and the Legal Discourse of Care Work

As noted above, the recognition that care is necessary to meet identified needs and the assumption of responsibility for such needs, including the determination of how to respond to the need, are critical aspects of practices of care-giving (Tronto 1993: 104). The reality in Malawi is, however, very different. My study shows how the physical act of care-giving is associated with the domestic private sphere and the community, where women provide most of the care.[8] Within the family and the community, women are perceived as care-givers and therefore associated with care work. The position is reinforced by the market and the state which relegate care-giving to the family and community.

The above can be explained partly based on the idea that the family is the natural site for care-giving.[9] Within the family, it is mostly the woman who is constructed as the care-giver. The construction of women as care-givers is justified on the basis of two related beliefs: the naturalness of women's ability to care for others and the socialisation of women as care-givers. A woman is perceived as best placed to look after children, the sick and the aged due to her natural ability to give birth and nurture her offspring. This 'nature' perspective is based on the belief that women have the hormones and instincts to be good providers of hands-on physical and emotional care and men do not (Cancian and Oliker 2000). Moreover, the 'natural' and 'socialisation' perspectives seemed to be mutually reinforcing. The belief that women are natural car-givers is passed on from one generation to another and ultimately becomes the norm on which generations are socialised. It translates into a discourse that, in most cases, reduces or justifies gender differences by biological differences (Tamale 2004: 52). Care-giving is then undervalued because it is seen as natural, unskilled and a feminine activity. This general conclusion is similar to findings in other studies (Cancian and Oliker 2000: 9). Hence, the processes of naturalisation and socialisation of care-giving in Malawi reproduce perceptions and practices of gendered division of labour. This is then reinforced at family, community, market and state levels through legal discourses that undervalue care-giving as work.

Family and community legal normative systems – mostly involving initiation, wedding and funeral ceremonies – reflect the gendered discourse of care-giving in Malawi. Such systems embody a discourse of the naturalness of women as care-givers. For example, the initiation ceremonies emphasise the future role of girls as good wives, mothers and women capable of taking care of their families and community. They are then groomed into this role by being given household chores related to such roles. Similarly, care-giving to the husband, children and other relatives is emphasised during marriage and child birth ceremonies. At the same time, through practice, people become socialised into this division of labour and act accordingly before being further regulated as such.

The legal protection of care-givers in this regard would require an appreciation of the important role of informal regulatory institutions at family and community

8 This is similar to findings from studies in other countries. See Sevenhuijsen et al. (2003: 299–321) on South Africa.

9 See similar findings by Cancian and Oliker (2000: 6) who also argue that this privatises care and perpetuates the distinction between the private and public nature of care.

level as reflected in the various ceremonies. Re-socialisation of the division of labour to emphasise the importance of care work is a step towards its recognition.

The social construction of womanhood, based on the gendered division of labour and care, is replicated in the state and market legal normative orders. Within the state and market, legislation embodies constructions of care in a similarly gendered and undervalued manner. Employment law in Malawi provides a good example of the gendering practice of law within the state and the market. For example, the Employment Act of 2000 provides for aspects of employment that include social responses to risks faced by employees. These, in the context of the discussion here, include maternity leave, maximum working hours, consideration to those with family responsibilities, sick leave and benefits including disability benefits. Maternity leave is available to women for a minimum of two months and there is further protection from dismissal due to maternity and punitive penalties for breach of the provision under Sections 47, 48 and 49 of the Employment Act. In practice, it is mostly those in government and statutory corporations or those working for large private firms that have access to maternity leave.

The Act also provides, in Section 37, for maximum working hours for employees, which would potentially allow men and women to engage in care work outside the workplace. There is also provision for non-discrimination of those with family responsibilities among other factors (Section 5). However, this has not yet been fully tested to see if it can be extended to cases related to care responsibilities. Time taken out for family responsibilities may be unpaid as no protection is expressly provided for in this regard within the Act. There may be no express motivation, therefore, to male employees to take leave based on family responsibility.

In practice, my field data show that, in the urban areas, it was mostly women who take leave from their employers to take care of the sick. Most male participants indicated that they never ask for leave from work if their wives were sick or during maternity, as female relatives would be expected to assist. In fact, most of my informants who were employed and received regular salaries were not aware of the provision on family responsibilities and when informed about these, were sceptical that their employers would allow them time off for family responsibilities. In addition to these cultural constraints, there are no serious enforcement mechanisms to ensure compliance beyond individual action that may be commenced by the affected woman. Thus, a thorough review of court records at the Industrial Relations Court of Malawi failed to discover a single case brought by women employees to enforce any of the provisions of the Act, although at the time of the review the Act had been in force for five years.[10]

Furthermore, there are no direct correlative provisions in Malawi to maternity leave such as paternity leave for men, which would enable them to take leave and provide physical care to the child and mother. The lack of provision for paternity

10 This may be attributed to a fear of losing jobs or lack of access to court. Both factors have been raised in other studies in Malawi. See Kanyongolo and Makuta (2000).

leave in the legislation can arguably be said to have been deliberate. During the drafting of the Employment Act, there were debates on whether paternity leave should be included or not.[11] The general consensus from both women and men was that the provision must not be included. Reasons for the exclusion included that most men do not take care of their wives and babies, and according to most women, paternity leave could only be abused by men who would use the time for other activities like beer drinking and not caring for their wives.

The discourse in this legislation, therefore, went a long way towards recognising maternity-related contingencies and protecting women from dismissal during such times. However, by failing to provide for paternity leave, it reinforces the social role of women as care-givers. The exclusion of paternity leave, based on a majority's view, shows not only the gendering practice of law, but also the interplay between state legislation and cultural norms with which the majority are socialised. It is imperative therefore that regard be given to the policies and legislation on care work.

Policies, Guidelines and Legislation on Care Work

Most of the formal regulation of volunteer care work is in the form of policies and guidelines, with limited enforcement mechanisms. The National Community Home Based Care (NCHBC) Policy and guidelines were produced in 2005, on the basis of the 2003 National HIV/AIDS Policy, with the overall objective of providing standards for the provision of quality care for the chronically and terminally ill, including risk groups and other vulnerable groups in the home and community (Ministry of Health 2005b). The policy applies to the public sector, private health facilities, non-governmental, faith-based and community-based organisations as well as all individuals who provide care as health workers or volunteers.

The NCHBC's objectives include the following: promoting availability, access and utilisation of quality and comprehensive care for the chronically and terminally ill; strengthening the capacity of individuals, families and communities and institutions to deliver safe and quality community and home-based care services; strengthening coordination and collaboration amongst NCHBC implementing institutions; and providing research and delivery of evidence based community based care services. The guiding principles for the NCHBC policy include a holistic approach in care provision, meaningful involvement of people living with HIV/AIDS at all levels and programme stages, sustainability through active community participating, capacity building including gender mainstreaming at all levels, promoting and protection of human rights of patients and care providers, including health workers, partnership, coordination and sharing of evidence based practices, care of carers and good governance, transparency and accountability.

11 I was personally involved in the revision process and attended most of the consultation meetings.

The policy is, however, yet to be translated into legislation. Most of the care-givers in my study were not aware of these policies, and hence unable to demand for implementation.

Unlike the formal labour market, there is limited formal regulation of labour relations in the informal sector generally and care work in particular. Labour-related legislation such as the Employment Act (2000), the Occupational Health and Safety Act (1997) and Workers' Compensation Act (2000) all regulate employment related relations and exclude unpaid labour relations. The Occupational Health, Safety and Welfare Act 1997, for example, provides for safety at work with specific duties for both employers and employees. And the government provides oversight over these duties. Thus, similar health and safety legislation could easily be promulgated for care-givers. Further, the Workers' Compensation Act of 2000 provides for compensation of all workers injured at work without proof of fault. The Workers Compensation tribunal is responsible for processing and assessment compensation. The Act is under review, with proposals to include a general compensation fund. This fund could again easily be extended to cover volunteer care-givers.

Moreover, the Constitution of Malawi makes provision for fair and safe labour practices. Section 31 of the Constitution states that, 'every person shall have the right to fair and safe labour practices and to fair remuneration'. The provision applies to all persons involved in labour relationships. Care work, whether paid or not is a form of labour. It is therefore arguable that all care-givers are entitled to fair and safe labour practices. The Constitution further provides for the right of workers to form trade unions. Initially there was resistance from the office of the Registrar of Trade Unions to register informal sector workers' unions. However, after complex negotiations between workers and trade union representatives, the registrar registered one trade union for informal workers. This therefore opens the door for care-givers to form a trade union in order to collectively bargain for minimum standards and improvements in their working conditions.

One major drawback, however, is that Malawi has not passed enabling legislation to translate and ensure care-givers' enjoyment of the right to fair and safe labour practices in the same way as it has done in relation to other workers, especially those in paid employment. I therefore argue that in view of the many challenges narrated by care-givers in this study, it is high time that the state passed specific legislation to protect volunteer care-givers. Since this group of workers may not fit in existing legislation that applies to formal labour and other employer–employee relationships, I therefore propose that Malawi should enact a special Volunteer Workers Act which will address the more specific needs of care-givers. Such an Act would specifically legislate on care-givers' minimum working hours, health and safety at work and access to compensation from the state-run Workers Compensation Tribunal in case of injury or infection from diseases. The enactment of such legislation would require concerted lobbying of government, especially legislators, by the care-givers themselves and organisations that work with care-givers.

Conclusion

The preceding sections of this chapter establish quite clearly the importance of volunteer care work to most communities in Malawi. Although the Malawi government provides free health care, the advent of the HIV/AIDS pandemic has put tremendous strain on the health care system. This has resulted in most people resorting to the family and community for their care needs much more than they did before. In most cases, it is women – who are not engaged in paid work – that are involved in care-giving at family and community levels. However, responses to HIV/AIDS have been skewed by a focus exclusively on the sick and others in need of care, and not on care-givers. This study shows how the skewed focus is partly due to the feminisation of care-giving, which has resulted in undervaluing and non-recognition of unpaid care work. Indeed, traditional norms and practices reproduce discourses that reinforce the undervaluing of care work. This is further reflected in market and state regulatory systems in Malawi.

It is clear that volunteer care-givers face a number of challenges and needs, most of which remain unmet. The challenges faced by volunteer care-givers include issues of health and safety and potential financial exploitation. There are limited responses by government, NGOs and communities to mitigate these challenges. Although, some of the responses are guided by government policy, the regulatory framework remains weak. The Malawi Constitution provides for the right to safe and fair labour practices for all persons. However, unlike the case with paid workers, there is no legislation that has translated this right into specific practical legal obligations in favour of unpaid care-givers. There is hence a need for specific legislation that provides for minimum standards of health and safety, including provision of work materials and psycho-social support, working hours and protection from exploitation and abuse. It is crucial that volunteer care work is recognised as a form of labour, albeit unpaid, that requires equal protection as other forms of labour and is properly regulated in similar terms to formal paid labour. This essay therefore calls for translation of care work related HIV/AIDS policies and guidelines into legislation specific to volunteer care-givers. And I have suggested that this may take the form of a Volunteer Workers Act, which would provide not only minimum enforceable rules but would also form a basis for more specific claims by care-givers – ultimately contributing to the effective legal protection and legal empowerment of care-givers in Malawi.

References

Action Aid Malawi, 2000. Strategies for Action: Home Based Care and Gender Study. Unpublished report.

Anderson, A. 2008. Palliative Care: A Field Guide for Community Home Based Care Volunteers. Lilongwe.

Cancian, F. and Oliker, S. 2000. *Caring and Gender*. New Delhi: Pine Forge Press/ Sage Publications.
Centre for Social Research, 1996. Community Health Volunteers. Zomba (Unpublished Research Report).
Daly, M. 2002. Care as a Good in Social Policy. *Journal of Social Policy*, 31(2), 251–70.
Kanyongolo, N. and Makuta, E. 2000. Employment and Human Rights in Malawi, Base Line Study, (Unpublished Research Report).
Lewis, J. 2002. Gender and Welfare State Change. *European Societies*, 4(4), 331–57.
Malawi Government, 2005. Malawi HIV /AIDS National Action Framework (NAF) 2005–2009. Lilongwe. Malawi.
Malawi Government, 2008. Malawi HIV and AIDS Monitoring and Evaluation Report. Lilongwe.
Ministry of Health, 2005a. Community Home Based Care Trainers' Manual. Lilongwe. Government of Malawi.
Ministry of Health, 2005b. National Community Home Based Care Policy and Guidelines. Lilongwe, Government of Malawi.
National Aids Commission, 2006. Trainers' Manual on Effective Management of HIV and AIDS Programme. Lilongwe, Government of Malawi.
National Aids Commission, 2007. HIV & Syphilis Sero-survey and National HIV Prevalence and AIDS Estimates Report. Lilongwe, Government of Malawi.
National Economic Council, 2000. Adaptive Strategies and Coping Mechanisms: The Effect of HIV/AIDS on the Informal Social Security System in Malawi. Lilongwe: National Economic Council.
Robinson F. 2006. Beyond Labour Rights: The Ethics of Care and Women's Work in the Global Economy. *International Feminist Journal of Politics*, 8, 321–42.
Sevenhuijsen, S., Bozalek, V., Gous, A. and Minnaar-Mcdonald, M. 2003. South African Social Welfare Policy: An analysis using the ethic of care, *Critical Social Policy*, 23(93), 299–321.
Tamale, S. 2004. Gender trauma in Africa: Enhancing women's links to resources. *Journal of African Law*, 48(1), 50–61.
Tronto, J. 1993. *Moral Boundaries: A Political Argument for an Ethic of Care*. London: Routledge.
Umoyo Network, 2000a. Assessment of Home Based Care Services in Malawi. Blantyre: Umoyo Networks Project.
Umoyo Network, 2000b. Assessment of Persons Living with HIV/AIDS Community-Based and Networking Organisations in Malawi, Blantyre: Umoyo Networks Project.
VSO-RAISA, 2007. Advocacy Strategy Document 2007–2010: Reducing the Burden of HIV and AIDS Care on Women and Girls. Lilongwe.

Chapter 10

The Right To Water: An Inquiry into Legal Empowerment and Property Rights Formation in Tanzania[1]

Ellen Hillbom

Introduction

The legal empowerment approach is a recent attempt to be specific about the role of institutions for the eradication of poverty. This is a broad concept that includes not only the national formal judicial system in a country, but all formal and informal institutional structures providing the rules of the game of human interaction in any given society. The approach has invited a lot of debate as to what the role of the law is in relation to other institutional structures, how the concept of empowerment is to be understood and how the two enhance the process of poverty reduction and economic development (Moore 2001; Bruns 2007; Banik 2008; Sengupta 2008; Singh 2009). In this chapter, I will discuss legal empowerment as it was summarised and presented by the Commission of the Legal Empowerment of the Poor (hereafter CLEP) in its final report *Making the Law Work for Everyone* (2008).

According to CLEP, four billion people around the globe are presently excluded from the rule of law. This exclusion disempowers the poor and perpetuates poverty. And the remedy is a transformation of society including comprehensive legal, political, social and economic reforms whereby the poor are legally empowered. A well functioning rule of law is the foundation on which all institutional structures promoting economic growth and development rests, including commodity and financial markets, business and labour contracts, and fiscal policies. With the rule of law working for all members of society, all individuals can theoretically reach their full potential as economic actors, and resources will be allocated with maximum efficiency. This provides the poor with the opportunity to work their way out of poverty. However, for future legal structures to be successful in caring for the interests of the poor, they have to be involved as co-designers (CLEP 2008).

---

1 The research for this chapter was conducted within the Lund University Initiative on Legal Empowerment of the Poor.

The focus of this chapter is on one of the four pillars of legal empowerment, namely property rights.[2] To CLEP the promotion and protection of property rights is key to poverty reduction and economic growth and it is assumed that it is generally the poor who are lacking the legal support for their property. Legal protection of assets is regarded as the first concern of the poor and such protection can secure livelihoods and provide incentives for productive investments (CLEP 2008: 51). The first aim is therefore to critically examine the basic assumptions on which CLEP builds its policy recommendations in relation to the formation of property rights and I wish to investigate how it differs from past and current development policy agendas.

The main contributor to the property rights debate in CLEP has been the Peruvian economist Hernando de Soto, and in order to better understand the commission's arguments on processes of property formation and the outcome of having legally protected assets, I will examine some of de Soto's work on the subject. This includes *The Mystery of Capital* (2000), where he argues that legally protected formal property rights are central for the promotion of economic growth and development. I wish to critically examine de Soto's theory and investigate what is new in his claims regarding the relationship between legally regulated formal property rights, market transactions and economic growth.

Thus, the applicability of CLEP's policy recommendations and de Soto's theory will be scrutinised using alternative theory and a case study. One of the greatest challenges for poverty reduction in the world today is the issue of how to achieve agricultural development in sub-Saharan Africa. Despite considerable achievements in promoting global development in the past five decades, 75 per cent of the world's poor live in rural areas. And rural poverty rates in sub-Saharan Africa remain among the highest in the world with an average of 51 per cent, while the absolute number of rural poor in the region has reached almost 250 million (World Bank 2007: 45). If CLEP and de Soto are to truly contribute to development policy and theory, their recommendations ought to also be of relevance to the agrarian sector in Africa. Hence, a second aim of the chapter is to relate CLEP and de Soto to a specific case of property rights formation and power struggles over agricultural resource in a rural sub-Sahara African setting, namely irrigation water among the Meru of Tanzania.

As irrigated land productivity is more than double that of rain-fed land, water is a key resource for future agriculture production and productivity increase. However, only four per cent of agricultural land in sub-Saharan Africa is under irrigation (World Bank 2007: 9). Understanding the fundamental principles behind well functioning property rights regimes appears therefore crucial for the achievement of quantitative and qualitative improvement of irrigation resources in Africa. The Meru farming system shares great similarities in physical as well as in social organisation features with a number of historical and contemporary irrigation

2 The other three pillars are: access to justice and the rule of law, labour rights and business rights.

systems in East Africa (Sutton 1990; Spear 1997). Such shared characteristics include intense farming methods, intercropping practices, gravity irrigation, low levels of technology and communal ownership of resources combined with private user rights. As the area is not unique in its allocation and management of agricultural resources, it is an interesting case that can constitute the basis for generally valid conclusions on how water resources for irrigation are allocated, controlled and managed.

I start with a brief background to water as an agricultural resource, a presentation of the case study area and an account of the empirical material. Thereafter, I will critically discuss the recommendations of the CLEP Report and de Soto's previous work on property rights formation and its applicability to the agrarian sector in sub-Saharan Africa. I will then examine the essence of legal protection of property rights and legal pluralism, including diverse arguments for private property rights as the most appropriate for creating sustainable economic growth. This is followed by an investigation into the pre-conditions for, and potential of, market transactions and an analysis of the complexity of power and exclusion in Tanzania.

Background

Clear definitions of property rights governing the distribution, allocation and management of water resources are often fundamental to the value of land and real property in agricultural societies (CLEP 2008: 36). In many instances, water is foremost an economic good, and it is becoming increasingly valuable in economic terms as it is being overused and misused, resulting in alarming worldwide scarcity. Water consumption is, consequently, often regulated by economic incentives (Kay et al. 1997). However, water is also a life-supporting natural resource and is regularly treated as a public good. Further, the economic and social aspects of life in developing countries are usually not neatly separated in public and private distinctions and property rights institutions contain both.

The sensitivity of allocation and governance of water resources is further complicated by the natural characteristics of water as a non-fixed resource. The seasonal aspect of water, for example, means that when the demand is the greatest, the supply is usually the lowest. Data availability on seasonal flows in rivers and irrigation furrows and the potential seepage and evaporation from open water sources is also often limited in developing countries. Before existing amounts are mapped and known, it is difficult for government officials to fairly allocate water rights. In this context, de Soto (2000) claims that measuring assets is not a problem for setting up secure property rights, but insufficient data easily leads to conflicts over distribution and excessive exploitation of scarce resources. As the state moves in to be the principal guardian of all national water resources, it needs correct information in order to serve diverse economic interests such as agriculture, industry, hydropower, and urban areas (Chenje and Johnson 1996). Instead, poor information about water recourses has resulted in situations where the total amounts stated in water rights actually can exceed availability in the river. Seasonality further adds to the challenge making it necessary to have flexibility in property rights institutions governing water resource (Carlsson 2003).

The Case

The Meru of Tanzania inhabit the southern and eastern slopes of Mount Meru, an extinct volcano 4,565 metres above sea level in the northern part of the country (see Map 10.1). Their area covers roughly 50 sq. km. and is located five kilometres east of the Arusha town. The mountain slopes have fertile soils of volcanic origin and the area has a tropical climate moderated by altitude and a bi-modal rainfall pattern with an average precipitation of more than 1,300 millimetres per annum, although there are significant local and seasonal differences (Assmo 1999: 78–9; Larsson 2001: 112).

During the 19th and towards the beginning of the 20th centuries, the Meru became increasingly geographically locked in. In the 1830s, the Arusha people arrived and settled on the mountain slopes to the west. And with the establishment of the German colonial administration in the 1890s, land on Mount Meru above 1,600 metres was declared a forest reserve while at the same time land to the south of Meru was allocated to European and South African settlers. These boundaries were not significantly changed by the take-over of either the British colonial administration in the 1920s or the independent government in 1961. Due to geographic limitations, the Meru developed strategies for improving land productivity through intensification of farming methods, including the construction of irrigation furrows (Spear 1994: 3; Larsson 2001: 102–3). The first furrows were established towards the end of the 19th century. Irrigation was originally intended foremost to increase security, making smallholders less dependent on seasonal rains, and to save on labour efforts (Puritt 1977: 93; Larsson 2001: 185). Due to intensification of farming methods resulting from population growth and increasing land scarcity, the need for irrigation water has steadily escalated in the area over the last century. The demand has further increased in the past two decades, especially on the lower slopes, where rainfall is more erratic and scarce (Carlsson 2003; Larsson 2001).

General information on the historical background, legislation, government policies and registration of water rights was collected in 1998, through interviews with government employed water officers at national, regional and district levels; representatives of NGO supporting irrigation furrows in Meru as well as water users and oral history key informants in Meru.

In September 2000, the Malala River was selected for a further in-depth study. The river has a history of more than 100 years of continuous construction and expansion of irrigation furrows and it covers multiple agricultural practices and property rights institutions. There are eight irrigation furrows along the river, five of them constructed by Meru smallholders and three constructed by immigrant white estate owners. Three of the furrows are shared by more than one water rightholder,

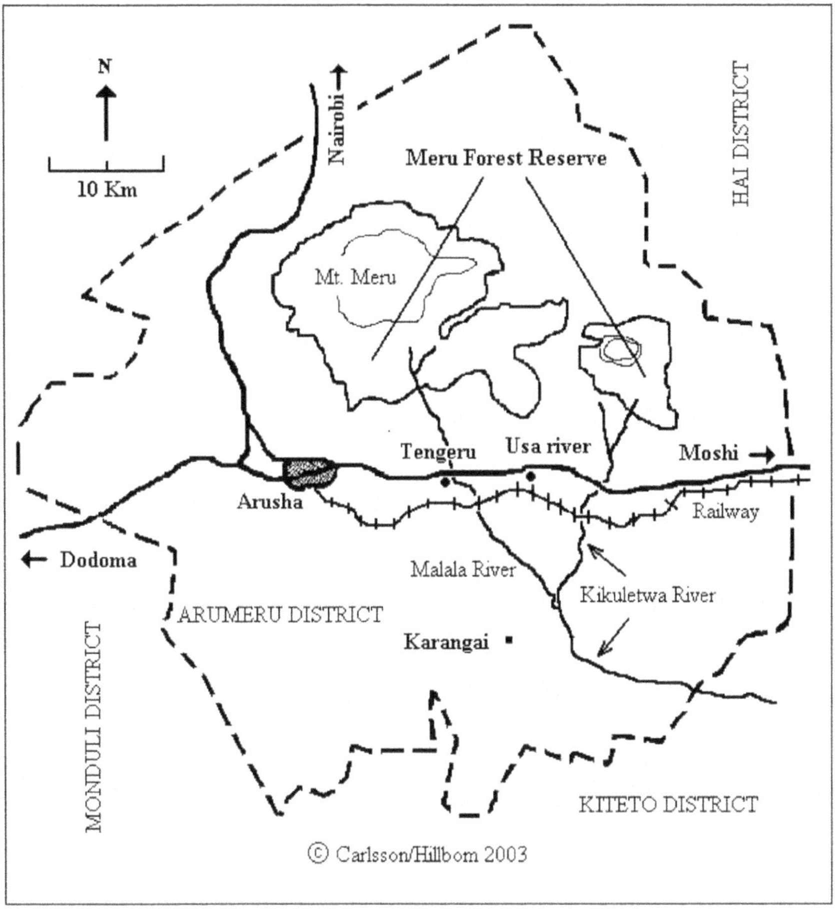

Map 10.1 Arumeru District and Malala River

Source: Carlsson (2003: 76).

and in an extreme case, there are as many as five water right holders sharing one furrow. Out of the total of 15 water rights, i.e. documented allocation sanctioned by the state, ten are held by formally recognised water committees with smallholders as members. The remaining five water rights are held by three estates, one catholic mission and one former estate that is today a Ministry of Agriculture Training Institute. Seventy nine smallholders, sharing communally owned furrows, were interviewed representing a mix of wealth, gender, marital status and age. Another six estates holding private water rights were included in the sample. The outcome of the first two studies was a doctoral thesis on property rights formation and long-term property rights change.[3] Follow-up studies were conducted in November

3 See Carlsson (2003).

2007 and September 2009 with the purpose of mapping changes in property rights institutions. They included return visits to meet government officials and NGO representatives in Arusha as well as interviewing key informants, water committee members and village officials in Meru. The purpose was to map and analyse any changes in property rights regimes in the case area and this chapter is based on the results of the follow-up studies.

Legally Protected Formal Property Rights

There is a general agreement on the necessity of having secure property rights to encourage economic activities leading to growth and development. The disagreement comes with the debate on whether or not there are alternatives to private rights that can still hold a sufficient amount of security to satisfy the needs of the property holder. In the writings of de Soto (2000; 2008), the need is dictated by the potential gains of creating capital that can lead to improved incomes for the individual, and economic growth and development for society at large. De Soto makes a simplified distinction between formal rights, backed up by a judicial system supported by the national authorities, and informal rights that are supported by social structures outside the formal legislation. This is an over-simplification because it ignores the existing variations in property rights and presupposes that there can only be one formal judicial system at a time. It thus condemns legal pluralism, without understanding the inherent complexities.

The true benefit of 'property' is the right that people hold over the future incomes provided by an asset. Thus, property rights award individuals the long-term benefit from a natural resource, or any other asset, which others are excluded from (Bromley 1997). All property is thereby subject to different forms of social recognition such as monitoring and enforcement, exclusion, social acceptance of claims, and external authorities. It is made up of the relationship between people in relation to an asset (Hodgson 1988). Further, having a right is closely connected to the issue of enforcement because, unless a right is temporarily taken by force, it is something that the individual holds with the support of an authority system. The authority system – that defends the right on behalf of the property holder – can be the government of a local village or a national government (Agarwal 1994: 1459; Bromley 1997: 3).

The current complex property rights systems found in rural sub-Saharan Africa includes several characteristic features. First, there are four categories of property rights: *private* (characterised by partial or full concentration of benefits and costs assigned to an individual), *state* (the public sector or the government is responsible for management of resources), *communal* (a group of individuals – sometimes as large as the whole community, sometimes small and exclusive – hold the exclusive right over a resource), and *open access* (rights are left unassigned, and there is an absence of property relations). Second, distinctions can be made between *ownership*, *user rights* and *access*. Although ownership usually carries with it stronger rights concerning utilisation than is the case with user rights, there is no definite correlation between the two. Meanwhile, the term 'access' signifies an informal concession being a socially rather than judicially recognised and enforceable right. Third, legally recognised formal rights are termed *de jure* rights, and in property rights theory it is generally taken for granted that *de jure* rights give an indisputable legitimacy to a claim. A *de facto* right is rather a presentation of the right as it is accepted and controlled in real life, and it often depicts an adaptation to social requirements or is the result of property holders not enforcing their rights.

In addition to the above, there are, in most African countries, two or more competing judicial systems – statutory and customary law. Ever since the colonial days the agricultural sector has had to deal with the problems of legal pluralism. For example, although The Natural Water Supply Regulation Ordinance No. 4 in 1923 was the first legislation in Tanganyika (TNA 3495, Vol. I), it did not formulate any principles taking into account local conditions and, in their absence, English Customary Law was applied in the country. This statutory legislation primarily included regulations for water within the Crow Land, i.e. land occupied by the colonial administration or by settlers. While the law stated that customary law and customary rights were recognised, these were not specified. As in other British colonies, the idea was to separate 'Crown Land' and statutory law from 'native reserves' occupied by the African population, which were allowed to be governed by local Customary Law (Kanthack 1936; TNA 471/w.2/8 Vol. I: 4–5). Hence, a dual legal system, governing the allocation and management of water, was created.

Among scholars there has been great concern with turning customary rights into statutory rights. The argument has been that in such a process the wealthy farmers would be given an unfair opportunity to use their knowledge about the administrative procedures involved. The losers would be poorer smallholders, women, and other groups with weaker economic, social and political power, who may be currently better protected by customary structures and social networks (Agarwal 1994; Toulmin and Quan 2000; Chimhowu and Woodhouse 2006). In addition to claims that an individualisation of communal customary rights leads to exclusion of socially and economically weak groups, some question whether registration of statutory rights would really result in increased investments and improved productivity (Migot-Adholla et al. 1991). It is thus argued that the causal relationship between tenure system and investments are much more complex than just a dichotomy between the formal and the informal. It is instead argued that the relationship must be understood in the context of various institutions controlling labour and land (Place and Keijiro 2002). One way forward, as Deininger (2003) argues, could therefore be the formalisation of existing communal customary rights, which could in the future lead to private property rights.

Government officials in the Northern Province realised as early as in the 1920s that the existing legislation was unsatisfactory in terms of solving problems of legal rights to water in a situation of high demand relative to supply that caused scarcity. The need for a more elaborate legal and administrative machinery, to deal with issuing and monitoring water rights and to prevent abuse, became increasingly obvious especially in areas such as Meru with a higher population density and where Africans smallholders and European settlers were to share water resources. When the new Water Ordinance of 1948 was finally brought into effect in 1954, it, however, lacked any profound reform and legal pluralism causing water conflicts remained (TNA 471/w.2/8 Vol. I). Although the colonial authorities passed a final water ordinance in 1959, in practice the power to grant property rights to water and water ways, and the control over water works continued throughout the colonial era to be divided between the colonial administration and the local African authorities (ibid.).

The first post-independence water legislation in Tanzania was the Water Utilization Act No. 42 (1974), which was rather a continuation of the previous colonial legislation. In the first decades after independence, the government officials were more concerned with land reforms in the form of a rearrangement of land ownership (principally the creation of *ujamaa* villages) and devoted far less time to dealing with the development and distribution of water resources.[4] Water, together with all other natural resources, was nationalised and placed under the jurisdiction of the national government and hence officially an end was put to the dual system of shared jurisdiction between tribal and colonial authorities. The new national jurisdiction did not, however, solve the issue of the dual property right system since old customary rights that had been issued by tribal leaders continued to exist side by side with statutory rights issued by the colonial administration. Statutory water rights, was easily registered with the new authorities while the customary rights were recognised in principle. The challenge was to register all customary rights with the new administration and thereby to gain knowledge and control over them.

Although it has been the intention of the post-independence authorities for several decades, many water sources that were granted customary rights – among them traditional irrigation furrows in Meru – have only recently been registered or remain unregistered. This poses a problem for the local authorities when they are to consider applications for construction of additional furrows. Slowly the number of furrows registered with the national authorities has increased and at present all furrows except one along the Malala River were registered with statutory, formal water rights.

It is important to recognise customary law as a formal legislation in the Native reserves during the colonial era as African smallholders in Meru obeyed the formal legislation and obtained legally protected formal property rights. After Independence, customary rights were recognised in statutory legislation and management of furrow, and allocation of water resources were delegated to water committees regulated by their own by-laws. And the current drawn-out process of registering smallholder furrows has not been due to the escape of smallholders from

4 Due to population density and farming of coffee as a perennial crop, *ujamaa* villages were never established in Meru.

the formal to the informal sector, but more the result of a weak state's problems in reaching out with legislation and policy to its citizens. Legal pluralism is thus not about the formal versus the informal, but of competing judicial systems that the state has been unable to merge.

Private Versus Communal Property

De Soto (2000) does not argue for legally formalised and secure property rights of any sort, but private property rights specifically. His claim that legally protected formal private property rights to assets is a development towards more efficient property rights structures allowing for secure ownership, market transactions, contracting, and so on, has been argued before in both theory and policy. For example, Aristotle (384–322 BC) wrote that a privatisation of communally held resources would give the right incentive structure to create an efficient and sustainable economy and that private property should therefore be encouraged (cited in Landreth and Collander 1994: 27). He also outlined a scenario where a resource is used as communal property by individuals who are all driven by utility maximising behaviour and who will in time exploit the resource beyond the optimal level for sustainability (Buchanan 1993: 1–2). This argumentation coincides with the concept of 'the tragedy of the commons' popularised by Garrett Hardin (1968), which has influenced international development policy throughout the twentieth century. The tragedy is that when there are no rules and regulations governing the natural resources the result will be overuse and collapse of the resource.

Advocating for privatisation of non-regulated natural resources as the only way to achieve economically efficient incentive structures, and mixing up communal property rights with open access, has continued. Harold Demsetz (1967) claims that the process of changing the property rights structure is initiated when the gains from an internalisation of externalities become larger than the cost of realising the internalisation. He refers to the transformation of non-exclusive resources into private and state ownership. Demsetz did not make a distinction between non-exclusive and communally held resources and setting up exclusive communal property was not considered an option. Steven Cheung (1970) and Yorum Barzel (1989) also understood communal ownership as free and non-regulated access for all members of a community. This pre-conception had implications for their further arguments on the opportunity of contracting. They departed from an assumption of financially and socially independent actors seeking maximum gains and entering into specific clear-cut contracts of their own free will.

Unfortunately, there is a great difference between such actors and African subsistence smallholders depending on social networks for opportunities and assistance. The advocates for private property have, for decades, been criticised by those adhering to a different understanding of how property rights regimes, and specifically communal property rights regimes can be successful. Although communal resources that are regulated poorly, or not at all, run a great risk of ending up in a 'tragedy of the commons' scenario, extensive fieldwork from around the world has shown that communal property rights regimes can be successful as a whole even if there are individual free-riders. Exercising one's rights to communally held natural resources is generally neither automatic nor without restrictions and principles guiding communal property rights regimes seldom imply free access for all community members to resources. Instead, communal property rights are conditioned and rights are limited and the scarcer the resource the stricter it is being governed (Dahlman 1980; Ostrom 1990; Andelson 1991; Bromley 1992; Peters 1994; Adams 1997; Carlsson 2003). The dichotomy between private as successful and communal as failure has proven to be far too simplistic. It appears that the CLEP report has taken consideration to some of the above critique in that the definition of 'formalisation' is a lot less rigid when compared to de Soto's original writings. For example, it is emphasised that there must be a system encompassing both collective and individual rights as well as a recognition of the importance of customary rights (CLEP 2008; Singh 2009).

The agenda of centralised authorities changing existing local property rights regimes from above, as advocated by both CLEP and de Soto, is not new to the African continent. Already in the 1930s, several colonial administrations showed concern regarding the property rights structures governing agricultural resources in African communities. It was argued that existing property rights did not offer smallholders the incentives neither for surplus production nor environmentally sustainable farming methods (Sumberg 1998). These arguments were frequently repeated during the last decades of colonial rule and resulted in several large-scale attempts at introducing changes in existing property rights regimes – the most well known example being land tenure reform in Kenya in the 1950s (Musembi 2007).

With the introduction of Structural Adjustment Programmes (SAP) in the 1980s, resource management was affected by universal arguments and trends related to the privatisation of all sorts of property and the deregulation and liberalisation of the agricultural sector. Policymakers began to consider privatisation of natural resources, particularly land, to be essential for the provision of the right incentives for farmers to invest in agriculture and for creating credit markets (Friis-Hansen 2000). As the privatisation policy promoted by the World Bank became increasingly criticised in the 1990s, it ceased to be central to the Bank's policy recommendations. The Bank's privatisation efforts showed meagre results just as the case had been in earlier attempts by largely disconnected central authorities to impose top-down institutional change (Musembi 2007; Assies 2009). The realisation that there was no empirical evidence that strict privatisation by itself automatically leads to increased private investments, influenced policy recommendations. However, a property rights focus remained, implying that a change in property rights structures governing natural resources in sub-Saharan African countries was necessary for the achievement of growth in the agricultural sector (Friis-Hansen 2000). Moreover, the CLEP report (2008) shows that there is still a belief in contemporary policy recommendations in the importance of the formalisation of property rights, although there is some recognition of the fact that any such attempt would need to be adjusted to existing local conditions.

As the establishment of irrigation furrows coincided with the colonisation of the Meru area, property rights structures and management systems have from the start been influenced by external forces. The Meru Paramount Chief, the *Mangi*, was put in charge of administering Meru land, first by the German, and later by the British, colonial administration. Consequently, those who constructed furrows on Meru land during the colonial era had to approach the *Mangi* as they were responsible for allocating rights to construct irrigation furrows and making sure that the channels' did not interfere with the agricultural activities of other farmers.

The first wave of smallholder furrows where constructed in the late nineteenth and early twentieth century and property rights were developed along two different paths. One scenario was that the construction was initiated by a leading figure in the village who would get villagers involved in the project. In return for the labour put into construction and maintenance work, farmers received a share of the water according to established schedules. The communal effort turned the furrow into communal property although the initiator could acquire the position of water committee chairman. In other cases the construction was undertaken by a village strong man who used paid labour and the furrow was then considered to be the property of that individual. There were, however, restrictions to his ownership as any farmer living along the stretch of the furrow who wanted access to water could approach the 'owner' and ask for allocations. It was socially unacceptable for the owner to refuse such a request from a smallholder living along the stretch of the furrow. In return for the use of water, farmers would pay the owner compensation in the form of gifts (Spear 1996: 221).

The African smallholder furrows were never registered with the colonial administration and have in rare cases remained unknown to government officials to this day. As long as they have not been registered, they have also not obtained formal water rights according to national statutory law. Instead they have continued to hold customary water rights given to them by the Mangi in his capacity as the administrator of the Native Reserve

Meanwhile, estate owners also constructed irrigation furrows around the same time using labour from their farms or by digging the channel system in a joint venture with neighbouring Meru smallholders. Depending on the arrangements around the construction, they considered part or the whole of the furrow to belong to them as private property. Unlike the Meru, the estate owners turned to the colonial administration in order to obtain permission to construct furrows and receive a water right for the furrow. Their private rights were later recognised by the independent government.

Independence meant the nationalisation of all natural resources and tribal authorities such as the *Mangi* lost their power to approve the construction of irrigation furrows. Further, all existing furrows became the property of village authorities established by the national government during the 1960s and the 1970s. The new *de jure* state ownership, however, meant no changes in *de facto* property rights institutions. Village authorities delegated water allocation and management to existing water committees who continued with the previous principles of communal ownership and private user rights. Although village authorities were consulted for the construction of new furrows, these were not registered with any district or regional water authorities. It is only in the past two decades that the Tanzanian government has shown interest in formalising water rights in Meru as part of developing water basin policies. Moreover, smallholders have begun appreciating the gains of having their furrows registered with national authorities and thereby obtaining statutory formal property rights. According to local water users, however, the formalisation of property rights has not, however, changed the by-laws of the individual furrows.

The set-up from the start was then two parallel property rights regimes – customary communal furrows owned and managed by the local smallholders and estate furrows held as private property according to statutory law. Such elaborate and competing property rights structures are common in many societies with furrow irrigation (Adams 1990). Neither of these regimes has over the years *de facto* been affected by changes in legislation or policy and their rationales have remained the same. Further, despite the fact that Meru is an area experiencing significant changes in relative prices between factor endowments due to population increase and land scarcity (Larsson 2001), there have been no grassroots initiatives to privatise irrigation resources. In the midst of policy changes, farm intensification, agricultural development and improved standards of living traditional communal property rights to irrigation resources has remained strong in Meru (Carlsson 2003; interviews with water users 2007, 2009). It appears thus that in this case the advocates for privatisation cannot explain the rationales of property formation.

Market Transactions

To CLEP (2008) and de Soto (2000, 2008), legally protected formal property rights are a pre-condition for market interaction and access to credit. Functional property rights institutions allow land, houses, moveable property, equity shares, and ideas to be transformed into assets that can be bought and sold at rates determined by market forces. De Soto's main concern is to provide the poor with the opportunity to use their assets as collateral in market transaction, thereby creating capital, which he claims is only possible if assets are fixed in a formal property system. He argues that formal property representation is a concept that goes beyond the physical possession of an object; it is the representation of specific qualities associated with the asset that enables property to be transformed into capital using the market as the mediator.

The claim, that successful market exchange is dependent on good institutions, has been made before (Kherralah 2000; North 2005) including the importance of optimal information transmission and a framework for mediating transactions and transferring of property rights (Coase 1988). One key explanation given for market failure in rural sub-Saharan Africa is that the institutional structure is unsuccessful in meeting these requirements, which in turn results in high marketing and transaction costs (Barrett 2008; Shiferaw et al. 2008: 26). Some have argued that the development of good market institutions depends on active government involvement and trade promoting policies in order to rectify the inability of the local development of creating market transaction (North 1987; Bardhan 1989). Such a top-down approach coincides well with the general assumptions of CLEP and de Soto that a benevolent government is needed for setting up legally protected formal property rights.

In recent years alternative options to traditional theories on market transactions have been developed. These are options where water is treated primarily as an economic good instead of a public good and where legally protected formal property rights play a key role, but where property rights are not necessarily privately owned. There is a significant and growing academic literature presenting research on how water markets are increasingly being relied upon to allocate water resources in various regions of the world (Michelsen et al. 2000; ; Bjornlund 2003; Zekri and Easter 2005). In fact, many countries have, during the last two to three decades, shifted their water policies away from 'command and control' constraints to relying on market mechanisms to manage and distribute water resources. The shift can be traced back to the revived belief in market led development as opposed to state led development that emerged with neo-liberal political trends in the 1980s. This shift took place both within economic theory and development policy and was effectuated via projects run by UN organisations, the World Bank and the OECD. As water resources were over-used, policymakers saw a need to search for a maximum use of limited resources using market forces. It was hoped that increasing economic costs would motivate farmers to either optimise irrigation or sell off their water rights (Bjornlund 2003). Still, in many developing countries local communities have been hesitant towards developing markets for permanent water rights, while markets for short-term leases of water allocations have become more common (Bjornlund 2003; Zekri and Easter 2005).

Within the policy domain, alternatives to market exchange of privately owned agricultural resources have also evolved. One such alternative is the creation of Green Water Credits (GWC). Green water represents 60 per cent of global fresh water flows and is defined as water held in the soil and available to plants, primarily rainwater. GWC is a pro-poor market based mechanism to support sustainable water and soil use. According to the concept, down-stream water users compensate up-stream water users for water management services. In more extensive schemes it would be possible to design a global facility with the help of international funding. At the local level the GWC system is expected to provide incentives for good soil management, which in turn would improve the percolation of green water into the ground thereby recharging blue water resources in groundwater and streams. Further, GWC could offer alternative sources of incomes to smallholders up-stream (Dent 2005) and have recently been tested in Kenya's Upper Tana catchment with some positive results. Within the pilot project, the GWC has enabled tradeoffs between upstream land use and downstream water availability and regulation, and developed practical ways to appraise costs and benefits (ISRIC 2010).

Groundwater and streams are termed blue water. Payments for environmental services (PES) have been suggested as one way of combining the goals of poverty reduction and sustainable use of natural resources, including blue water. PES schemes are defined as voluntary transactions of environmental services between buyers and suppliers. There is hope that up-stream land and water holders can increase their income through PES as they receive payments from among others, down-stream large scale farmers, urban dwellers and hydropower dam owners. PES-schemes can be designed in various ways, depending on the local conditions (Wunder 2008), but are still fairly untested. Empirical studies of attempts in Africa, Asia and Latin America show mixed results in obtaining economic and environmental sustainable management of blue water resources combined with poverty reduction (Wunder 2008; Jack 2009; Quintero et al. 2009).

Returning to the Tanzanian case, there is no selling and buying of water rights for irrigation in Meru and there are no institutionalised water markets. As was stipulated by CLEP and de Soto, the local property rights regime – made up of communal ownership of irrigation furrows and private user rights to irrigation water – is an important part of the explanation. All smallholders who can be reached by the furrows are welcome to join the water committees, and as long as they abide by the by laws of the furrow, they can ask for water allocations. Consequently, there are other ways for smallholders to get access to water than purchasing water rights in the market. Further, within this system there are few opportunities for a smallholder to amass water rights. Allocations are distributed fairly equally among water committee members, although there are instances of rule breaking, including theft, and preferential treatment. The existing communal property rights regime was created with the intent of granting opportunities for agricultural production to many rather than turning water into capital for the few. Risk spreading and secure access to water has hence been prioritised over opportunities for wealth maximisation.

Modest change is, however, occurring and we can speculate as to where these trends are heading. Instead of institutionalised exchange of ownership of water rights, there are temporary instances of water allocation rentals. Water committee members – who are unable to make use of their water allocations, for example due to old age or off-farm engagements – can delegate the allocation and in return are compensated in cash, kind or labour. There are both economical and physical constraints to these transactions as the smallholder buying such a temporary allocation has to be someone who concentrates his/her efforts in agricultural resources and lives along the same stretch of the furrow. Nonetheless, these new opportunities could in the long run mean a modest concentration of water in the hands of the more entrepreneurial smallholders. Secure rights protected by local authorities are necessary pre-conditions for these exchanges. However, it is not the expansion of market transaction that is driving the process of concentration of property rights, but rather factors, such as increasing landlessness, participation in the water committee activities and renting of allocations.

Bringing Power Back In

Possibly the most serious critique against both CLEP (2008) and de Soto (2000) is that the complexities of power struggles over resources are unaccounted for (Cousins 2009). In *The Mystery of Capital* (2000) de Soto makes a point of going back the experiences of the European occupation of the North American continent. He argues that policymakers and politicians of today can learn from the US experience when squatters where fighting to have their claims to the land accepted and formally registered with state agencies, thereby receiving legally protected formal rights. The European migrants were invited by the US government to settle on land that was owned by no-one (claims of Native Americans were not recognised) and squatters could therefore count on the support of the government. The situation, claims de Soto, is the same in developing countries today where rural and urban squatters alike need to have their property recognised by the law. By assuming a situation of excess land combined with the presence of a benevolent government de Soto paints the picture of a win-win situation and the complexities of power and exclusion are consequently ignored. I believe, such an analysis has numerous flaws.

The history of factor endowments in Africa south of the Sahara has generally been one of abundance of land and scarcity of labour (Iliffe 1995). Since the start of a general rise in population on the continent from roughly the 1930s, land, however, has become less abundant and labour less scarce. Smallholders in rural areas are now no longer staking claims to unoccupied land. Instead, they are often fighting to get access to resources that have already been appropriated. In their fight over resources it is, further, far from the general case that smallholders have the support of the government. They are often in direct confrontation with a land owning elite who have been given legally protected formal property rights according to statutory law. In the case of estates, many property rights may go back to the colonial era; others have been awarded since Independence. These estates are often important to the national economy as they produce cash crops and thereby contribute to national export earnings. Therefore governments usually prioritise property rights claims by estate holders over smallholders. It is thus not only a fight over resources between estates and smallholder, but also one between statutory and customary rights. It is furthermore a struggle within customary property rights institutions – between the wealthier and the poorer smallholders (Berry 1993, 2002; Odgaard 2003; Peters 2004).

As assumed by CLEP and de Soto, the poor are usually the ones without formal property rights to the resources they need to move out of poverty. If public policy is concerned with promoting the rights of the poor, it would require having the political will to also exclude other groups no matter how politically or economically powerful they are. In the US case it was about distribution of resources; in contemporary rural Africa it is about re-distribution of resources and therein lies an enormous difference.

Once there is recognition that a win-win situation cannot be expected and that a re-distribution in favour of the poor is required, then there is a considerable amount of academic literature to draw on. Although there is a difference between inequality and poverty (Singh 2009), the literature on equity also states that inequality perpetuates poverty and redistribution is necessary for poverty reduction. The call for a relatively equal distribution of natural resources within the agricultural sector rests on the argument that there is a causal relationship between equity and agricultural development leading to improved incomes and living standards for the rural population (Berry and Cline 1979; Cornia 1985; Deininger and Squire 1996; Kay 2001; Griffin et al. 2002). The rationale is that the larger the holding of the resource, the lesser the value per unit for the property holder who instead attempts to increase output per labour unit, as labour in this case is the evasive production factor. Meanwhile, the situation is the opposite for the smallholder who relies on family labour and on increasing output per resource unit. As the relative factor price of agricultural resources increases, the resource holder will intensify farming methods, which in turn leads to an increase in land productivity and a decrease in labour productivity. In societies with abundant labour and scarce agricultural resources and capital, total factor productivity should increase after redistributive reform since smallholders all in all utilise resources more efficiently than larger ones (Cornia 1985; Deininger and Squire 1996; Griffin et al. 2002).

An unequal distribution of agricultural resources in turn reflects an institutional inequality that characterises society at large (Engerman and Sokoloff 2002; World Bank 2005). In societies with institutional inequality, government policies tend to favour elites in various ways while denying the majority of the population equal opportunities. Groups and individuals with wealth and high social status influence institutions and distort them in their favour, further enriching themselves. Political and economic inequality, thus, go hand in hand and unequal political power leads to an institutional structure that perpetuates inequalities in power and wealth (World Bank 2005: 107–8). The property rights reforms suggested by CLEP and de Soto entails, in reality, taking on a power struggle against such structural inequality and most likely also against the interests of those controlling the government. It is hence suggested by critics that the CLEP report (2008) avoids the complexities of state led redistribution of resources by instead advocating market-assisted mechanisms. The market is preferred compared to compulsory acquisition as it is less politically sensitive, but unfortunately it has also proven to be prone to elite capturing (Assies 2009). Further, such factors as the ability to utilise a positions of power to bypass the rule of law as well as struggles between the classes are underestimated by CLEP and de Soto (Cousins 2009).

Negotiability within the customary property rights system is possibly slowing down the process of exclusion (Berry 2002; Odgaard 2003). Meanwhile, negotiability is also part of a process of increased exclusion and polarisation (Peters 2004). It is a general trend on the African continent that the present elite have continued to support and maintain the customary institutional system. The consequence has been considerable and growing inequality, a polarisation process within the framework of prevailing customary property institutions (Platteau 1996; Ribot 2000).

In Meru, the number of water users has increased as has the demand for and scarcity of water, but the property rights regimes remain intact, functioning according to the old model of communal furrows and private user rights where farmers along the furrows can get access to water in return for contributions in money, kind and labour. The system has been non-exclusive, and it has been, and continues to be, of an open attitude so that farmers find it easy to gain user rights and access. Here, the poor manage to continue to access a scarce resource and the room for negotiations within customary property rights institutions have not been overly negative.

The explanation for this does not lie in an inherent African unwillingness to privatise, because there has been a parallel *de facto* privatisation of land in Meru. Instead, our understanding of the process should be based on the practical difficulties with exclusion along such a long waterway (Ostrom 1990), and on the community's acceptance that access to irrigation water is the key to the existence and survival of many farmers. The water committees are, however, facing an increasing number of difficulties in managing the furrows and dividing the water and, as a result, the by-laws of each furrow are becoming more detailed and more effort is put into enforcement.

The only real example of how population increase has altered property rights institutions is in the case of private irrigation furrows owned by estate holders, which are slowly being taken over by communities of African smallholders and thereby becoming *de facto* communal property. Contrary to orthodox property rights theory, the increase in resource users and the resulting augmented price of water have not led to privatisation attempts, but rather to a *de facto* de-privatisation of water sources. The explanation for this development is the same as the one telling us why African furrows have not become more exclusive – monitoring and enforcing property rights are extremely difficult and African smallholders consider themselves to be entitled to access irrigation water for their survival. When the demand for water could not be met by an increased supply of water resources, it instead turned into a demand for institutional change giving smallholders access to already existing irrigation furrows.

The Meru case is particularly interesting since agricultural resources held as private property with the legal protection of formal statutory law are gradually being lost in a power struggles with customary communal property rights institutions. Partly, this is then a case that is in complete opposition to the theoretical assumptions and policy recommendations of CLEP and de Soto. Meanwhile, the winners of this power struggle are the poor smallholders who benefit by taking over estate resources. In that sense it is an example of the readjustment of property rights institutions in accordance with aspirations of legal empowerment of the poor and pro-poor reforms. Smallholders are gaining because legally protected formal property rights are not respected and their gain is impossible without a power struggle over resources.

Conclusion

Throughout this chapter, I have shown that the policy recommendations of CLEP and the grand theories of institutional change for economic development presented by de Soto resonates with both colonial and World Bank policy as well as institutional and property rights theory. Indeed, the basic idea – that the promotion of legally protected formal private property rights brings efficient and sustainable use of resources – has been heard since the days of Aristotle and it has been intensively debated by scholars and policymakers during the last five to six decades. There is agreement on the importance of the rule of law in general, and secure property rights in particular, for long-term economic growth and development as well as for the eradication of poverty. However, the conclusions and the remedies of CLEP and de Soto echoes old statements rather than providing a new level of understanding of what good institutions really are and how they develop. The CLEP response to this critique would probably be that previous theories on property rights have been focussed on governing natural resources, while legal empowerment is a larger concept embracing all aspects of society (Singh 2009).

I have argued that CLEP's policy recommendations and de Soto's grand theory are both stuck in old tracks. Much research has been produced on legal pluralism, the possible success of communal property rights regimes, alternative forms of exchange other than transactions in traditional markets as well as the complexities of redistribution of resources. The empirical case of property rights institutions governing irrigation resources in Meru, Tanzania has been used here as an illustration of the shortcomings of CLEP and de Soto as well for presenting the usefulness of alternative analytical frameworks. It is time to evolve the concept of legal empowerment beyond CLEP and to expand our understanding of the principles of property rights formation beyond de Soto.

References

Adams, W.M. 1990. How beautiful is small? Scale control and success in Kenyan irrigation. *World Development*, 18(10), 1309–23.

Adams, W.M., Watson, E.E. and Mutiso, S.K. 1997. Water, rules and gender: Water rights in an indigenous irrigation system, Marakwet, Kenya. *Development and Change*, 28(4), 707–30.

Agarwal, B. 1994. Gender and command over property: A critical gap in economic analysis and policy in South Asia. *World Development*, 22(10), 1455–78.

Andelson, R.V. (ed.) 1991. *Commons without Tragedy: Protecting the Environment from Overpopulation – A New Approach*. London: Shepheard-Walwyn.

Assies, W. 2009. Legal empowerment of the poor: With a little help from their friends. *Journal of Peasant Studies*, 36(4), 909–24.

Assmo, P. 1999. *Livelihood Strategies and Land Degradation: Perceptions among Small-scale Farmers in Ng'iresi Village, Tanzania*, Department of Geography, University of Göteborg, Series B, no. 96.

Banik, D. 2008. Rights, Legal Empowerment and Poverty: An Overview of the Issues, in *Rights and legal Empowerment in Eradicating Poverty*, edited by D. Banik. Farnham: Ashgate Publishing, pp. 11–30.

Bardhan, P. 1989. The new institutional economics and development. *World Development*, 17(9), 1389–95.

Barrett, C.B. 2008. Smallholder market participation: Concepts and evidence from Eastern and Southern Africa. *Food Policy*, 33, 299–317.

Barzel, Y. 1989. *Economic Analysis of Property Rights*. Cambridge: Cambridge University Press.

Berry, A. and Cline, W.R. 1979. *Agrarian Structure and Productivity in Developing Countries.* Baltimore: John Hopkins University Press.

Berry, S. 1993. *No Condition is Permanent: The Social Dynamics of Agrarian Change in Sub-Saharan Africa*. Madison: The University of Wisconsin Press.

Berry, S. 2002. Debating the land question in Africa. *Comparative Studies in Society and History*, 44(4), 638–68.

Bjornlund, H. 2003. Efficient water market mechanisms to cope with water scarcity. *Water Resource Development*, 19(4), 553–67.

Bromley, D.W. (ed.) 1992. *Making the Commons Work: Theory, Practice, and Policy*. San Francisco: ICS Press.

Bromley, D.W. 1997. Property Regimes in Environmental Economics, in *The International Yearbook of Environmental and Resource Economics 1997/1998: A Survey of Current Issues*, edited by H. Folmer and T. Tietenberg. Cheltenham, UK and Lyme, USA: Edward Elgar.

Bruns, B. 2007. Irrigation water rights: options for pro-poor reform. *Irrigation and Drainage*, 56, 237–46.

Buchanan, J.M. 1993. Property as guarantor of liberty, in *Property Rights and the Limits of Democracy*, edited by C.K. Rowley. Aldershot: Edward Elgar.

Carlsson, E. 2003. *To Have and to Hold: Continuity and Change in Property Rights Institutions Governing Water Resources among the Meru of Tanzania and the BaKgtala in Botswana, 1925–2000*. Lund Studies in Economic History, 28. Stockholm: Almqvist & Wiksell International.

Chenje, M. and Johnson, P. (eds) 1996. *Water in Southern Africa*. Maseru/Harare: SADC/IUCN/SARDC.

Cheung, S.N.S. 1970. The Structure of Contract and the Theory of a Non-exclusive Resource. *Journal of Law and Economics*, 13(1), 49–70.

Chimhowu, A. and Woodhouse, P. 2006. Customary vs. Private Property Rights? Dynamics and trajectories of vernacular land markets in sub-Saharan Africa. *Journal of Agrarian Change*, 6(3), 346–71.

CLEP (Commission on Legal Empowerment of the Poor) 2008. *Making the Law Work for Everyone*. New Jersey: Toppan Printing Company America Inc.

Coase, R.H. 1988. *The Firm, the Market and the Law*. Chicago: The University of Chicago Press.

Cornia, G.A. 1985. Farm size, land yields and the agricultural production function. An analysis for fifteen developing countries. *World Development*, 13(4), 513–34.

Cousins, B. 2009. Capitalism obscured: the limits of law and rights-based approaches to poverty reduction and development. *Journal of Peasant Studies*, 36(4), 893–908.

Dahlman, C.J. 1980. *The Open Field System: A property rights analysis of an economic institution*. Cambridge: Cambridge University Press.

Denninger, K. 2003. *Land Policies for Growth and Poverty Reduction*. Washington, DC: World Bank.

Deininger, K. and Squire, L. 1996. New Ways of Looking at Old Issues: Inequality and Growth. Washington: World Bank mimeo.

Demsetz, H. 1967. Towards a theory on property rights. *The American Economic Review*, 56(2), 347–59.

Dent, D. 2005. Green Water Credits. Presentation at the FAO/Netherlands Conference on Water for Food and Ecosystems: Make it Happen!

De Soto, H. 2000. *The Mystery of Capital: Why Capitalism Triumphs in the West and Fails Everywhere Else*. London: Black Swan Books.

De Soto, H. 2008. Are Africans Culturally Unsuited to Property Rights and the Rule of Law? Some Reflections based on the Tanzanian Case, in *Rights and Legal Empowerment in Eradicating Poverty*, edited by D. Banik. Farnham: Ashgate Publishing, pp. 155–74.

Engerman, S. and Sokoloff, K. 2002. Factor endowments, inequality, and paths of development among new world economies. *Economia*, 3(1), 41–108

Friis-Hansen, E. (ed.) 2000. *Agricultural Policy in Africa After Adjustment*. Copenhagen: CDR Policy Paper, Centre for Development Research.

Griffin, K., Khan, A. and Ickowitz, A. 2002. Poverty and the distribution of land. *Journal of Agrarian Change*, 2(3), 279–330.

Hardin, G. 1968. The Tragedy of the Commons. *Science*, 162, 1243–8.

Hodgson, G.M. 1988. *Economics and Institutions: A Manifesto for a Modern Institutional Economics*. Cambridge: Polity Press.

Iliffe, J. 1995. *Africans: The History of a Continent*. Cambridge: Cambridge University Press.

ISRIC2010.PolicyBrief,http://www.isric.org/isric/webdocs/docs/PolicyBrief11web.pdf Accessed 25 August 2010.

Jack, B. Kelsey 2009. Upstream-downstream transactions and watershed externalities: Experimental evidence from Kenya. *Ecological Economics*, 68: 1813–24.

Kanthack, F.E. 1936. *Report on the Control of the Natural Waters of Tanganyika and the Framework of a Water Law on Which Such Control Should be Based*. Dar es Salaam: Government Printer.

Kay, C. 2001. *Asia and Latin America's Development in Comparative Perspective: Landlords, peasants, and industrialization*. The Hague: ORAPS WP Series: 336.

Kay, M., Franks, T. and Smith, L. (eds), 1997. *Water: Economics, Management and Demand.* London: E & FN Spon.

Kherralah, M. 2000. Access of Smallholder farmers to the Fruits and Vegetables Market in Kenya. International Food Policy Research Institute Working Paper.

Landreth, H. and Colander, D.C. 1994. *The History of Economic Thought.* Third edition. Toronto and Boston: Houghton Mifflin Company.

Larsson, R. 2001. *Between Crisis and Opportunity: Livelihoods, diversification, and inequality among the Meru of Tanzania*, Lund Dissertations in Sociology No. 41, Sociologiska institutionen, Lunds universitet.

Michelsen, A.M., Booker, J.M. and Person, P. 2000. Expectations in water-right prices. *Water Resource Development*, 16(2), 209–19.

Migot-Adholla, S., Hazell, P.B., Blarel, B. and Place, F. 1993. Indigenous Land Right Systems in Sub-Saharan Africa: Constraint on Productivity?, in *The Economics of Rural Organizations: Theory, Practice, and Policy*, edited by K. Hoff, A. Braveman and J.E. Stiglitz. Oxford: Oxford University Press.

Moore, M. 2001. Empowerment at last? *Journal of International Development*, 13, 321–29.

Musembi, C.N. 2007. De Soto and land relations in rural Africa: Breathing life into dead theories about property rights. *Third World Quarterly*, 28(8), 1457–78.

North, D.C. 1987. Institutions, transaction costs, and economic growth. *Economic Inquiry*, 25(5), 419–28.

North, D.C. 2005. *Understanding the Process of Economic Change.* Princeton: Princeton University Press.

Odgaard, R. 2003. Scrambling for land in Tanzania: Processes of formalisation and legitimisation of land rights, in *Securing Land Rights in Africa*, edited by T. Benjaminsen and C. Lund. London: Frank Cass.

Ostrom, E. 1990. *Governing the Commons: The Evolution of Institutions for Collective Action.* Cambridge: Cambridge University Press.

Peters, P. 1994 *Dividing the Commons: Politics, Policy, and Culture in Botswana.* Charlottesville and London: University Press of Virginia.

Peters, P. 2004. Inequality and social conflict over land in Africa. *Journal of Agrarian Change*, 4(3), 269–314.

Place, F. and Keijiro, O. 2002. Land tenure systems and their impact on agricultural investments and productivity in Uganda. *The Journal of Development Studies*, 38(6), 105–28.

Platteau, J-P. 1996. The evolutionary theory of land rights as applied to sub-Saharan Africa: A critical assessment. *Development and Change*, 27(1), 29–86.

Puritt, P. 1977. The Meru of Northeastern Tanzania, in *The Chagga and Meru of Tanzania*, edited by S. Falk Moore and P Puritt, Ethnographic Survey of Africa, East Central Africa 18, International African Institute, London.

Quintero, M., Wunder, S. and Estrada, R.D. 2009. For services rendered? Modelling hydrology and livelihoods in Andean payments for environmental services schemes. *Forest Ecology and Management*, 258, 1871–80.

Ribot, J, 2000. Decentralization, Participation, and Representation: Administrative Apartheid in Sahelian forestry, in *Development Encounters: Sites of Participation and Knowledge*, edited by P. Peters. Cambridge: Harvard University for HID.

Sengupta, A. 2008. The Political Economy of Legal Empowerment of the Poor in *Rights and Legal Empowerment in Eradicating Poverty*, edited by D. Banik. Farnham: Ashgate Publishing, pp. 31–46.

Shiferaw, B., Obare, G. and Muricho, G. 2008. Rural market imperfection and the role of institutions in collective action to improve markets for the poor. *Natural Resource Forum*, 32, 25–38.

Singh, N. 2009. Fighting rural poverty, inequality and low productivity through legal empowerment of the poor. *Journal of Peasant Studies*, 36(4), 871–92.

Spear, T. 1994. *Land, Population, and Agricultural Development on Mount Meru*. BIEA Conference on the Growth of Farming Communities, Cambridge University, 1994.

Spear, T. 1996. Struggles for the Land: The Political and Moral Economies of Land on Mount Meru, in *Custodians of the Land: Ecology and Culture in the History of Tanzania*, edited by G. Maddox, J. Giblin and I.N. Kimambo. London: James Currey Ltd, pp. 213–40.

Spear, T. 1997. *Mountain Farmers: Moral Economics of Land and Agricultural Development in Arusha and Meru*. Oxford: James Currey.

Sumberg, J. 1998. Mixed farming in Africa: The search for order, the search for sustainability. *Land Use Policy*, 15(4), 293–317.

Sutton, J. 1990. *A Thousand Years of East Africa*. Nairobi: British Institute in Eastern Africa.

TNA (Tanzania National Archives) TNA 3495 Vol. 1. 1922. Natural Water Supply Ordinance.

TNA (Tanzania National Archives) TNA 3495/2. 1923. *Ordinance No. 4 of 1923*.

TNA (Tanzania National Archives) TNA 471/w.2/8 Vol. I. 1955–58. *Water Ordinance and Water Court Matter*.

Toulmin, C. and Quan, J. 2000. *Evolving Land Rights in Africa*. London: IIED.

World Bank 2005. *World Development Report 2006: Equity and Development*. Washington, DC: World Bank.

World Bank 2007. *World Development Report 2008: Agriculture*. Washington, DC: World Bank.

Wunder, S. 2008. Payments for Environmental Services and the Poor: Concepts and Preliminary Evidence. *Environment and Development Economics*, 13, 279–97.

Zekri, S. and Eatser, W. 2005. Estimating the potential gains from water markets: A case study from Tunisia. *Agricultural Water Management*, 72, 161–75.

Chapter 11
Rights, Legal Empowerment and the Informal Economy in Africa: Concluding Remarks

Dan Banik

An effort to provide a summary of the discussions in the preceding chapters of this volume may not adequately capture the rich analytical insights that my co-authors have offered. Nonetheless, and at the risk of oversimplification and repetition, I wish to briefly draw your attention to four broad sets of conclusions.

First, it is time to move away from simply being concerned with definitions and issues of identification to one where there is a recognition of the rapid growth and importance of the informal economy in the lives of the poor and an understanding of the *process* that continues to produce, maintain and increase informality in developing country settings. Moreover, the emphasis must now shift from establishing the linkages between the informal and the formal to analysing the exact nature of such relationships – how, when and why such relationships are exploitative, discriminatory and exclusionary, but also mutually beneficial, in nature. Most importantly, policymakers must show increased interest in understanding what motivates people, not just the poor, to continue to operate in the informal economy. Thus, policies must be designed to pay adequate attention to improving human capabilities, challenging power relations, and supporting the ability of the poor to shape their own life trajectories. This requires good institutions and understanding how such institutions can be developed.

Second, once the above is recognised, and a correct diagnosis of the problems arrived at, the authorities will be better capable of formulating and implementing specific initiatives to improve the well-being of individuals and groups who remain highly vulnerable to poverty and deprivation. Responses to problems of the poor that find themselves entrenched in the informal economy will depend on how social, economic and political actors understand the causes of its existence and the potential benefits of addressing needs and challenges in informal economy. In other words, improving the well-being of the poor also entails making convincing arguments to the society at large about the benefits of doing so, i.e. elites, who often benefit from a thriving informal economy and may resist attempts to change the status quo, must be convinced that it may also be in their interest if the government were to undertake reforms in unregulated areas. However, this would require a fundamental shift in the manner in which workers in the informal economy are perceived by influential actors in society – i.e. changing stereotyped perceptions of workers as lazy, ignorant, undeserving, and prone to adopting strategies that involve theft, violence and social chaos. And identifying the underlying causes that explain the continued preference of informal services by large groups in society – including use of a particular language and terminology that the poor do not understand and complex procedures that limit access to vital services – will improve the ability of the poor to claim their rights and hold their leaders to account when such rights are violated. Thus, simply providing a legal identity may be insufficient, if broader issues to improve access to justice remain unaddressed.

Third, domestic regulations of labour markets and social protection provisions in Africa continue to prioritise the formal economy. Here the role of historical factors, including political repression and social and economic exclusion, that explain spatial isolation of certain groups in the informal economy, appears crucial. The net result is that the poor continue to live in, and/or are confined to, particular parts of a city or region (e.g. townships in South Africa). Such prioritisation of the formal economy has to change and policies must be geared towards addressing the newer realities of causalisation and externalisation of the labour force. Moreover, labour law institutions in most African countries require radical reform, which must be followed up by increased allocation of financial resources that will enable their personnel to be adequately trained, vigilant and perform their duties without falling prey to corruption. Similarly, existing legislative frameworks must be interpreted to encompass actors and activities in the informal economy.

Governments must consider the possibilities of introducing new legislation in areas where existing legislation in inadequate, particularly in relation to social protection of unpaid workers and vulnerable groups in the population. While such attempts may include a financial component (e.g. providing wages for certain types of activities that were previously undertaken on a voluntary basis), the case studies in the volume show that being treated with dignity and respect is what matters most for the poor.

Simply introducing new legislation, without empowering labour institutions to effectively implement resulting policies, is another area of concern. And any measure that is justified on the basis of promoting greater institutional efficiency – such as sub-contracting intermediaries to provide services and terminating the direct employment relationship that workers previously enjoyed vis-à-vis the state – must be undertaken with great caution and awareness of the possible erosion of core labour standards that follow from short-term contracts. The issue at hand is to ensure clear lines of accountability so that governments cannot absolve themselves of all responsibility when the rights of workers are routinely violated by contractors working for the government. In this respect, important lessons can be drawn from India, where the efforts of successive labour commisions and the recent recommendations of the National

Commission for Enterprises in the Unorganised Sector India (NCEUS) that are increasingly putting pressure on central and state governments in the country to give the informal sector increased priority and attention in agenda-setting.

Fourth, and finally, this volume has tried to further elaborate on the links between democracy and development in Africa with an examination of the role of political parties, trade unions and civil society organisations to aggregate and articulate issues that concern people in the informal economy. As some of the case studies show, even when a particular policy appears to have been successfully implemented, there is no guarantee that this actually results in an improvement in the well-being of intended beneficiaries. Politicians are concerned with visible action, and in their quest to please their constituents, the importance of consulting affected groups and listening to the views of their representatives, may be compromised in the quest for speedy interventions. Therefore, the *process* of consultation, dialogue and trust can be just as important as the final *outcome*. The key here appears to be able to reach an acceptable level of agreement with intended beneficiaries on the merits of a particular intervention without jeopardising overall policy objectives.

As many of the chapters in the book highlight, interventions by civil society organisations have had some success in helping informal businesses better access, and benefit from, formal markets. Thus, barriers to enter the formal markets in certain sectors may be lowered for informal businesses and value chain management practices – that analyse the process of raw materials making their way to the final product – can help identify important, profitable and longer-term employment security for actors in the informal economy. For example, producers, through non-profit intermediaries, can provide information about markets, the types of products that are in demand and then help secure bulk orders, while at the same time helping to limit risks involved. In some cases, civil society organisations can help promote social dialogue and issue-based bargaining, which can lead to considerable improvements in elementary facilities for actors in the informal economy such as the provision of drinking water and increased police presence in unsafe areas. However, large parts of the African continent face a representational gap, and 8 out of 10 workers do not belong to a work-related organisation to undertake collective bargaining. And even when such organisations exist, we need to better understand why trade unions and even NGOs sometimes prefer to avoid certain issues that affect particular groups of people. While there are many reasons for this, one explanation that has been highlighted in this book relates to the practical challenges that civil society organisations face in organising groups such as domestic workers, who may be 'hidden' from public life.

Index

Bold page numbers indicate figures, *italic* numbers indicate tables.

For Product Safety Concerns and Information please contact our EU representative GPSR@taylorandfrancis.com
Taylor & Francis Verlag GmbH, Kaufingerstraße 24, 80331 München, Germany

www.ingramcontent.com/pod-product-compliance
Ingram Content Group UK Ltd.
Pitfield, Milton Keynes, MK11 3LW, UK
UKHW011004180926
475701UK00004B/559

* 9 7 8 1 4 0 9 4 1 1 1 9 2 *